EMPOWERING
EDUCATION

EMPOWERING EDUCATION

Critical Teaching for
Social Change

IRA SHOR

The University of Chicago Press
Chicago and London

The University of Chicago Press, Chicago 60637
The University of Chicago Press, Ltd., London
© 1992 by Ira Shor
All rights reserved. Published 1992
Printed in the United States of America
01 00 99 98 97 96   5 4

ISBN (paper): 0-226-75357-3

Library of Congress Cataloging-in-Publication Data

Shor, Ira.
  Empowering education: critical teaching for social change/Ira
Shor.
     p.   cm.
  Includes bibliographical references and index.
  I. Critical pedagogy—United States.   I. Title.
LC196.5.U6S56   1992
370′.973—dc20   92-6237
                                                          CIP

Contents

Acknowledgments   vii

Introduction   The First Day of Class: Passing the Test   1

1   Education Is Politics: An Agenda for Empowerment   11

2   Problem-Posing: Situated and
Multicultural Learning   31

3   Three Roads to Critical Thought: Generative,
Topical, and Academic Themes   55

4   Critical Dialogue versus Teacher-Talk: Classroom
Discourse and Social Inequality   85

5   Rethinking Knowledge and Society: "Desocialization"
and "Critical Consciousness"   112

6   Democratic Authority: Resistance, Subject Matter,
and the Learning Process   135

7   Critical Teaching and Classroom Research: An
Interdisciplinary Field for Activist Learning   169

8   Becoming an Empowering Educator: Obstacles
to and Resources for Critical Teaching   200

9   "The Third Idiom": Inventing a Transformative
Discourse for Education   237

References   265

Author Index   273

Subject Index   275

Acknowledgments

I would like to thank generous colleagues for their helpful and intelligent criticisms of the manuscript: James Berlin, Bill Bigelow, Linda Christensen, David Dillon, Nan Elsasser, Marilyn Frankenstein, Nathan Gover, Tom Heaney, Dan Moshenberg, Peter McLaren, Bertell Ollman, Michael O'Loughlin, Bob Peterson, and Nancy Schniedewind. In addition, Dee Tedick not only critiqued the manuscript well but offered new sources for me to follow. Also, Fred Pincus provided sociological background essential to my research, for which I am very grateful. Further, Mike Rose read the manuscript with great care and offered me sage advice on what to revise and refine. Finally, I want to thank Sarah Benesch for her many important suggestions along the way as I went from draft to draft.

Introduction

The First Day of Class:
Passing the Test

Like many kids, I loved learning but not schooling. I especially dreaded the first day of class. I would wake up early, jump nervously out of bed, and run to open the window. From my fifth-floor apartment in the South Bronx, where I grew up, I would lean out and see my old public school across Bruckner Boulevard, a street busy with a stream of traffic on the way to Manhattan. Sometimes, if I was lucky, a big gray fog bank rolled in from the Long Island Sound, covered the weedy flats behind the school where Gypsies camped and veterans once lived in Quonset huts, and swallowed P.S. 93. My dreams were answered. Miraculously, the school had disappeared.

Years later, as a college teacher, I was walking to the first day of my basic writing class. I had a black book bag on my shoulder, a lesson plan in hand, and butterflies in my stomach.

I entered B building on our concrete campus and climbed the stairs, passing students smoking and talking loudly to each other. My writing class was in room 321, a place I knew well, with its gray tile floor, cinder-block walls, dirty venetian blinds, fiberglass chairs, and cold fluorescent lights. Since I began teaching English at this low-budget public college in New York City in 1971, I had spent a few semesters in the long, narrow rooms of B building.

On this first day, I wondered what would happen in class. I always bring a plan and know what I want to do, but what would the students do? I had been experimenting for some time with "student-centered teaching," hoping to engage students in critical learning and to include them in making the syllabus. But they came to class wary and uninspired, expecting the teacher to tell them what to do and to lecture them on what things mean. I knew their intelligence was strong, but could I convince them to use their brains in school?

My confidence was shaken a little that first day when I reached the open door of B-321 and heard not a sound. Was this the right classroom? Had my room been changed at the last minute?

1

I took a step forward, peeked in the doorway, and saw twenty-four students sitting dead silent in two long rows of fiberglass chairs. They were staring straight ahead at the front desk. They were waiting for the teacher to arrive and do education to them, I thought to myself—one more talking head who would shellack them with grammar and knowledge.

Just then, as I stood in the doorway, all eyes turned in my direction. There were many eyes, but no smiles. New York, my home town, is famous for its tough faces, but these were some of the toughest I had ever seen on students. The class was made up mostly of young white men from Brooklyn, with some women and a few minority students. I looked away from their eyes, quietly took a breath, and strode to the desk, where I put down my shoulder bag and said, "Hello! Welcome to English One. My name is Ira Shor. Why don't we put the chairs in a discussion circle, to make it easier to talk to each other?"

No one moved. I wondered if I should give up on the circle. But maybe it was too soon to retreat. So I stepped forward and asked them once more to form a circle, but deep in my heart I asked myself if it was time to change careers. Should I go sell computers in the suburbs?

The students waited for me to make my move. I reached for one empty chair and turned it around, to confirm my resolve. Then I stood close to some students in the front row and gestured to help them turn their seats. Grudgingly, one, and then another, inched their chairs around into a loose circle, actually more like a wandering amoeba than a circle. The sound of the chairs banging and scraping was a relief from the silence.

I sat down in the circle. I said hello again and asked them to spend a few minutes interviewing each other and then to tell us something about their partners, so that we could get to know who was in the room. This was supposed to be an icebreaker. But some ice can survive August in New York. Their aggressive silence once again greeted my request, so I began pointing out partners for people to work with and nudged them to begin. A few did start talking in pairs, and then a few more, but their conversations crawled, then died.

I was getting impatient, which felt better than anxiety, and I decided to run at the problem instead of away from it. I followed an intuition to make their resistance itself the theme we talked about. I had been developing "critical teaching" and "dialogic pedagogy" that posed problems from student experience for class inquiry. I thought to pose the problem of their silence. Why not have a dialogue about the absence of dialogue? Would they be willing to communicate with me about why they weren't communicating? Who knew? Anyway, I was getting nowhere fast. Confronting their resistance to dialogue might warm up a critical discussion about our icy situation.

I took a small risk and asked them about their silence, saying something like this: "What's going on here? I walk in and nobody wants to move a chair or talk or relate to me. What's the story? You don't even know me. At least get to know me before you decide you don't want to talk. Maybe I'll do a lot of things to make you angry, maybe I won't. Now, who'll tell me why you're sitting so silent?"

After a moment that felt like an hour, one of the bigger guys in class suddenly spoke. His voice was loud and direct. I was so startled to hear even a word that I didn't catch what he said. "What was that?" I asked. He replied, simply, "We hate that test."

"What test?" I asked.

"That writing test," he answered.

"The one you took for the college?"

"Yeah."

"What's wrong with the test?" I asked him.

He looked me dead in the eye and answered, "It ain't fair." I glanced away and saw a few heads nodding in agreement, so I put the question to the class, "Is anyone else angry about the writing test?" Hands shot up around the room.

I should say here that soon after tuition was forced on the City University of New York for the first time in 129 years, in the fiscal crisis of 1976, standardized examinations in writing, reading, and math were also imposed. Since then, these examinations have been given to entering freshmen, producing an enormous amount of failure and frustration as well as a record-keeping nightmare and an expanding empire of remedial classes. More students have had to spend more time and tuition dollars in low-credit remediation, which delays their accumulation of course credits toward a degree. In a few years, the single remedial course in my English department of 1971 had grown to ten separate courses and a college testing program.

After a number of hands shot up in class when I asked if anyone else was angry at the writing test that had landed them in this basic writing course, I asked, "What's wrong with the test? Why is it unfair?"

To my amazement, this silent group began an avalanche of remarks. The students found their voices, enough to carry us through a ferocious hour, once I found a "generative" theme, an issue generated from the problems of their own experience. When I first said hello to them, no one wanted to speak. Now they all wanted to speak at once. My teaching problem shifted from no participation to wrestling with a runaway discussion. They began complaining in outbursts that confirmed each other's feelings. They interrupted each other. They spontaneously broke off into small groups that talked to themselves. It was dizzying until I managed to assert some order. What emerged was a collective sense that the imposed writing exam and this remedial class were unfair punishments.

To give some structure and depth to this perception, I asked them to write for a while, explaining why they thought the requirement was unfair and what should be done about it. I said something like this: "I agree with you that the exam is unfair. I also oppose it. But it's not enough to yell and complain. You have to take your ideas seriously, explain how you see the situation, and come up with an alternative you think makes more sense." I suggested they each write two pages or so about the writing exam. To my great relief, they agreed. For the next twenty minutes, the room was quiet and busy.

When they had finished rough drafts, I asked them to practice writing exercises I'd be asking them to do during the term, exercises which I will explain in a later chapter on the structure of "problem-posing dialogue." Basically, I said that they had powerful voices, as anyone could tell from the talk that had raged around the room a few minutes earlier. They had much to say, displayed broad vocabularies, and spoke fairly grammatically. I encouraged them to use the already existing good grammar in their speaking voices to help improve their less-developed writing hands. In this "voicing" exercise they read aloud their compositions singly or in pairs. By reading aloud slowly and carefully, they can become better editors of their written work, noticing and correcting the small errors usually left for the teacher to find. After voicing, I asked them to read their drafts in groups of three, to discuss the ideas, compare their criticisms, and choose one essay to read to the whole class for discussion. When they chose the material for class discussion, they were codeveloping the curriculum with me, a key idea for critical and democratic teaching, which I will be focusing on in this book. Students formed small groups and spent some time discussing their positions. The first session ended about then, and we picked up the project the next time the class met.

In the ensuing classes, I took notes as the students read their selected essays. Using my notes, I re-presented to them some of the key issues, so that they could reflect on their thoughts, which is one way to develop a critical habit of mind. As it turned out, that basic class evolved an alternative policy for the writing exam which they thought was more sensible and equitable. First, they disagreed with the fifty-minute time limit. They said that students should have as long as they needed to write the best essay they could. This sounded reasonable to me. The

fifty-minute limit is a bureaucratic convenience to control costs by fitting the test into a single class hour. If the time was open-ended, special
proctors would have to be hired to monitor the students. The time limit,
then, benefits the institution, not the students. A developmental writing process requires time to think over the issues, discuss them with
other people, write notes and rough drafts, share them with peers, get
feedback, do relevant reading, and make revisions. The administrative
time limit blocks this process. Further, the students thought that they
should not have required topics. In their opinion, they wrote at their
best not only when they had as much time as they needed but also when
they wrote about what they knew and liked. Sitting down to write about
themes out of the blue, like "Does TV make children violent?" may
make it harder for many of them to write at their best. They proposed
that the two prompts offered on the writing exam should be kept for
those students who wanted to use them, but the others should be free to
pick their own themes. Put simply, the prompt questions on the exam
are often experienced by them as issues without a context. Lastly, they
wanted the exam given at a different point in their academic lives. Many
had taken it in the spring or summer of their senior year in high school
when "senioritis" had set in, jeopardizing the seriousness with which
they do academic work. They thought the exam should be given in the
fall of their senior year, while they were still focused on schoolwork.

   Their policy proposals for the writing exam made sense to me. This
basic skills class of twenty-four students had been unable to pass an apparently simple writing exam, but they were able in a student-centered
classroom to critique the policy and come up with alternatives. The exercise was not only centered in their thoughts, language, and conditions, but it also focused their critical intelligence on an issue they had
not thought about in depth before. Though they had bad feelings
about the test and the remedial class, they had not reflected on the situation. They had simply acted out their bad feelings by refusing to participate in class. By reflecting critically on the problem, they went
beyond mere opinions or bad feelings.

   But some things did not work out well. For one thing, in this class,
student-centered teaching sometimes left me overtaken by events, trying to catch up with student expression. When students codevelop themes
for study and share in the making of the syllabus, the class dialogue
sometimes moves faster than I can understand it or organize it for academic study. Finding a generative theme, that is, a theme generated from
student conditions which is problematic enough to inspire students
to do intellectual work, can produce a wealth of student expression. I
listen carefully in class to students so that I can develop critical study

based in their thoughts, but I often need to go home to mull over what they said and to figure out what to do next. For example, in the exercise over the required writing examination, I would have liked a slower pace to give me time to find material on its history and to bring in articles and documents for the students to discuss. This would add outside texts to the critical dialogue in class, so that the students' essays would not be the only reading matter we examined. When projects emerge in-progress from student themes, the opportunity to deepen academic inquiry about them is often limited by the pace of student-centered dialogue. I kept this in mind for the next round of projects we undertook in this class, to make sure that reading matter would be built into the work.

A second problem was the small participation of the few minority students in class. I encouraged them to speak, met with them after class, and kept in touch with their work. They did their assignments but were reluctant to speak in class. As I will discuss later, this reluctance is understandable on a campus and in classes that are predominantly white and in an area where race relations are tense.

A third problem emerging from this project on the writing examination is that understanding reality is not the same thing as changing it. Knowledge is not exactly power. Knowledge is the power to know, to understand, but not necessarily the power to do or to change. The learning process we shared helped reduce the students' alienation from intellectual work. They gained an empowering relationship to the teacher, to writing, and to the act of studying. But while their writing and thinking developed, the testing policy remained the same. Literacy and awareness by themselves do not change oppressive conditions in school and society. Knowledge is power only for those who can use it to change their conditions.

To face this problem, I invited the class to consider acting on their new knowledge, perhaps to change their oppressive reality while also developing their thinking and writing. If they thought their policy proposals made more sense than the existing ones, why not publish them in the school newspaper, take them to the student government for support, and campaign for them among faculty and other students who might agree with them? I suggested that there were outside arenas where their proposals might have an impact.

A few mulled over my suggestion, but the group as a whole was unenthusiastic about becoming activist. They had never done anything like that before and were not yet ready to try it. In my heart and thoughts, I was a little disappointed but not surprised, given the conservative climate in the country, on our campus, and in their community. So I dropped my proposal, but I did mention that I would talk about their policies whenever I could in faculty meetings, because they were good ones.

For the rest of the term, that class took on ambitious projects. They formed project groups on such self-selected issues as abortion, child abuse, unemployment, education, women's equality, and drugs. Students chose which committee to join. I asked each group to do research and bring to class something for us to read on their theme, to make sure that this next round of projects would integrate outside texts into the discussion. I also brought in reading matter relevant to each of the themes. The groups did research, organized their work during class time and also outside, and then took over a class session. I had wanted them to chair the sessions, to develop their authority and leadership skills, but they were shy and inexperienced in running the class, so I had to sit with each committee and act as chair. During their sessions, the committees offered their readings for discussion, then posed a problem for the whole class to write on for twenty minutes, after which we did some literacy exercises and then had discussion. The committees took home the student papers after class, to read, respond to, and return next time. This way, they became readers and evaluators of each other's work. I read their papers as well, asked for some to be revised at home, and offered exercises when I noticed recurring writing problems in their essays.

I also led discussions on themes and readings of my own choosing. One topic was particularly challenging. I wondered if this basic writing class would participate in the nuclear arms debate then under way in many places but not visible at my college or in their communities. Around the world, many people were alarmed at the spread of nuclear weapons and at the vast sums spent on militarism. To raise this social concern with my students, I read with them various materials, including an excerpt from Thompson and Smith's *Protest and Survive* (1981), about the "destructivist" consciousness spreading as nuclear weapons became a way of life. They struggled with the conceptual frameworks, evaluating their own positions in terms of being destructivist or activist. In general, I was gratified by the seriousness with which they took on this difficult issue. My suggesting an outside social theme like the arms race did not silence the students. I did not lecture them on my point of view but followed the discussion format of their own project groups. During these weeks, one young veteran in class decided to write a critical narrative of his military service, which he had not examined before. He shared a strong essay with the class, which I later published in a professional volume of student writing.

Overall, the class developed an emotional tone which made it attractive. We laughed. We spoke about our differences. The students got down to work in class and organized trips to the beach after class. Attendance was high. I brought a colleague or two to sit in and enjoyed seeing the students emerge as distinct personalities as well as writers and thinkers. There were some memorable moments, too. When the women's group led class, several of the men said that women couldn't do men's work. One tall, muscular guy was especially angry at the city for lowering the physical strength standards for firefighters so that females could qualify. Some male students made the case that women were too weak and unmechanical to do the work of real men, like construction, truck driving, and so on. At that point, Marie, about twenty-two, turned to the men and announced that she was an auto mechanic. For weeks she had kept this to herself. She did not look like the men's idea of a mechanic, but she spoke with confidence when she said that she could tune a car better than any of the guys in the room and was ready to prove it. We looked at her in awed silence. None of the men took up her challenge. Marie's intervention was a real-life rebuttal to the men's sexist prejudice, coming at just the right time. It reminded me that the students are complicated people whose authentic personalities can emerge in the context of meaningful work.

Later on, Marie's authenticity left me in awed silence again. During the abortion committee session, one question was "What would you do if your teenage daughter came home one day and announced she was pregnant?" Students debated various answers. When I turned to a silent Marie and asked her opinion, she said without hesitation, "I'd break both her legs." The class roared with laughter at her matter-of-fact response. I was left speechless by her casual brutality, because I thought of her as a natural feminist who would have an enlightened opinion on teenage pregnancy. Instead, she stood by her position that her daughter would have two broken legs to go along with being pregnant. This reminded me again not to take students for granted. I learn a lot about them, but they are always capable of surprising me with something new. I was stumped by Marie's answer. Not knowing how to respond, I re-presented it to the class and was relieved that few people agreed with this mechanic's solution.

By the end of the term, six of the original twenty-four had dropped out of the class, and I was sorry to see them go. I had a chance to consult with some of them and got a feel for why they left. One student had no front teeth and was ashamed to talk in class. I told him he didn't have to, that he could talk to me in private until he felt ready to speak publicly. But then I discovered that he didn't want to write in class or out, because he was a poor writer. I worked tutorially with him, but he missed appointments and didn't hand in assignments. Apparently he had gotten through high school with very little expected of him, and now was unable to face a serious class. A couple of other students also dropped out when I expected them to rewrite poorly written work.

Eventually, sixteen of the eighteen remaining students passed the writing exam when they took it again at the end of the term. The two who failed made another try a week later. One was Tommy, a bright young guy who handed in work late all term. He was behind in his assignments but produced passing material when I pushed him to get the writing done. On the writing exam in class, he froze and handed in a blank booklet, something I had never expected. Afterwards, to prepare for the exam again, I counseled him on ways to get started when he felt a block. But he failed the test once more, didn't hand in all his missing course work, got an *F* for my class, and took a second-term basic skills class. After that, he finally passed the writing exam and went on to get a *B* in freshman composition.

The other student who failed the exam at the end of my course was Marie, the mechanic. I tutored her, too, before her next try at it. When we finished discussing her failed test paper, she stood up, shook my hand, and said, "Mr. Shor, I ain't gonna write no more comma splices." She then took the exam once more and failed yet again. Apparently resourceful, Marie managed to bypass the exam and another term of basic skills. Instead of prolonged life in the remedial empire, she found her way directly into freshman composition and got an *A*. The next term she took creative writing and got a *B*, all without having passed the entry exam in writing. Good for her. But I still wonder if she will break her future daughter's legs and if she was influenced by our discussion of militarism.

Because most students got through an exam that frustrated their progress in college, the overall results were acceptable to me, but I think many of them could have passed the first time if the test had been structured the way they wanted and if their education had helped them perform at their peak abilities. They also could have gone directly on to freshman composition and, like Marie, passed without the obstacle of remediation. Something is very wrong with their education when it suppresses instead of develops their skills and intellectual interests. They need a different kind of learning, critical and democratic, the kind that will be discussed in this book.

Some classes turn out well enough, like the basic writing group I've discussed here. Others don't. Some groups of students resist all term.

They remain too unhappy with education or too distracted by jobs, commuting, other courses, money problems, family life, or relationships to focus on learning.

Over the years, the classes that resist and those that open up have kept me asking what kind of learning process can empower students to perform at their best. Many teachers want a learning community in class that inspires students whose creative and critical powers are largely untouched. A democratic society needs the creativity and intelligence of its people. The students need a challenging education of high quality that empowers them as thinkers, communicators, and citizens. Conditions in school and society now limit their development. Why? How can that be changed? What helps students become critical thinkers and strong users of language? What education can develop them as active students and as citizens concerned with public life? How can I promote critical and democratic development among students who have learned to expect little from intellectual work and from politics? These are the questions underlying this book.

Education Is Politics
An Agenda for Empowerment

Schooling and the Politics of Socialization

What kind of educational system do we have? What kind do we need? How do we get from one to the other?

Can education develop students as critical thinkers, skilled workers, and active citizens? Can it promote democracy and serve all students equitably?

These big questions preoccupy many people because schooling is a vast undertaking and mass experience in society, involving tens of millions of people, huge outlays of money, and diverse forces contending over curriculum and funding. All this activity converges in schools, programs, and colleges, where each generation is socialized into the life of the nation.

About the role of education in socializing students, Bettelheim said near the end of his life, "If I were a primary-grade teacher, I would devote my time to problems of socialization. The most important thing children learn is not the three R's. It's socialization" (quoted in Meier 1990, 6).

He urged teachers to encourage students to question their experience in school: "You must arouse children's curiosity and make them think about school. For example, it's very important to begin the school year with a discussion of why we go to school. Why does the government force us to go to school? This would set a questioning tone and show the children that you trust them and that they are intelligent enough, at their own level, to investigate and come up with answers" (Meier 1990, 7). A school year that begins by questioning school could be a remarkably democratic and critical learning experience for students.

Bettelheim's concern for the critical habits of students also preoccupied Piaget, who emphasized the restraint and imposition in the socializing function of schools:

To educate is to adapt the child to an adult social environment. . . . The child is called upon to receive from outside the already perfected products of adult knowledge and morality; the educational relationship consists of pressure on the one side and receptiveness on the other. From such a point of view, even the most individual kinds of tasks performed by students (writing an essay, making a translation, solving a problem) partake less of the genuine activity of spontaneous and individual research than of . . . copying an external model; the students' inmost morality remains fundamentally directed toward obedience rather than autonomy. (1979, 137–38)

Piaget urged a reciprocal relationship between teachers and students, where respect for the teacher coexisted with cooperative and student-centered pedagogy. "If the aim of intellectual training is to form the intelligence rather than to stock the memory," Piaget wrote, "and to produce intellectual explorers rather than mere erudition, then traditional education is manifestly guilty of a grave deficiency" (1979, 51). The deficiency is the curriculum in schools, which he saw as a one-way transmission of rules and knowledge from teacher to students, stifling their curiosity.

People are naturally curious. They are born learners. Education can either develop or stifle their inclination to ask why and to learn. A curriculum that avoids questioning school and society is not, as is commonly supposed, politically neutral. It cuts off the students' development as critical thinkers about their world. If the students' task is to memorize rules and existing knowledge, without questioning the subject matter or the learning process, their potential for critical thought and action will be restricted.

In a curriculum that encourages student questioning, the teacher avoids a unilateral transfer of knowledge. She or he helps students develop their intellectual and emotional powers to examine their learning in school, their everyday experience, and the conditions in society. Empowered students make meaning and act from reflection, instead of memorizing facts and values handed to them.

This kind of critical education is not more political than the curriculum which emphasizes taking in and fitting in. *Not* encouraging students to question knowledge, society, and experience tacitly endorses and supports the status quo. A curriculum that does not challenge the standard syllabus and conditions in society informs students that knowledge and the world are fixed and are fine the way they are, with no role for students to play in transforming them, and no need for change. As Freire (1985a) said, education that tries to be neutral supports the dominant ideology in society.

No curriculum can be neutral. All forms of education are political because they can enable or inhibit the questioning habits of students, thus developing or disabling their critical relation to knowledge, schooling, and society. Education can socialize students into critical thought or into dependence on authority, that is, into autonomous habits of mind or into passive habits of following authorities, waiting to be told what to do and what things mean.

From another point of view, the politics of education have been discussed by Apple (1979, 1982, 1988), who emphasized two aspects of teaching which make it *not* neutral:

First, there is an increasing accumulation of evidence that the institution of schooling itself is not a neutral enterprise in terms of its economic outcomes. . . . While schools may in fact serve the interests of many individuals, empirically they also seem to act as powerful agents in the economic and cultural reproduction of class relations. . . . [Second], the knowledge that now gets into schools is already a choice from a much larger universe of possible social knowledge and principles. . . . Social and economic values, hence, are already embedded in the design of the institutions we work in, in the "formal corpus of school knowledge" we preserve in our modes of teaching, and in our principles, standards, and forms of evaluation. (1979, 8–9)

The contents included and excluded in curriculum are political choices while the unequal outcomes of education are not neutral either. But even though the subject matter and the learning process are political choices and experiences, Apple also observed that there was no simple socialization of students into the existing order and no automatic reproduction of society through the classroom. Education is complex and contradictory.

Questioning the Status Quo: The Politics of Empowerment

Education can be described in many ways. One way, suggested above, is to say that education is a contested terrain where people are socialized and the future of society is at stake. On the one hand, education is a socializing activity organized, funded, and regulated by authorities who set a curriculum managed (or changed) in the classroom by teachers. On the other hand, education is a social experience for tens of millions of students who come to class with their own dreams and agendas, sometimes cooperating with and sometimes resisting the intentions of the school and the teacher.

The teacher is the person who mediates the relationship between outside authorities, formal knowledge, and individual students in the classroom. Through day-to-day lessons, teaching links the students' development to the values, powers, and debates in society. The syllabus deployed by the teacher gives students a prolonged encounter with structured knowledge and social authority. However, it is the students who decide to what extent they will take part in the syllabus and allow it to form them. Many students do not like the knowledge, process, or roles set out for them in class. In reaction, they drop out or withdraw into passivity or silence in the classroom. Some become self-educated; some sabotage the curriculum by misbehaving.

To socialize students, education tries to teach them the shape of knowledge and current society, the meaning of past events, the possibilities for the future, and their place in the world they live in. In forming the students' conception of self and the world, teachers can present knowledge in several ways, as a celebration of the existing society, as a falsely neutral avoidance of problems rooted in the system, or as a critical inquiry into power and knowledge as they relate to student experience.

In making these choices, many teachers are unhappy with the limits of the traditional curriculum and do what they can to teach creatively and critically. Whether they deviate from or follow the official syllabus, teachers make numerous decisions—themes, texts, tests, seating arrangements, rules for speaking, grading systems, learning process, and so on. Through these practical choices, the politics of the classroom are defined, as critical or uncritical, democratic or authoritarian.

In class, as Apple suggested and as Giroux (1983) and Banks (1991) have also argued, the choice of subject matter cannot be neutral. Whose history and literature is taught and whose ignored? Which groups are included and which left out of the reading list or text? From whose point of view is the past and present examined? Which themes are emphasized and which not? Is the curriculum balanced and multicultural, giving equal attention to men, women, minorities, and nonelite groups, or is it traditionally male-oriented and Eurocentric? Do students read about Columbus from the point of view of the Arawak people he conquered or only from the point of view of the Europeans he led into conquest? Do science classes investigate the biochemistry of the students' lives, like the nutritional value of the school lunch or the potential toxins in the local air, water, and land, or do they only talk abstractly about photosynthesis?

Politics reside not only in subject matter but in the discourse of the classroom, in the way teachers and students speak to each other. The rules for talking are a key mechanism for empowering or disempowering students. How much open discussion is there in class? How much one-way "teacher-talk"? Is there mutual dialogue between teacher and students or one-way transfers of information from teacher to students?

What do teachers say about the subject matter? Do students feel free to disagree with the teacher? Do students respond to each other's remarks? Do they act like involved participants or like alienated observers in the exchange of comments in the classroom? Are students asked to think critically about the material and to see knowledge as a field of contending interpretations, or are they fed knowledge as an official consensus? Do students work cooperatively, or is the class a competitive exchange favoring the most assertive people?

In addition, the way classrooms, schools, colleges, and programs are governed is political. Is there a negotiated curriculum in class, or is a unilateral authority exercised by the teacher? Is there student, teacher, and parent co-governance of the institution or an administrative monopoly on power?

School funding is another political dimension of education, because more money has always been invested in the education of upper-class children and elite collegians than has been spent on students from lower-income homes and in community colleges. Moreover, testing policies are political choices, whether to use student-centered, multicultural, and portfolio assessments, or to use teacher-centered tests or standardized exams in which women and minorities have traditionally scored lower than men and whites.

In sum, the subject matter, the learning process, the classroom discourse, the cafeteria menu, the governance structure, and the environment of school teach students what kind of people to be and what kind of society to build as they learn math, history, biology, literature, nursing, or accounting. Education is more than facts and skills. It is a socializing experience that helps make the people who make society. Historically, it has underserved the mass of students passing through its gates. Can school become empowering? What educational values can develop people as citizens who think critically and act democratically?

Values for Empowerment

Empowering education, as I define it here, is a critical-democratic pedagogy for self and social change. It is a student-centered program for multicultural democracy in school and society. It approaches individual growth as an active, cooperative, and social process, because the self and society create each other. Human beings do not invent themselves in a vacuum, and society cannot be made unless people create it together. The goals of this pedagogy are to relate personal growth to public life, by developing strong skills, academic knowledge, habits of inquiry, and critical curiosity about society, power, inequality, and change.

The pedagogy described in this book is student-centered but is not permissive or self-centered. Empowerment here does not mean students can do whatever they like in the classroom. Neither can the teacher do whatever she or he likes. The learning process is negotiated, requiring leadership by the teacher and mutual teacher-student authority. In addition, empowerment as I describe it here is not individualistic. The empowering class does not teach students to seek self-centered gain while ignoring public welfare.

Students in empowering classes should be expected to develop skills and knowledge as well as high expectations for themselves, their education, and their futures. They have a right to earn good wages doing meaningful work in a healthy society at peace with itself and the world. Their skills should be welcomed by democratic workplaces in an equitable economy where it becomes easier each year to make ends meet. To build this kind of society, empowering education invites students to become skilled workers and thinking citizens who are also change agents and social critics. Giroux (1988) described this as educating students "to fight for a quality of life in which all human beings benefit." He went on to say, "Schools need to be defended, as an important public service that educates students to be critical citizens who can think, challenge, take risks, and believe that their actions will make a difference in the larger society" (214).

Further, McLaren (1989) discussed this pedagogy as "the process through which students learn to critically appropriate knowledge existing outside their immediate experience in order to broaden their understanding of themselves, the world, and the possibilities for transforming the taken-for-granted assumptions about the way we live" (186). Banks (1991) defined empowerment in terms of transforming self and society: "A curriculum designed to empower students must be transformative in nature and help students to develop the knowledge, skills, and values needed to become social critics who can make reflective decisions and implement their decisions in effective personal, social, political, and economic action" (131).

The teacher leads and directs this curriculum, but does so democratically with the participation of the students, balancing the need for structure with the need for openness. The teacher brings lesson plans, learning methods, personal experience, and academic knowledge to class but negotiates the curriculum with the students and begins with their language, themes, and understandings. To be democratic implies orienting subject matter to student culture—their interests, needs, speech, and perceptions—while creating a negotiable openness in class where the students' input jointly creates the learning process. To be critical in such a democratic curriculum means to examine all subjects and the learning process with systematic depth; to connect student individuality to larger historical and social issues; to encourage students to examine how their experience relates to academic knowledge, to power, and to inequality in society; and to approach received wisdom and the status quo with questions.

For this empowering pedagogy, I will propose an agenda of values, each to be discussed in detail, which describe it as:

• Participatory
• Affective
• Problem-posing
• Situated
• Multicultural
• Dialogic
• Desocializing
• Democratic
• Researching
• Interdisciplinary
• Activist

A Door to Empowerment: Participation

In elaborating these items, I start with the participatory value because this is an interactive pedagogy from the first day of class. Participation is the most important place to begin because student involvement is low in traditional classrooms and because action is essential to gain knowledge and develop intelligence. Piaget insisted on the relation of action to knowing: "Knowledge is derived from action. . . . To know an object is to act upon it and to transform it. . . . To know is therefore to assimilate reality into structures of transformation and these are the structures that intelligence constructs as a direct extension of our actions" (1979, 28–29). With a Deweyan emphasis, Piaget reiterated that we learn by doing and by thinking about our experience.

People begin life as motivated learners, not as passive beings. Children naturally join the world around them. They learn by interacting, by experimenting, and by using play to internalize the meaning of words and experience. Language intrigues children; they have needs they want met; they busy the older people in their lives with questions and requests for show me, tell me. But year by year their dynamic learning erodes in passive classrooms not organized around their cultural backgrounds, conditions, or interests. Their curiosity and social instincts decline, until many become nonparticipants. It is not the fault of students if their learning habits wither inside the passive syllabus dominant in education.

Participatory classes respect and rescue the curiosity of students. As Dewey argued, participation in school and society is crucial to learning and to democracy:

> There is, I think, no point in the philosophy of progressive education which is sounder than its emphasis upon the importance of the participation of the learner in the formation of the purposes which direct his activities in the learning process, just as there is no defect in traditional education greater than its failure to secure the active cooperation of the pupil in construction of the purposes involved in his studying. (1963, 67)

Dewey emphasized participation as the point at which democracy and learning meet in the classroom. For him, participation was an educational and political means for students to gain knowledge and to develop as citizens. Only by active learning could students develop scientific method and democratic habits rather than becoming passive pupils waiting to be told what things mean and what to do.

Politically, for Dewey, participation is democratic when students construct purposes and meanings. This is essential behavior for citizens in a free society. Dewey defined a slave as someone who carried out the intentions of another person, who was prevented from framing her or his own intentions. To be a thinking citizen in a democracy, Dewey maintained, a person had to take part in making meaning, articulating purposes, carrying out plans, and evaluating results.

Dewey's connecting of participation with democracy underscored the political nature of all forms of education. Rote learning and skills drills in traditional classrooms do more than bore and miseducate students; they also inhibit their civic and emotional developments. Students learn to be passive or cynical in classes that transfer facts, skills, or values without meaningful connection to their needs, interests, or community cultures. To teach skills and information without relating them to society and to the students' contexts turns education into an authoritarian transfer of official words, a process that severely limits student development as democratic citizens.

Free public schooling and low-cost mass higher education are often celebrated as triumphs of democracy. Why, then, does the traditional curriculum in these institutions tilt toward authority rather than to freedom, participation, and mutuality? Silberman (1970) blamed it on "mindlessness," on the thoughtless functioning of a bureaucratic education system. But more than carelessness and bureaucracy are at work here. Clark (1960, 1978) spoke of a "cooling-out process" in mass colleges that depresses the aspirations of non-elite students in an economy with limited rewards. In an unequal society, there is simply not enough to go around, and the bulk of students are encouraged to settle for less while blame is transferred from the college to them. Examining the economic system closely, Bowles and Gintis (1976) identified a "correspondence principle" between authoritarianism and inequality in the economy and in education. To them, schooling supports existing power and divisions in society by sorting students into a small elite destined for the top and a large mass destined for the middle and the bottom—an educational policy also studied carefully by Spring (1989) and by Oakes (1985). I would add that nonparticipatory education corresponds to the exclusion of ordinary people from policy-making in society at large. Students come of age in a society where average people do not participate in governance, in framing major purposes, in making policy, or in having a strong voice in media and public affairs. Banks do not hold elections on their investments or credit policies. Bosses and supervisors are appointed by owners and higher management; they cannot be voted in or out by the staffs below them. Hospitals are governed by appointed bureaucrats, not by delegates accountable to the clientele. General elections have become an alienating process that discourages people from voting, while politicians depend on the wealthy's contributions to finance their media campaigns. Expensive campaigns and restrictive electoral laws discourage new political organizations and thus protect the power of the two established parties. The mass media have become international conglomerates, detached from the communities they publish for or broadcast to.

About the weakness of democratic power in society, Apple comments: "To many people, the very idea of regaining any real control over social institutions and personal development is abstract and 'nonsensical.' In general . . . many people do see society's economic, social, and educational institutions as basically self-directing, with little need for their participation and with little necessity for them to communicate and argue over the ends and means of these same institutions" (1979, 163). In this social setting, passive curricula help prepare students for life in undemocratic institutions. Students do not practice democratic habits in co-governing their classrooms, schools, or colleges. There, they learn that unilateral authority is the normal way things are done in society. They are introduced in school to the reality of management holding dominant, unelected power. At the same time, they are told that they live in freedom and democracy.

While principals, teachers, and textbooks may lecture students on freedom, nonparticipatory classrooms prepare them for the authoritarian work world and political system they will join. In postsecondary education, nonparticipatory classes confirm the undemocratic experiences of adults in school and society. Teacher-centered curricula in the classroom and administration-centered power in the school or college reflect the reality of other social institutions. Traditional schools thus prepare students to fit into an education and a society not run for them or by them but rather set up for and run by elites.

Many students do not accept these limits, which is why teachers often face resistance in the classroom. Many teachers also refuse to be undemocratic educators, which limits the extent to which the official syllabus and authority can be imposed on students. In this conflicted setting, the empowering educator transforms the teacher's unilateral authority. She or he offers a participatory process to students with little experience in democratic learning, in institutions generally hostile to challenges to authority.

Participation challenges the experience of education as something done to students. This is key to the passivity and resistance produced by the traditional syllabus: education is experienced by students as something done to them, not something they do. They see it as alien and controlling. To reverse this passive experience of learning, education for empowerment is not something done by teachers to students for their own good but is something students codevelop for themselves, led by a critical and democratic teacher. Participation from the first day of class is needed to establish the interactive goals of this pedagogy, to shake students out of their learned withdrawal from intellectual and civic life.

That learned withdrawal evolves in traditional schooling as students spend thousands of hours hearing lectures, instructions, rules, interpretations, information, announcements, grade reports, exhortations, and warnings. Many withdraw from intellectual work because they are told so much and asked to think and do so little. Rote drills drain their enthusiasm for intellectual life, as do short-answer exams and standardized tests. These familiar methods disable their intellects in a process I call endullment, the dulling of students' minds as a result of their nonparticipation.

Resisting Endullment: The "Performance Strike"

In school and society, the lack of meaningful participation alienates workers, teachers, and students. This alienation lowers their productivity in class and on the job. I think of this lowered productivity as a performance strike, an unorganized mass refusal to perform well, an informal and unacknowledged strike.

Nonparticipatory institutions depress the performance levels of people working in them. Mass education has become notorious for the low motivation of many students (and the burnout of many teachers).

Large numbers of students are refusing to perform at high levels, demoralizing the teachers who work with them. At times, performance strikes become organized resistance to authority, with leadership and articulate demands. But most often the students' refusal to perform appears as low motivation, low test scores and achievement, and a "discipline problem." These manifestations of the performance strike keep authority at bay in class. They are ways to refuse cooperation with a system that invests unequally in students and denies them participation in curriculum and governance.

In classrooms where participation is meager, the low performance of students is routinely misjudged as low achievement. But the actual cognitive levels of students are hard to measure in teacher-centered classrooms where students participate minimally. An accurate picture of what students know and can do is possible only when students really want to perform at their best. In a participatory process, where students codevelop the course, teachers can learn better the actual cognitive levels of students from which to design forward development. Until students experience lively participation, mutual authority, and meaningful work, they will display depressed skills and knowledge, as well as negative emotions. Teachers will be measuring and reacting to an artificially low picture of student abilities.

This is where the affective value of empowerment, second on the agenda defined above, crosses paths with the first value of participation. Participation provides students with active experiences in class, through which they develop knowledge that is reflective understanding, not mere memorization. Further, participation sends a hopeful message to students about their present and future; it encourages their achievement by encouraging their aspirations. They are treated as responsible, capable human beings who should expect to do a lot and do it well, an affective feature of the empowering classroom that I will have more to say about shortly.

A participatory pedagogy, designed from cooperative exercises, critical thought, student experience, and negotiated authority in class, can help students feel they are in sufficient command of the learning process to perform at their peak. From Dewey to Piaget to Freire, many educators have asserted that learning works best when it is an active, creative process (Bissex 1980; Smith 1983; Wertsch 1985). The National Institute of Education (1984) cited student involvement as the most important reform needed in undergraduate education: "There is now a good deal of research evidence to suggest that the more time and effort students invest in the learning process and the more intensely they engage in their own education, the greater will be their growth and achievement, their satisfaction with their educational experiences, and their persistence in college, and the more likely they are to continue their learning" (17). The NIE urged faculty to use more "active modes of teaching" instead of the familiar lecture method. In another report, the Association of American Colleges (1985) also focused on student participation in learning, departing from the conservative demands for more testing and traditional content that dominated the 1980s: "The prevailing spirit of pedagogy should reduce the possibilities for passivity in students and authoritarianism in faculties. Students should undertake a variety of pedagogical approaches—seminars, lectures, research, field study, tutorials, theses" (26). This study identified key interdisciplinary themes rather than narrow content as the foundation for undergraduate study, thus challenging the drift in the 1980s toward transferring more official information to students.

To take participation into an empowering terrain, I would add that the more involved the student, the more he or she wrestles with meaning in the study, exercises his or her critical voice in a debate with peers, and expresses his or her values in a public arena, where they can be examined and related to conditions in society. This is what Giroux (1988) emphasized as the "public sphere" of education, or education as an activity that could invigorate the life of a democracy if it became critical and empowering. When education is a participatory sphere of public life, meaning and purpose are constructed mutually, not imposed from the top down as orthodoxies. The participatory classroom is a "free speech" classroom in the best sense, because it invites all expressions from all the students. An empowering class thrives on a lively exchange of thoughts and feelings. The way students speak, feel, and think about any subject is the starting point for a critical study of themselves, their society, and their academic subjects.

Participatory learning also opens the possibility of transforming the students'-powers of thought. For Freire, "transformation is possible because consciousness is not a mirror of reality, not a mere reflection, but is *reflexive and reflective* of reality" (Shor and Freire 1987, 13). When we participate in critical classes, we can go beyond merely repeating what we know or what we have been taught. We can reflect on reality and on our received values, words, and interpretations in ways that illuminate meanings we hadn't perceived before. This reflection can transform our thought and behavior, which in turn have the power to alter reality itself if enough people reconstruct their knowledge and take action. Freire explained the process: "As conscious human beings, we can discover *how* we are conditioned by the dominant ideology. We can gain distance on our moment of existence. . . . We can struggle to become free precisely because we can know we are not free! That is why we can think of transformation" (Shor and Freire 1987, 13). Human beings are capable of overcoming limits if they can openly examine them. The participatory class offers that possibility.

Integrating Cognitive and Affective Learning

As I have said, participation involves affective as well as cognitive development. Empowering education is not only rationalistic, as Peter Elbow (1986) argued in a critique of Freire's work. Contrary to Elbow's reading, critical learning in this model is emotional as well as rational. Critical thought is simultaneously a cognitive and affective activity. But if empowering education involves both intellectual and emotional elements, so does traditional, teacher-centered education. In its own way, the standard syllabus is also jointly rational and emotional. This is true because education is a social experience, as Dewey (1963) understood it, not a moment of disembodied intellect. Learning cannot be reduced to a purely intellectual activity. It is more than a mental operation and more than the facts or ideas transmitted by books or lectures. Education is a complex experience of one kind or another. As an experience of human beings in a specific community at a certain moment in history and in their lives, it is a social interaction involving both thought and feeling.

The difference between empowering and traditional pedagogy has to do with the positive or negative feelings students can develop for the learning process. In traditional classrooms, negative emotions are provoked in students by teacher-centered politics. Unilateral teacher authority in a passive curriculum arouses in many students a variety of negative emotions: self-doubt, hostility, resentment, boredom, indignation, cynicism, disrespect, frustration, the desire to escape. These student affects are commonly generated when an official culture and language are imposed from the top down, ignoring the students' themes, languages, conditions, and diverse cultures. Their consequent negative feelings interfere with learning and lead to strong anti-intellectualism in countless students as well as to alienation from civic life.

The competitive practices and emotions dominating traditional education also interfere with the cognitive development of many students. Sapon-Shevin and Schniedewind (1991) point to this affective and cognitive impact of competition on students:

The typical classroom is framed by competition, marked by struggle between students (and often between teacher and students), and riddled by indicators of comparative achievement and worth. Star charts on the wall announce who has been successful at learning multiplication tables, only children with "neat" handwriting have their papers posted for display. . . . Competition encourages people to survey other people's differences for potential weak spots. . . . We learn to ascribe winner or loser status based on certain perceived overt characteristics, such as boys are better at math. . . . The interpersonal outcomes of competition—rivalry, envy, and contempt—all encourage blaming the loser and justifying their "deserved" fate. (164–65)

They conclude that "this competitive orientation leads to isolation and alienation" among students, encouraging a handful of "winners" while depressing the performance of the many, especially female students and minorities, who withdraw from the aggressive affect of the classroom.

In class, then, teacher-centered competitive pedagogy can interfere with the positive feelings many students need to learn. The authoritarian traditional curriculum itself generates bad feelings which lead many students to resist or sabotage the lessons.

In contrast, an empowering educator seeks a positive relationship between feeling and thought. He or she begins this search by offering a participatory curriculum. In a participatory class where authority is mutual, some of the positive affects which support student learning include cooperativeness, curiosity, humor, hope, responsibility, respect, attentiveness, openness, and concern about society. There are, of course, conflicts in empowering classrooms, chiefly among students with different values and needs, and between students and the teacher in the negotiation of meaning and requirements. In addition, the participatory class can also provoke anxiety and defensiveness in some students because it is an unfamiliar program for collaborative learning and for the critique of received values and taken-for-granted knowledge.

I will have more to say on student resistance to empowering classes in a later chapter, because the positive affect sought by critical teachers is not a simple objective. For now, I want to suggest that conflicts cannot be prevented and cannot always be negotiated successfully even in a participatory classroom. But a democratic and cooperative process provides the best chance for the constructive resolution of conflict between teachers and students, as Schniedewind and Davidson (1987) and Sapon-Shevin and Schniedewind (1991) have argued in their reviews of classroom research and in their models for cooperative learning. In a participatory, collaborative class, conflicts and complaints can be expressed openly and negotiated mutually, which increases the possibility of solving them or at least maintaining a working relationship in the group. In teacher-centered classes, student alienation is provoked and then driven underground, where it becomes a subterranean source of acting out. The traditional learning process lacks a mutual dialogue through which all sides can negotiate their positions. This bottling up of bad feelings undermines the transfer of knowledge in the official syllabus.

The affective atmosphere of a participatory classroom also aims for a productive relationship between patience and impatience. On the one hand, the critical teacher has to balance restraint and intervention. She or he must lead the class energetically while patiently enabling students to develop their thoughts, agendas, and abilities for leading. The teacher has to offer questions, comments, structure, and academic knowledge while patiently listening to students' criticisms and initiatives as they codevelop the syllabus. The patient critical teacher is also impatient to propel students' development so that they take more responsibility for their learning. This tension between patience and impatience also suggests an evolving willingness in students and teachers to study deliberately while desiring to act critically on the knowledge gained. As Freire pointed out, the "patiently impatient" student or teacher does not act unilaterally or impulsively. But neither does she or he reflect forever. Patience and impatience are part of the challenge of gaining critical knowledge and using it to transform learning and society. Put simply, it takes impatience with the way things are to motivate people to make changes, but then it takes patience to study and to develop the projects through which constructive learning and change are made.

Further, regarding the affective side of empowering pedagogy, in Freire's conversations with Myles Horton, the legendary founder of the Highlander School in Tennessee, both men insisted on the relationship of play and joy to critical thought and social change. Here they are talking about the labor workshops at Highlander in the 1930s, which included role-playing about workplace grievances and about organizing strikes:

Myles: We tried to involve everybody in singing and doing drama and dancing and laughing and telling stories because that's a part of their life. It's more of a holistic approach to education, not just a bunch of unrelated segments. The way people live was more important than any class or subject that we were dealing with. . . . They had that learning experience, making decisions, living in an unsegregated fashion, enjoying their senses other than their minds. . . .

Paulo: No matter where this kind of educator works, the great difficulty (or the great adventure!) is how to make education something which, in being serious, rigorous, methodical, and having a process, also creates happiness and joy. . . .

Then for me one of the problems we have as educators in our line is how never, never to lose this complexity of our action. . . . I cannot understand a school which makes children sad about going to school. This school is bad. But I also don't accept a school in which the kids spend all the time just playing. This school is also bad. The good school is that one in which in studying I also get the pleasure of playing. (Horton and Freire 1990, 168–72)

The denial of positive feelings begins in the traditional curriculum, not in critical programs oriented for empowerment. This state of bad feeling was confirmed by John Goodlad (1984) in an eight-year study of schools in the United States. Goodlad found many problems, among them a remarkable lack of positive emotions in the classroom. Twenty-five years earlier, Jerome Bruner (1959) had toured American classrooms, where he found a similar lack of passion for learning.

In traditional classes, affective and cognitive life are in an unproductive conflict. Students learn that education is something to put up with, to tolerate as best they can, to obey, or to resist. Their role is to answer questions, not to question answers. In passive settings, they have despairing and angry feelings about education, about social change, and about themselves. They feel imposed on by schooling. They expect to be lectured at and bored by an irrelevant curriculum. They wait to be told what to do and what things mean. Some follow instructions; others go around them; some manipulate the teacher; still others undermine the class. In such an environment, many students become cynical, identifying intellectual life with dullness and indignity.

To help move students away from passivity and cynicism, a powerful signal has to be sent from the very start, a signal that learning is participatory, involving humor, hope, and curiosity. A strong participatory and affective opening broadcasts optimistic feelings about the students' potential and about the future: students are people whose voices are worth listening to, whose minds can carry the weight of serious intellectual work, whose thought and feeling can entertain transforming self and society.

Student Participation and Positive Affect: The Teacher's Role

The teacher plays a key role in the critical classroom. Student participation and positive emotions are influenced by the teacher's commitment to both. One limit to this commitment comes from the teacher's development in traditional schools where passive, competitive, and authoritarian methods dominated. As students, teachers learned early and often that to be a teacher means talking a lot and being in charge. Prior school experiences leave teachers with what Giroux (1983) called "sedi-

mented" histories and Britzman (1986) "institutional biographies"—
the values layered into professional behavior from years of traditional
education. The heart of the problem is that teachers are taught to lecture and give orders. These old habits have been overcome by many
creative and democratic teachers now practicing in the classroom, but
the change is not easy.

To help myself and the students develop participatory habits, I begin
teaching from the students' situation and from their understanding of
the subject matter, in line with Bettelheim's suggestion that students
should start out by questioning the material and the process of schooling. I often ask students to tell me in writing why they took the class,
what they want from it, and what suggestions they have for running it
or improving their education at the college. In a Utopian literature class
I teach, a student once suggested that there should be no required attendance in our class or in others. She argued that attending class in her
other courses had been a waste of time because she was able to do the
work on her own. Instead of responding immediately, I posed her ideas
back to the class, to see what other students thought. Some agreed with
her strenuously, saying that they should not have to come to class if they
could do the work on their own. I then asked, "Is there nothing special
to be gained by students and teachers meeting in class to talk over ideas?
How often in life do you set aside time just for intellectual growth?"
They were not impressed. They reported being bored and silenced by
didactic lectures in classes where teachers raced to cover the material
and ignored their questions. They were convinced that if they could
copy a friend's class notes, read the textbook, and talk to each other on
the phone, they would get just as good an education as they got by coming to class. Their alienation from the traditional learning process sur-
faced early and became the starting theme for negotiating our own
class. I argued for required attendance because I was, as I told them,
committed to a mutual learning community, a concept I briefly explained, but I offered them the right at any moment to complain, object, protest, and announce that they were bored, impatient, angry, or
unhappy with the process. I said that when they felt bad about the class,
they should speak up, explain why, and suggest a change in the day's
work or the syllabus, which we would then discuss. After debate, students accepted my proposal for required attendance but built into it al-
lowable absences and lateness. In the following months, they asserted
their protest rights a few times and stopped class dialogue that bored
them. They also complained to me outside class individually and in a
special "after-class" group I set up to discuss the work of the session, to

evaluate the learning under way, and to make changes for the next class. I will have more to say in a later chapter about this special group, as a means to democratize authority, but I can report here that it stimulated an unusual amount of participation.

In the first session of an introduction to journalism class, to encourage immediate participation and questioning I routinely ask students to define what "news" means to them and to write down questions they have about the news. Their definitions and questions launch our class discussion, not a lecture by me. I record their questions and statements, collate them, and then re-present them for students to decide which are the most important. Here are some key questions chosen by one class as their starting issues for class discussion:

• Is there a body that regulates the ethics of newspapers? Why isn't the media more accountable for its actions? How can one be certain that the news is accurate?

• Why are the owners of news media allowed to set the tone and make their papers or stations slanted?

• If it's true that news media lean to the left or the right wing, isn't it likely that those presenting the dominant opinion are the more successful? If so, how do opposing views survive?

• What can journalism teach me if I don't go into the field?

• Is TV news driven by entertainment values? Is that happening more as people go directly into TV without having training in print?

Their questions provided some wonderful launching pads for our study. Instead of answering their questions in brief lectures, I posed them one by one, so that students could participate more, answer their peer's questions as best they could, practice thinking out loud, and display what they already knew—all this before I provided any academic response. The syllabus was built upward from student responses instead of downward from my comments. This political change of direction in the making of a democratic curriculum is a way to authorize students as co-developers of their education. With some authority, they can feel co-ownership of the process, which in turn will reduce their resistance.

In another class, a literature course on the American Dream, I began by asking students to write their definitions of the American Dream and a short essay on whether they believed in it or not. The class held divided views on this issue and debated their differences. Their compositions became the initial texts for class discussion and for entry into literary works. Again, I did not begin by lecturing on the subject, for I did not want to pre-empt their participation or thinking by giving them a definition of the American Dream. Further, I avoided communicating my own affect in relation to the theme. By keeping my emotion and intellect low-profile, I tried to avoid provoking their desire to copy my words and values for a good grade. After they had established their own positions, I joined in the discussion with mine.

In short, their words and their ideas are the points from which the class begins a critical journey forward. For me to provide lectures first would risk provoking passivity or hostility in students. It would also cheat me and the students from making contact in class with student subjectivity—their real language, feelings, and understandings. The participatory opening draws out students' knowledge, literacy, and affect toward academic work. I need exposure to these factors as the base on which to structure the subject matter. In traditional classrooms, teachers routinely begin by defining the subject matter and the proper feeling to have about the material rather than by asking students to define their sense of it and feeling about it, and building from there.

Overall, it would be hard to exaggerate the crucial role participation plays in the teacher's attempt to encourage positive feelings toward learning. In participatory, cooperative classrooms, the walls between teacher and students have a chance to become lower. Freire referred to the separation of teachers and students as the first obstacle to learning. To bring them together, teachers can identify themes and words important to students and ask them to be coinvestigators of that material with the teacher. Freire (1970) argued the case for coinvestigation: "Through dialogue, the teacher-of-the-students and the students-of-the-teachers cease to exist and a new term emerges: teacher-student with students-teachers. . . . They become jointly responsible for a process in which all grow" (67). Participation and affective growth are not, of course, brought about by lecturing students on the value of participation and good feelings. The class hour itself is structured so that students reflect on meaningful questions and influence the direction of the syllabus.

While a participatory classroom cannot transform society by itself, it can offer students a critical education of high quality, an experience of democratic learning, and positive feelings toward intellectual life. That experience may spread through many classrooms if enough teachers undertake it as a project in a single institution. In turn, if participatory approaches become a leading response to student alienation and teacher burnout, the progressive impact of democratic learning may be felt broadly in education, and eventually outside education, by orienting students to democratic transformation of society by their active citizenship. The more widespread the practice of participatory empowerment in classrooms and schools, the greater will be the challenge to unilateral authority in and out of educational institutions. As teachers see other teachers and students experimenting, more may be encouraged to test participatory empowerment in their own classrooms, and in the process promote the positive emotions that students need in order to embrace critical and democratic learning as the politics of their education.

Problem-Posing

Situated and Multicultural Learning

2

The Teacher as Problem-Poser

To build an empowering program, the participatory and affective values discussed in the last chapter are foundations for teacher-student cooperation. Another means to engage students in critical and mutual learning can be found in the third value on the agenda, problem-posing. In this chapter, I will survey some aspects of problem-posing and will later offer a detailed model for using it in the classroom.

Problem-posing has roots in the work of Dewey and Piaget, who urged active, inquiring education, through which students constructed meaning in successive phases and developed scientific habits of mind. They favored student-centered curricula oriented to the making of knowledge rather than to the memorizing of facts. Many educators have agreed with this dynamic approach, including Freire, who evolved from it his method of "problem-posing dialogue." In a Freirean model for critical learning, the teacher is often defined as a problem-poser who leads a critical dialogue in class, and problem-posing is a synonym for the pedagogy itself.

As a pedagogy and social philosophy, problem-posing focuses on power relations in the classroom, in the institution, in the formation of standard canons of knowledge, and in society at large. It considers the social and cultural context of education, asking how student subjectivity and economic conditions affect the learning process. Student culture as well as inequality and democracy are central issues to problem-posing educators when they make syllabi and examine the climate for learning.

Freire (1970) used his well-known metaphor of "banking education" to contrast the politics of traditional methods with problem-posing. Banking educators treat students' minds as empty accounts into which they make deposits of information, through didactic lectures and from commercial texts. The material deposited in students is drawn from the "central bank of knowledge." The central bank in any society is a meta-

31

phoric repository of official knowledge. As a store of cultural capital, the central bank is comprised of the standard syllabus in schools and colleges; traditional canons in academic disciplines; established scientific and technical knowledge; "correct usage" considered to be standard for writing and speaking; and works of art canonized as models of aesthetic excellence. It is material selected by those with the power to set standards. A good example of a central bank of knowledge is the sixty-four-page list of items appended to E. D. Hirsch's *Cultural Literacy* (1987), and his two subsequent volumes, the *Dictionary of Cultural Literacy* (1988) for adults, and *A First Dictionary of Cultural Literacy* (1989) for children. From these lists, Hirsch codified facts that he said every American ought to know and developed his findings into grade-by-grade curriculum guides. Coupled with his promotion of Standard English as the only dialect worth studying, Hirsch thus provided a Eurocentric canon of information, works, and usage for teachers to transfer to students.

Hirsch and other traditionalists like Bloom (1987) and Ravitch and Finn (1987) present standard canons of knowledge as universal, excellent, and neutral. They do not present them as historical choices of some groups whose usage and culture are privileged in society. Instead, the central bank is delivered to students as a common culture belonging to everyone, even though not everyone has had an equal right to add to it, take from it, critique it, or become part of it. This body of knowledge, according to its supporters, is society's essential facts, artifacts, words, and ideas. But at root, the central bank underlying the standard curriculum is a deficit model for most students. It represents them as deficient, devoid of culture and language, needing to be filled with official knowledge. The transfer of this knowledge to students is thus a celebration of the status quo which downplays nontraditional student culture and the problem of social inequality.

In contrast, problem-posing offers all subject matter as historical products to be questioned rather than as universal wisdom to be accepted. From this perspective, the central bank is viewed as exclusionary rather than inclusive. From a critical point of view, existing canons of knowledge and usage are not a common culture; they have ignored the multicultural themes, idioms, and achievements of nonelite groups, such as women, minorities, homosexuals, and working people. The empowering teacher who denies universal status to the dominant culture also denies emptiness in students. They are not deficits; they are complex, substantial human beings who arrive in class with diverse cultures; they have languages, interests, feelings, experiences, and perceptions. The responsibility of the problem-posing teacher is to diversify subject matter and to use students' thought and speech as the base for developing critical understanding of personal experience, unequal conditions in society, and existing knowledge. In this democratic pedagogy, the teacher is not filling empty minds with official or unofficial knowledge but is posing knowledge in any form as a problem for mutual inquiry.

Before Freire coined his banking metaphor and his proposal for problem-posing, Dewey offered the metaphor of "pouring in" to criticize the practice of filling students with information and skills. "Why is it," he asked, "in spite of the fact that teaching by pouring in, learning by a passive absorption, are universally condemned, that they are still entrenched in practice?" (1966, 38). Decades after he first asked the question, classes that poured a traditional syllabus into students still predominated in the school system, according to studies by Goodlad (1984) and Boyer (1984). At the turn of the century, Dewey answered his own impatient question about pouring prescribed content into students. He found that schools lacked the "agencies" or the means for experiential, interactive education. They needed programs, methods, equipment, and facilities built around active learning, where students would draw conclusions in their own words from observation, analysis, experimentation, and experience. Besides the lack of agencies that Dewey noted, there is also political opposition to student participation because it challenges power relations in school and society. In this regard, Freire's contribution was the problem-posing approach, a mutual process for students and teachers to question existing knowledge, power, and conditions.

Freire shared Dewey's impatience with passive lecturing and his insistence that learning required participation and inquiry. He developed Dewey's critique of schooling by emphasizing how the banking or pouring-in method is authoritarian politics. Because it deposits information uncritically in students, the banking model is antidemocratic. It denies the students' indigenous culture and their potential for critical thought, subordinating them to the knowledge, values, and language of the status quo. Writing before he stopped using only *man, men,* and the masculine pronouns when referring to people in general, Freire elaborated on the term *liberation:*

Authentic liberation—the process of humanization—is not another deposit to be made in people. Liberation is a praxis: the action and reflection of men upon their world in order to transform it. Those truly committed to the cause of liberation can accept neither the mechanistic concept of consciousness as an empty vessel to be filled, nor the use of banking methods of domination (propaganda, slogans—deposits) in the name of liberation. (Freire 1970, 66)

In banking education, knowledge and society are assumed to be fixed and assumed to be fine the way they are. By limiting creative and critical questioning, the banking model makes education into an authoritarian transfer instead of a democratic experience. Any material imposed by authority as doctrine stops being knowledge and becomes dogma. Critical learning and democratic education end where orthodoxy begins.

Against orthodoxy, problem-posing asserts that standard knowledge in the central bank is not neutral but is rather a means through which the status quo tries to promote and protect its position. When official canons are challenged by new paradigms, movements, or curricula, there is often a bruising battle between contending forces, not a welcoming of the new material that challenges the interests represented by the old. The hostile reception in the mass media and in academic circles in the United States to feminist and multicultural studies since the 1960s exemplifies the political nature of apparently neutral knowledge. Banks (1991) reflected on the conflict over knowledge which had been under way in the United States for several decades:

> The demand for a reformulation of the curriculum canon has evoked a concerted and angry reaction from established mainstream scholars. They have described the push by ethnic and feminist scholars for a reformulation of the canon as an attempt to politicize the curriculum and to promote "special interests." Two national organizations have been formed . . . to resist the efforts by ethnic and feminist scholars to reformulate the canon and to transform the school and university curriculum so that it will more accurately reflect the experience, visions, and goals of women and people of color. (127)

Banks was referring to the Madison Center and to the National Association of Scholars as well as to the "political correctness" campaign launched by academic and media conservatives in the late 1980s. Existing orthodoxies resist change because the standard curriculum represents more than knowledge; it represents the shape of power in school and society. Curriculum is one place where the dominant culture can either be supported or challenged, depending on the way knowledge is presented and studied.

Knowledge has always been a place where forces contend for power, as Galileo discovered in his conflicts with the Vatican, as slaveholders in the American South understood when they made it illegal to teach slaves to read or write, and as the Bush White House demonstrated when it imposed strict censorship on the coverage of the Gulf War. In no society is knowledge a neutral terrain. Because some groups in history have had the power to establish standard knowledge and standard usage, these canons need to be studied critically, not absorbed as a bogus common culture.

The problem-posing approach views human beings, knowledge, and society as unfinished products in history, where various forces are still contending. Freire emphasized problem-posing as a democratic way for students to take part in the contention over knowledge and the shape of society:

> Problem-posing education affirms men as beings in the process of *becoming*—as unfinished, uncompleted beings in and with a likewise unfinished reality. . . . The banking method emphasizes permanence and becomes reactionary; problem-posing education—which accepts neither a "well-behaved" present nor a predetermined future—roots itself in the dynamic present and becomes revolutionary. . . . Whereas the banking method directly or indirectly reinforces men's fatalistic perception of their situation, the problem-posing method presents this very situation to them as a problem. (1970, 72–73)

This does not mean that students have nothing to learn from biology or mathematics or engineering as they now exist. Neither does it mean that students reinvent subject matter each time they study it or that the academic expertise of the teacher has no role in the classroom. Formal bodies of knowledge, standard usage, and the teacher's academic background all belong in critical classrooms. As long as existing knowledge is not presented as facts and doctrines to be absorbed without question, as long as existing bodies of knowledge are critiqued and balanced from a multicultural perspective, and as long as the students' own themes and idioms are valued along with standard usage, existing canons are part of critical education. What students and teachers reinvent in problem-posing is their relationship to learning and authority. They redefine their relationships to each other, to education, and to expertise. They re-perceive knowledge and power. As allies for learning and for democracy in school and society, they stop being adversaries divided by unilateral authority and fixed canons.

Thus, in problem-posing, students don't reinvent biology or engineering or literature each time they study them, and they don't throw grammar and the teacher out of the room; but they do study biology, engineering, literature and grammar in a critical context with a teacher who practices democratic authority and who deploys a multicultural syllabus. They ask why the official textbook and syllabus are organized the way they are and how this knowledge relates to their community cultures and to conditions in society. They ask why the books and readings in the syllabus were chosen and what readings are left out of the official texts. Critical students want to know what they are not being taught as well as what they are being told. They do not wait for the teacher to "do" education to them. They frame purposes and codevelop the syllabus and the learning process.

For example, in a problem-posing class that is studying the muscles of the human hand or the structure of the eye, these bodies of knowledge will be offered in a context that is functional to student life and work and that reveals critical problems in society. First, the teacher would ask students what questions they have about the subject matter. Their questions or issues are the starting points for discussion. In a class studying the hand and the eye in the context of designing office furniture and computers, the class could then interview clerical workers at the school or college, to ground the course in the furniture and the computers at use in their immediate situation. The teacher might introduce the history of clerical work as low-paid women's employment. The medical effects of long-term exposure to video display terminals would be one area of research included in this design class, and another would be hand ailments arising from repetitious functions, like keyboard operations to enter data. I am suggesting here a critical context in which technology design and knowledge of the hand and the eye would be studied sociologically and historically, not just technically, for the purpose of making people-centered furniture and computers.

Moreover, problem-posing computer science would integrate questions like these into the syllabus: Who controls the design, functioning, and marketing of computers? Which groups in society use them for what purposes? Which groups lack them? What would enable computer-deprived groups to use them? What is the impact of computers on employment (for example, industrial and clerical computerization replacing workers and enabling close surveillance of remaining employees by management)? How do computers promote or diminish democracy in society and at work?

A problem-posing health science class could begin by asking students to define the difference between health and illness, in their own words, and trace the process by which human beings go from one condition to the other. The students could list the health issues most important to them. Their definitions and questions would comprise the basic material of the syllabus. To develop a critical study of health in society, the problem-posing teacher could go on to ask: Why is there so much diabetes, cancer, and heart disease in the United States? What is the typical diet like, and how does it affect these diseases? What local environmental conditions are implicated in causing them? What groups have special interests in maintaining the current diet and current environ-

mental conditions? Does the school (or college or office) cafeteria practice healthy menu making and sound environmental policies in regard
to waste management?

In still other disciplines, such as engineering, urban sociology, or architecture, a problem-posing teacher could ask: Why do we have so
many expressways in our cities instead of expanded mass transit?
Which groups tend to live or go to school near expressways? How does
this college's (or school's) buildings differ from those in private institutions? How many square feet and dollars per student are community
colleges budgeted compared to the allotments for elite public and private campuses? How does this affect the design of buildings and the
learning that goes on in them?

Problem-Posing in Practice

To speak more concretely about problem-posing, I can report in some
detail on a freshman writing class I taught at my mostly white college in
New York City.

I began in a participatory and critical way by posing the subject matter itself as a problem. The course was offered to help students become
good writers, but rather than lecturing on what that involved or meant,
I asked them to first establish their understandings of it.

On the opening day of class, I asked students, "What is good writing?" and suggested they write a reply of a few sentences. After students wrote their definitions of good writing, the next problem I posed
was, "How do you become a good writer?" Once again, students wrote
replies individually. I then asked them, "What questions do you have
about good writing?" to which they responded by listing one or two
questions. Last, I asked, "What are the hardest and easiest things for
you as a writer?" I was writing my own answers as students composed
theirs, but I did not read mine right away.

From the start, I wanted students to be active and thoughtful. A participatory class begins with participation. A critical and empowering
class begins by examining its subject matter from the students' point of
view and by helping students see themselves as knowledgeable people. I
wanted them to take, from day one, a critical attitude toward their
knowledge, their writing habits, and their education. The foundation
of the syllabus would be their words, understandings, self-respect, and
desire to learn more. I hoped they would recognize that they were already writers who knew some important things about writing, even before the teacher told them anything. They were not cultural deficits.
They could examine what they knew by taking an inquisitive attitude
towards knowledge and experience, which is why I wanted them to raise

their own questions about good writing. I hoped to animate their intelligence, their writing habits, and some good feelings about being in the class.

After students had replied to my questions, I asked them to read over what they had written to see if they wanted to make corrections or changes. This brief attention to their writing helps initiate a deliberate attitude toward their written work. Following some individual attention to their essays, I asked them to read their replies in pairs to notice how similar or different their answers had been. This practice helps develop peer relations without teacherly supervision; it promotes student autonomy and a learning community in class. I then asked students to read their responses to the class as I repeated the original questions one by one. Following that, I led a dialogue on each question.

The students' replies provided us with interesting material to discuss. Some students said that good writing is correct spelling and punctuation. Others said it is having a good beginning and sentences that keep the reader interested. Still others suggested that good writing means not repeating yourself and knowing what you want to say. Another group indicated that good writing means a well-organized essay with lots of examples. Besides analyzing these positions, we discussed their advice about how to become a good writer, advice which varied from suggestions to learn how to spell to ideas for doing more reading in order to gain a big vocabulary. Then we went on to their questions, which were also interesting. They wanted to know how to begin writing an essay, how to avoid boring your reader and repeating yourself, how to organize material, and how to use criticism from a teacher. As we discussed their statements, I brought in my definition of good writing, my perspective on how people become good writers, my own list of the hardest and the easiest things for me when I write, and my questions about good writing. My aim was to merge my thinking into an ongoing dialogue that had begun from their points of view.

Instruction in writing began with this participatory approach. It continued in a student-centered way as I used their questions about good writing as starting points for more exercises—"How do you begin writing an essay?" for instance. Instead of delivering a lecture about good writing or assigning exercises in grammar or providing a model essay for students to imitate, I presented good writing as the first problem to write on and discuss, drawing out their words and perspectives as initial texts for discussion and more writing. This class began from their own starting points, which I re-presented to them as further problems for writing and debate.

As they wrote from week to week on other themes, I used their compositions as texts for a classroom workshop on writing, photocopying selected papers through which to study such items as paragraphing, sentence boundaries, word choice, developing ideas, and organizing an essay. I asked them to write down the social issues most important to them and to bring in news articles about them, as their self-selected themes and reading material. I photocopied some of their readings for class discussion and compiled a list of their themes in ballot form. They voted on which we should take up in class. I then re-presented their most popular themes (such as "personal growth") in a long process of writing, reading, discussion, and critical inquiry.

In another instance of problem-posing, this one in a mass media class, I did not begin with a traditional lecture on the structure and politics of media organizations. Instead, I asked students to write what the phrase "mass media" meant to them, so that they would begin by reflecting on their knowledge in their own idiom. As in the freshman writing class, the subject matter of the course became the first problem for students to write on and discuss with peers, and the class began with student-centered material, not teacher-centered texts. I wanted them to establish their voices as the linguistic milieu into which my own academic voice would enter. My discourse joined a dialogue already in progress rather than having the class start from a teacher-centered presentation that might very well silence the students.

After they read their definitions of mass media to themselves and made whatever changes they wanted, and then in groups of two had some collaborative discussion, they read aloud so that we could have a dialogue on their material, during which I read my definition, comparing my ideas to theirs. They defined mass media as the TV stations or newspapers that send out news and entertainment to big audiences. My own definition covered some academic ground that the students had missed, like defining delivery systems and distinguishing between commercial and noncommercial media, as well as drawing attention to small alternative media versus big mainstream media. Thus I offered some basic academic material that entered a dialogue stemming from the students' voices and perceptions. Then I asked them to write down their questions about the media, which I used as the first issues for our inquiry. Among their questions, some asked more than once included "Who controls the media?" "How is the front page decided?" and "Should the media be allowed to invade a person's privacy?"

After a number of class sessions devoted to their questions, I took the initiative to teach the form of daily newspapers interactively and critically. I brought in copies of major New York City dailies and displayed the sections into which each paper is divided, asking the students to name them and their contents—national news, local news, sports, and so forth. I drew special attention to the business news section in every paper. I asked them to name some business news reporters they knew from TV, which a few could identify. Less familiar to them was the half-hour Nightly Business Report on public TV in our area, on an allegedly noncommercial network that has heavy corporate sponsorship, some advertisements, and two weekly business programs as well. Then I posed a problem: "Why does every major newspaper have a business section while none has a labor report? Why is there daily coverage of business news in papers, TV, and radio, but no special sections devoted to labor and trade unions?" Not only do major news organizations and public TV cover business news, but the largest circulating daily paper in the United States, the *Wall Street Journal,* specializes in business news. There is no "labor daily" to match it even though most Americans work for a living and few own businesses or actively trade stocks. "Why do major news media cover business in such detail but not labor?"

I posed the problem but did not lecture on it. Instead, I asked students to write their responses individually. They read them to each other in small groups of three or four to discuss their analyses before each group reported to the whole class for dialogue, reading statements from their groups one at a time for discussion. This problem of pro-business coverage in the major media was truly news to them. They had read their daily papers for years without knowing that labor news was virtually ignored. Now they saw a bias behind the apparently neutral news of the day. The absence of labor reporting left a gap in their knowledge of society, one not visible to them until it was revealed in class.

The students' analyses of why news media covered business and not labor were the starting points for discussion. Some said that few readers would be interested in labor news because work is boring, workers have no power, and labor is a special interest group in society; some said that all people are interested in business news because business is powerful and money interests everybody; some said labor unions give workers the labor news they need in their own publications; some said the mass media are big businesses that don't want the American people to like or to know about unions, strikes, and boycotts, for fear more people would join them, start them, or support them. For each student hypothesis, I re-presented the contending opinions for dialogue, which included my own statements on the issue. After prolonged discussion, I proposed that the class divide into project groups and that each group design a labor news section suitable for a major daily paper in New York. The class accepted this proposal and went to work for over a month, eventually producing models of labor news that I mailed to the editors of New York dailies for their comments.

The students in that media class learned subject matter through student-centered problem-posing in a critical dialogue, not through my lecturing them in a banking fashion. But while I did not lecture students on pro-business coverage, neither did I stay silent. In my remarks in the ongoing dialogue, I did not follow commercial texts on mass media, which generally play down political issues related to corporate power in society. Had I tried to be a "neutral" teacher who ignored the pro-business bias of news organizations, I would have cheated students of a chance for critical thinking about the real world they live in. For a teacher or syllabus to ignore business bias would have been just as political in orientation and less scientific; that would have meant avoiding criticism of the way power actually operates in the media to create manipulative images of the world. A media class that ignores the question of bias in the news misleads students into thinking that what they hear, see, and read is devoid of ideological content. Such a class disempowers student perception of their society while protecting the powerful media from critical scrutiny. A syllabus without critical questions is not neutral or apolitical. In fact, it supports the status quo by not questioning it.

Students in the media class gained a critical perspective on their TV, radio, and daily papers. They had for years been reading the major dailies and listening to TV news, but they had not perceived an anti-labor tilt in these media. When I posed it as a problem, they had a chance to see one structure in society for what it is.

In science, a problem-posing approach could take a debate form. A science class could present controversies in the field and in society. Students could examine competing interpretations of the origins of the universe, the causes and treatments of AIDS, the policy conflicts over energy sources and global warming, or the debates over the health hazards of exposure to low-level radiation or to electromagnetic fields generated by power lines. By presenting science as debates, controversies, and competing interpretations, the critical teacher would pose the subject matter as a problem for students to think through rather than a bland official consensus for them to memorize.

Science classes could begin actively with such questions as "What is biology?" or "What is chemistry?" or "What is geology?" This would enable students to write their definitions of the subject matter before a teacher preempts their thought and language with a didactic lecture. The students could also be asked to write down what they already know about biology or chemistry, and whether they are currently using biology or chemistry in their lives. Further, students might develop agendas of questions and issues in biology that interest them. From the way students define the field, characterize it as part of their lives, and pose their own questions about the subject matter, the science teacher would become educated about the particular group she or he is teaching and could design a curriculum built from what students offered.

Science could also be structured around some particular situations and experiences of students. Adolescent body chemistry could be integrated into junior high or secondary school science. At those levels and in elementary school, too, students could study the school cafeteria's menu and the students' favorite snacks to discover the nutritional value of these foods. In addition, a participatory science curriculum could ask students to grow plants, flowers, and food grains in class, from vegetation local to the area as well as from far away, to integrate geography with botany. They might visit neighborhoods to study the vegetation growing outdoors, which would lead to the question of why wealthy areas often have more trees and shrubs than do poorer sections. Students could compare the sweet soda they drink to tap water, to learn the metabolic consequences of their liquid intake. They could test tap water from school and from their homes to do chemical analyses of the contents, coordinated with a study of how pollutants enter the local water supply. They might compare local tap water to the bottled waters sold in stores to see what chemical differences there are. Such a participatory scientific study of chemistry could lead to the question of who buys bottled water. It could branch out into a study of soft-drink ads, so that students could redesign them with new information about what these liquids do to the body. Their critical scientific ads on soft drinks could be displayed around the school as a health campaign. From a study of soda and water in school and at home, a junior high or secondary class could go on to examine the air and soil. In high school, where teenage alcoholism and drug use are problems, students might also study beer, wine, liquor, and narcotics to learn about their chemical contents and their effects on the body. Lastly, a study in secondary science classes of sexually transmitted diseases would integrate biochemistry into student conditions, absorbing the ordinary concerns of everyday life into academic study just as academic study becomes absorbed into daily experience.

Situated Knowledge in Problem-Posing

For further definition of problem-posing, I will turn to Auerbach and Wallerstein, who adapted Freire's use of pictured scenes from daily life, called "codes" or "codifications," to develop language skills, job competencies, and critical thinking in English as a Second Language classes:

The goal of problem-posing dialogue is critical thinking and action, which starts from perceiving the social, historical, or cultural causes of problems in one's life. . . . The first step in promoting action outside the classroom is to transform education inside the classroom. Our role as teachers is to create a safe environment in which students can express opinions and, most importantly, generate their own language materials for learning and peer-teaching. (1987, vii)

Though their book focuses on critical literacy for adult ESL classes, it is generally instructive about student-centered problem-posing. They suggest three basic steps: listening to students to learn about key issues in the community, dialoguing on these themes, and figuring out ways to act on problems discussed.

By posing problems rather than by giving answers, their approach begins in a participatory way. By including an action phase, they make action a legitimate result of learning. Further, by defining the learning process as problem-posing rather than as problem-solving, their teaching goes beyond simplistic questions and short answers. Problem-*solving*—how to fix a down computer or soundproof a school near an expressway—has a useful place in education. Problem-solving skills and information, in critical contexts related to student life and society, are meaningful parts of education. But even useful skills and information, when studied abstractly and through lectures, will invite boredom and resistance.

Problem-*posing* goes deeply into any issue or knowledge to indicate its social and personal dimensions. A good example of in-depth problem-posing is an ESL unit from Auerbach and Wallerstein called "Getting through the Day" (1987, 72–90). It begins with a picture code showing three shopwomen working at sewing machines. Just above them is a bulletin board with restrictive notices: "no smoking, no eating or drinking, no talking, no music." Standing over the women while they work is a male supervisor. A lit cigarette dangles from his lips while he examines the work of one of the women.

To problematize this pictured work situation, the teachers use five groups of gradually more challenging questions. They start by asking students for simple descriptions of what they see in the picture, who the people in the scene are, and what they are doing. The second level of questions asks students to project what the women and men feel and think in the situation. Students are asked if the workers or the supervisor should be allowed to smoke. Third, the deepening theme asks students to discuss how this situation relates to work they used to do in their native countries and to work they are doing now in the United States. This locates the problem in their lives, but the question is also critical and egalitarian because it asks "Do supervisors have rules at your job? What happens if they break them? Have you ever gotten in trouble for breaking a rule? . . . Was it *fair* or *unfair?*" The last two ranks of questions generalize the problem by asking why there are work rules, does everyone follow the same rules, what are rules for management, and what should you do if you or if a supervisor breaks a rule?

The students are not drilled in grammar, lectured about job rules, or scolded about the work ethic. They are not blamed for workaday infractions. Language study does not refer dishonestly to a glamorized picture of work. The problems of inequality and undemocratic authority on the job are raised directly. To make the problem of democracy even more concrete, the unit goes on to list typical rules at work which students judge as applicable or not to their jobs and as fair or unfair. Then there are activities related to calling in sick, to responding to fair and unfair discipline, and to violations by an employer. The unit concludes with readings in workers' rights to organize and in peer interviews of people who have tried to change conditions on their jobs. This unit offers an example of how problem-posing can be used in a structured and participatory classroom. The format here merges language instruction, academic content, and daily experience. Empowering knowledge is sought by questioning rules, work relations, and daily episodes often taken for granted.

Starting from the Everyday to Know and Overcome It

Themes and words from daily life are strong resources for problem-posing. The turn toward student language and perceptions makes this pedagogy a *situated* model of learning, the fourth value in the agenda. The problem-posing teacher situates learning in the themes, knowledge, cultures, conditions, and idioms of students. In the situated style of Auerbach and Wallerstein's curriculum, subject matter and literacy skills are structured into the students' conditions and ways of knowing.

Situated teaching avoids teacher-centered syllabi and locates itself in the students' cultures. But while a situated curriculum is one way for the teacher to practice democratic authority, this is not a static entrapment in what students already know and say. What students bring to class is where learning begins. It starts there and goes places. Where does it go? Empowering education in this model adapts the subject matter and learning process to the students so as to develop critical dimensions missing from their knowledge and speech. A goal in this curriculum is to marry critical thought to everyday life by examining daily themes, social issues, and academic lore. This approach contrasts with traditional pedagogy, which expects the students to adapt uni-laterally to the standard curriculum, with its academic themes and for-mal language of both teacher and texts. Commenting on situated pedagogy in a program in Scotland, Kirkwood and Kirkwood (1989) reported that

it encourages [students] to become curious, critical and creative. It begins with their existing ways of seeing, including felt needs, but doesn't simply cater to those needs. It helps people both to articulate and to change their values (133). Some people admitted they were alarmed at being asked to contribute to discus-sion in learning groups right from the start. They felt sure no one would be interested in their views or hearing about their experiences. When they did risk speaking, they were delighted to be taken seriously. (121)

By starting from the students' situation, problem-posing increases their ability to participate, because they can begin critical reflection in their own context and their own words.

In addition, empowering pedagogy is situated in the political climate of the agency, institution, or community in which the class is offered. It is not invented abstractly by the teacher according to what he or she imagines is good for the students or the locale. Instead, the empower-ing teacher researches her or his situation so as to develop as much crit-ical learning as possible under the current conditions. Where the open-ings are for critical projects is an experimental question. Teachers find them through projects that aim at the limits of what is possible. I will have more to say on failure and success in these projects in a later sec-tion on teacher-student resistance to transformation. Here I would like to offer an example of situated problem-posing applicable to the ele-mentary grades.

To teach children about social issues, Ooka Pang (1991) focused on situating the theme of justice in the elementary curriculum. This is a good theme to choose, she wrote, because kids have a strong interest in this idea: "Children often can be heard saying 'But that's not fair.' They understand the importance of dealing equitably with each other" (190). Her approach begins by lifting the word "justice" out of the Pledge of Allegiance recited daily in class, a device that encourages students to extraordinarily reexperience the ordinary. When an everyday habit be-comes the subject of unusual scrutiny, it can raise awareness about the meaning of experience. Ooka Pang then asked students for synonyms of "justice." Students responded with "being equal," "fair play," and "playing fair and square." The playground is one obvious place to go to next in a discussion of justice, Ooka Pang suggested, to ask children about the concept there, but since she wanted to situate it in society as well, she integrated a discussion of health care in the community with the concept of justice:

Very young children can learn what health care is by discussing health care at home, visiting the school nurse, and so forth. At this level, they can discuss justice as meaning everyone gets treated by the nurse or by someone at home when needed. In math, story problems can sensitize children to health care costs. Children can then examine which jobs in the community provide health insurance and which do not, and what kinds of people occupy which jobs. Older children can find out what provisions there are in the community for health care for poor people. Some of their own families may use such services. (1991, 190)

From this integration of health care and justice, Ooka Pang suggested, students can draw on their experience in their communities and examine "the extent to which justice is actually carried out, and how they could act on behalf of it" (190). They started from routine experiences such as the pledge and the playground, and then moved outward to apply the concept of justice to their experiences in society through health care. This illustrates one student-centered way to integrate a social theme with critical thinking at the elementary level.

The Situation of Diversity: Problem-Posing and Multiculturalism

By situating critical study in student experience and language, problem-posing is also multicultural, the fifth value in the agenda offered in the first chapter. Student speech, community life, and perceptions are foundations of the curriculum. Empowering pedagogy develops classroom discourse from the students' cultural diversity.

To see how situated programs respect and use student culture, I can refer to Freire's literacy project in northeast Brazil (Brown 1987). In the 1950s and early 1960s, Freirean literacy teams situated instruction in the words and experiences of the students, who came from peasant or worker backgrounds. The literacy teachers did not invent thematic material on campus and then take it to a neighborhood class. They did not impose a standard text or a basal reader designed far away. Instead, these projects developed curricula from student culture by researching local issues and language in the students' communities. From the many linguistic and sociological items researched in students' neighborhoods, the educators selected some key concerns—generative themes expressed through single generative words. They are called generative words because they are generated from student culture and also because their polysyllabic structure make them suitable for generating new words by breaking up and recombining their syllables. Further, they are provocative themes discovered as unresolved social problems in the community, good for generating discussion in class on the relation of personal life to larger issues. They are key words through which a critical literacy about self in society may be gained; they are all words and themes indigenous to the student culture.

The generative words used variously to instruct the preliterate students in Brazil included such items as slum, land, food, work, salary, vote, profession, government, brick, sugar mill, and wealth. For situated pedagogy, the choice of words and themes is as crucial to the program as the process by which the curriculum discovers these items. Community research by teachers, with students as coinvestigators, established a student-centered, democratic process through which a literacy program was built from the bottom up rather than from the top down. Student subjectivity was the starting point but not the end. Freire's program aimed to develop critical thought and action around themes identified in everyday life, so that by learning to read and write, the students would also be gaining the power to critique and act on their conditions. In my adaptation of this pedagogy for a postliterate, mostly white urban group of working college students in New York City, my classes have started at the level of generative themes, bypassing the need to gain basic literacy through learning and recombining single generative words. The generative themes emerging in my classes from student culture have most often related to sex, abortion, drugs, family, education, careers, work, and the economic crisis.

By situating critical inquiry in student culture, the generative-theme approach also reflects Deweyan progressive education. Dewey advised teachers to begin instruction with the most experiential materials and to gradually structure in conceptual understanding and academic knowledge:

The educator cannot start with knowledge already organized and proceed to ladle it out in doses (82). Anything which can be called a study, whether arithmetic, history, geography, or one of the natural sciences, must be derived from materials which at the outset fall within the scope of ordinary life experience. When education is based in theory and practice upon experience, it goes without saying that the organized subject-matter of the adult and the specialist cannot provide the starting point. Nevertheless, it represents the goal toward which education should continuously move. (Dewey 1963, 83)

Freire offered a similar theory for problem-posing: "We are advocating a synthesis between the educator's maximally systematized knowing and the learner's minimally systematized knowing—a synthesis achieved in dialogue. The educator's role is to propose problems about the codified existential situations in order to help the learners arrive at a more and more critical view of their reality" (Freire 1985b, 54–55). Dewey said that the structured subject matter of the teacher is the scientific knowledge which students would eventually gain but from which they could not start. Freire also saw the teacher's systematic knowledge and critical habits of mind as goals for students, but he added a political emphasis on the relation of knowledge and everyday conditions to power in society. Critically examining the politics of structured knowledge was an important emphasis to Freire, who asserted that no knowledge is neutral.

When problem-posing situates itself in the language and perceptions of the students, their diverse cultures are built into the study. When students see their words and experiences in the problems posed, the power relations of study are allied to their interests. It becomes easier for them to understand the meaning and purpose of intellectual work. Studying is no longer submitting to a dull imposition of an alien culture. Based in the diversity of students, including gender diversity, the multicultural class challenges the subordination of some groups in school and society and orients the curriculum to equality. To make some of these goals concrete, I will talk about two teaching experiences.

The first is from a college-based writing class in the Virgin Islands, reported by Elsasser and Irvine (1987). As writing teachers to Afro-Caribbean students, they taught the community idiom, Creole, and Standard English simultaneously. They did not install white English as the preferred idiom in the classroom. Instead, they developed bilingual literacy and a political awareness of the relationship between the dominant and the community languages. To challenge the subordinate position of Creole, the teachers asked the students in this basic writing class to develop a written form, or orthography, for their spoken language. With an orthography, Creole and those who speak it could have a stronger political position in society, because the white version of English would no longer be the only written language. In written form, Creole might develop as a rich medium for politics, business, journalism, and science. Elsasser and Irvine's approach challenged the politics of language in the islands, which had established Creole as a subordinate idiom for daily talk, inferior to the written English left behind by the former colonial masters.

Students in their writing class had failed a required freshman entry examination in written Standard English. To begin the course, the instructors posed a problem situated in the students' reality: "Why don't we have the skills to pass the writing exam?" This question opened the way for student participation and even provoked an outburst. In writing and discussion, the students vented their frustration at the writing test. They offered various explanations for their failure, from their perception that they never learned "good English" in school or at home to their suggestion that they did badly because they spoke "broken English," Creole. The problem of Standard English versus Creole emerged as a predominant issue, a generative theme coming out of the students' reflections on their experience. Elsasser and Irvine isolated it for deeper inquiry.

They invited an Afro-Caribbean linguist, Vincent Cooper, to class, to speak on the history, structure, and politics of language in the Caribbean. The students were taken by this attention to their language problems. Cooper spoke in a community oratorical style which galvanized the class. By the example of his speech as well as by his analysis, he showed how Creole could assume a position competitive with traditional academic discourse. He demonstrated the potential of community discourse and showed students that the conflict between their home language and the academic idiom might not require them to deny their linguistic roots.

Cooper's presentation of Creole as a rule-governed language gave it a stature and legitimacy that enlarged the students' perceptions. With some background in the history and nature of Creole, they began writing and studying in both Standard English and Creole. About a student who wrote an essay in Creole challenging landlords' abuse of poor tenants, Elsasser and Irvine said, "When he learned that he could write forcefully in his native language, Creole, he and other students in an experimental writing course took the first step in challenging assumptions that had relegated Creole to oral use in limited contexts and had created silence in English courses" (129).

Elsasser and Irvine went on to conclude that "we find their reluctance to write directly attributable to the denigration of their native language and to their conviction that they do not, in fact, possess a true language but speak a bastardized version of English" (1987, 137). In another context, Selase Williams (1991) drew a similar conclusion about the denigration of African-American speech in American schools:

Imagine the impact on one's self-esteem and self-concept to discover that the language that is spoken in your community and which you embrace as part of your identity is nothing more than an inferior copy of someone else's language. Imagine further that, no matter how hard you try to master the "superior" language, elements of your own language keep creeping in. (208)

Williams defined some rule-governed aspects of African-American English and reported successful bidialectal approaches to teaching community language and Standard English at the elementary and secondary levels. At the college level, Elsasser and Irvine recommended a dual teaching approach that can empower a multicultural language class: provide a framework to distinguish Creole and English as separate, rule-governed linguistic systems; address the power relations inherent in language choices and language attitudes; and integrate the study of Creole and writing in Creole with academic research and writing skills. Their class in Creole and Standard English is an example of multicultural language arts seeking a critical and democratic balance between community speech and the dominant usage, without denying either (see Cummins 1989 for more analysis of this approach).

The Elsasser-Irvine experiment is instructive about multicultural teaching, which is also a form of egalitarian language arts. For an example of a multicultural curriculum that tries to establish equality among cultural groups, I can report on efforts at the Fratney School in Milwaukee. Started in 1988 by a coalition of parents, community activists, and teachers, the hope was for "a decent school that children want to attend, based in an integrated neighborhood, teaching children to be bilingual in Spanish and English, using cooperative and innovative methods, governed by a council of parents and teachers," according to one of the founders (Peterson 1989a, 28). After community pressure on the Milwaukee school authorities, a hundred-year-old elementary school building was reopened as The Fratney School/La Escuela Fratney. As told by teacher-activist Peterson, "The proposal called for the creation of a kindergarten through 5th grade school that was a two-way bilingual, multicultural, whole language, site-based managed school. . . . While each student learns to read first in their mother language, they are also learning a second language. The goal is that by the end of the fifth grade, the children will be bilingual and biliterate" (1989a, 27–28).

Students study their own culture and that of the other students different from them. They undertake a cross-cultural study of the other groups in the community—white, Black, Hispanic, Asian—and all students learn English and Spanish. Further, this curriculum is thematic rather than fact-driven. The classwork revolves around cross-cultural themes, among them Our Roots in the Community, Native American Experience, Peace Education and Global Awareness. The teaching methods include cooperative learning, democratic discipline, and students' participation in peer groups and in decision making.

In its first year, the school had three hundred children in this program—42 percent black, 37 percent Hispanic, and 21 percent white/other, with nearly 90 percent qualifying for federal free lunches. The innovative government of the school included five parents, five teachers, one community representative, the principal, a delegate from the school staff, and a student. As this school invented itself, Peterson (1991) reported that the pieces were slowly falling into place after five years of ups and downs. Still, this experiment faced the problems of sustaining parental involvement, reeducating teachers who have practiced only traditional methods, overcoming budget crises, and orienting students to cooperative, multicultural values in a society of racist divisions, sexist stereotyping for boys and girls, self-reliant careerism, and competitive learning styles.

To gain support for their experiment, some of Fratney's teachers did more than experimental teaching and development of multicultural curricula. They engaged in citywide school politics to organize other parents and teachers for student-centered policies. By connecting the classroom, the school, the community, and the city, Peterson and other activists in the Rethinking Schools group in Milwaukee faced the reality that education is politics and that the fate of student learning is decided in more places than the classroom (Peterson 1989b, 1991).

Situated Learning and Transformation

Situated, multicultural pedagogy increases the chance that students will feel ownership in their education and reduces the conditions that produce their alienation. In the case of women, minorities, and non-elite whites, who comprise the majority of students, democratic education should reflect their culture, conditions, needs, and history. Doing so will encourage their participation in intellectual study. But participation is a means, not an end, in this program for empowering education. There is a challenging goal to the participatory process I am suggesting: to discover the limits and resources for changing self and society.

In the Elsasser-Irvine class, the situated limit at the College of the Virgin Islands was the students' failure on the required writing examination in Standard English. This circumstance was embedded in a larger political limit: a society that established colonial white English as superior to Creole. The students had already spent a number of years in a traditional school system. Traditional language classes had failed to develop their command of Standard English. Blaming the system of education and the elitist language policies in school and society instead of blaming the students, Elsasser and Irvine offered the class an empowering program.

To pass the college entry examination in Standard English, the Afro-Caribbean students developed their home language into written forms and examined the politics of language, from which they gained the desire and the knowledge to overcome the writing exam. Their basic writing class challenged the elite prejudice in school and society against Creole, the language of their everyday life. The students created an orthography for their indigenous speech while critically studying the official idiom of Standard English. In the process, they developed critical and creative abilities that had eluded them before.

If those students were to go on to change the language policies of their institution or of their island's school system, or if they campaigned for linguistic equality for Creole in society, they would carry forward into the larger public arena the democratic lessons of a single classroom. By themselves, breakthroughs in single classrooms or with small groups of students do not end the undemocratic conditions in school and society. Those conditions cannot be changed by a lone critical syllabus. They have to be challenged in arenas outside the classroom, as the Milwaukee teachers in the Rethinking Schools group demonstrated. They understood that a limit on their dreams for a multicultural community school was the fiscal and education policy decided by distant authorities, which led some of them to campaign outside their school and their community for the changes needed to protect the classroom.

In a larger arena for change, inventing spoken Creole as a written language was the democratic project Freire proposed for the newly liberated African nation of Guinea-Bissau in the 1970s, when the government there asked his help in its literacy program (Freire 1978; Freire and Macedo 1987; Freire and Faundez 1989). About the low status traditionally ascribed to everyday language, Freire said that "Creole, the medium of expression of those colonized, was always viewed by the colonialists as something inferior, ugly, poverty-stricken, incapable, for example, of conveying scientific or technological ideas, as if languages did not change historically in step with actual developments in the forces of production" (Freire and Faundez 1989, 117). Freire urged that Creole become a national language, not the Portuguese of the former colonial masters, in newly freed Guinea-Bissau. He recommended the development of a written system for the language used in everyday life and said that with an orthography and with economic development, Creole could emerge as a language with dimensions in science and technology. The new regime decided to use Portuguese, a choice that limited the impact of its literacy program. In a small way, the Elsasser-Irvine experiment confirmed Freire's hopes for the potentials of community speech, because their Afro-Caribbean students did develop their spoken Creole into a written instrument.

Elite prejudice against the language of everyday life also limits working-class, poor, and minority students in the United States mainland. Standard English, a dialect not used by most people in daily life, dominates the academic, political, media, and business worlds. Williams (1991) posed the problem of the clash between everyday speech and the official standard: "One of the new realities which America is going to have to accept is the fact that few Americans, regardless of their ethnolinguistic background, speak a variety of English that closely resembles the written standard. One of the answers to the question 'Why can't Johnny read?' is that Johnny speaks a variety of English that is not represented on the written page" (214).

In the States, one approach to developing everyday language into a critical discourse is the classroom work of Linda Christensen, a high-school English teacher from Oregon. In a moving account, she reports on efforts to develop the students' command of two idioms, their "home" language and the "cash" language (Standard English):

They write stories. They write poems. They write letters. They write essays. They learn how to switch in and out of the language of the powerful. . . . We ask: Who made the rules that govern how we speak and write? . . . Who already talks and writes like this? Who has to learn how to change the way they talk and write? Why? . . . We read articles, stories, poems written in Standard English and those written in home language. We listen to videotapes of people speaking. Most kids like the sound of their home language better. . . . We talk about why it might be necessary to learn Standard English. . . . Asking my students to memorize the rules without asking *who* makes the rules, *who* enforces the rules, *who* benefits from the rules, *who* loses from the rules . . . legitimates a social system that devalues my students' knowledge and language. (1990, 38–40)

Christensen's bidialectical class reflects the approach used by Elsasser and Irvine, but in this case with white and minority nonelite students in the United States. Their critical study of everyday idioms and correct usage encouraged students to question the social system behind their language problems in school. Instead of blaming themselves, they learned that the problem of doing well in school is a problem of an unequal society that devalues the idioms spoken by ordinary people. With a critical and multicultural pedagogy, the students can gain a self-supporting awareness of undemocratic language policies. They can study correct usage while also validating their own dialects, in a process which questions fairness and democracy in the status quo.

Democratizing the Educator: Teachers Learn
from Student Learning

To make problem-posing work, the teacher needs to listen carefully to students to draw out the themes and words from which critical curricula are built. Student participation provides the raw material for the inquiry. As the teacher observes students in class, reads their writing, and holds dialogues with them, he or she perceives many suggestive threads which have to be fashioned into a problem for the next phase of inquiry.

This reflexive teaching, where the teacher poses questions, listens carefully, and re-presents to students what they have said for further reflection, is adaptable in academic courses, not only in literacy classes. In academic, scientific, or technical courses with bodies of knowledge to cover, the teacher also needs to hear student voices as soon as possible, to reverse passivity and to provoke involvement, to learn the cognitive and affective levels of the class into which a serious study is situated. Few students will learn academic material if it is lectured at them in a manner designed simply to transfer information. As I suggested earlier, subject matter is best introduced as problems related to student experience, in language familiar to them.

A participatory classroom offers chances to hear the largely silent voices of students from which teachers learn how to integrate subject matter into their existing knowledge. Students routinely hold back their voices as a means of resisting traditional classrooms where authority is unilateral and where they lack an inspiring life of the mind which speaks to their dreams and needs.

Changing power relations in the classroom through problem-posing reduces the need for students to resist learning. More students can embrace education without fear of boredom or of a cultural invasion by an elite, remote curriculum. The empowering classroom can open their voices for expression rarely heard before. Their voices are an untapped and unexpected universe of words rich in thought and feeling. From it, students and teachers can create knowledge that leaves behind the old disabling education in a search for new ways of being and knowing.

Three Roads to Critical Thought
Generative, Topical, and Academic Themes

3

Subject Matter and Problem-Posing: Thematic Options

Critical-democratic pedagogy situates curriculum in issues and language from everyday life. Generative themes make up the primary subject matter; they grow out of student culture and express problematic conditions in daily life that are useful for generating critical discussion. About generative themes from student experience, Freire said that they are "weighted with emotion and meaning, expressing the anxieties, fears, demands, and dreams of the group" (quoted in Cox 1990, 78). Generative issues are found in the unsettled intersections of personal life and society. Based in such experiences as voting, working, housing, community activity, they are student-centered foundations for problem-posing. What I want to name and explore in this chapter are two other thematic approaches important for an empowering process, the topical theme and the academic theme.

The topical theme is a social question of key importance locally, nationally, or globally that is not generated directly from the students' conversation. It is raised in class by the teacher. The academic theme is also material brought to the discussion by the teacher, not generated from student speech, but its roots lie in formal bodies of knowledge studied by specialists in a field.

In a problem-posing class, the teacher chooses a topical theme for critical study with great care. The teacher's choice of an outside theme is delicate because it must fit into a mutual curriculum. He or she has to use it in ways consistent with the student-centered discourse and the democratic process. The topical theme fits when it is relevant to the work in progress, when it is introduced as a problem for cooperative study in class, and when it is in an idiom students can understand. If these minimal conditions are *not* met, the topical theme can convert a participatory class into a teacher-centered experience for students. The risk is that outside themes brought in by the teacher will change democratic relations into unilateral authority, replacing mutual inquiry with one-way teacher-talk.

Critical teachers are willing to take the risk of introducing topical themes because student conversation and thought often do not include important issues in society. In some cases, a topical theme can be treated in the media and still not enter student speech, as was the case of the Savings and Loan scandal or the wars in Central America in the 1980s. These events received considerable media attention but were largely absent from the talk and writing of the students in my classes, at a mostly white working-class campus. Other social issues outside the speech and thematic universe of my students are the urban housing policies that help produce homelessness ("planned shrinkage," "tax breaks for co-op and condo conversions," and "gentrification"); hunger and its roots in various corporate-government policies ("soil bank," "cash crops" that discourage the growing of food); unemployment resulting from corporations moving jobs to cheap labor areas in the South or to antiunion countries abroad in search of lower wages and taxes ("runaway plants" and "deindustrialization"); tax giveaways to corporations to keep them from leaving ("abatements"); the politics of "big oil" that discourage alternative energy and mass transit (little research and development money for solar or wind power); the big business of militarism (high Pentagon spending despite the end of the cold war); secret United States government aid to right-wing guerrillas around the world; government surveillance of dissident groups and censorship of war coverage; and tax loopholes for the wealthy and for corporations. These concerns affect the quality of life and the standard of living of my students, as well as the quality of democracy, but they are rarely themes they talk about, think about, or act on. When posed as social problems in class, topical themes add critical potential to students' thought and action.

In some cases, like discrimination based on sex, race, age, or class, students at my college have often experienced the issue. Many of them are women subjected to lower pay and sexual harassment on the job, or minorities facing discrimination in hiring and housing, or entry-level young workers paid a substandard minimum wage, or working collegians treated with contempt when they apply to medical school from a "no-name" college. The topics can exist as unexamined student experience, not yet reflected on in conversation or grasped critically in relation to the larger society. By introducing topical themes, a critical teacher gives these social experiences a depth, articulation, and visibility missing in student culture.

On the one hand, a topical theme is a teacher's thematic intervention based on her or his critical knowledge of society at large and the students' experiences in it. On the other hand, the topical theme emerges from the teacher's perception of the learning process and what social issues are appropriate for the next phase of inquiry. The teacher's choice adds to those social concerns already spoken about and chosen by students in democratic classes, where the teacher asks students to suggest themes they want to study.

When selected by the teacher, the topical theme lacks the subjectivity of an issue generated from the students' conversation. Because the topical theme originates at some distance from daily talk, it must be presented in a meaningful context related to the students' situation and to the ongoing curriculum. Further, the topical theme must also be open to rejection by students. A topical theme, to be critical and democratic, cannot be an isolated exercise or unchallenged lecture by the teacher. This is the crucial way it differs from teacher-centered subject matter in traditional classrooms. The topical theme is a part of a syllabus students can reject or amend as they exercise their democratic rights. The critical-democratic class is a negotiated experience where students have protest rights, unlike the syllabus set unilaterally by teachers in traditional courses.

Critical teachers offer students a topical thematic choice which they can accept or reject. If they do accept a social topic for study, it offers the chance of expanding their development in ways closed off by the traditional syllabus and by the dominant media, which generally discourage the critical thought and democratic participation of students and citizens. By encouraging critical development, the topical theme challenges the politically limited content of mass education and mass media. It invites students to make contact with issues kept in the shadows or excluded from their attention, especially in regard to unequal power relations in society, so that they can decide whether to think about and act on them.

By giving students more choices for their learning and action, topical themes add political diversity to the subject matter in education. By increasing diversity, topical themes strengthen the democratic learning process. Democracy thrives on the widest flow of ideas and the broadest points of view in public circulation. Topical themes enhance education as a "democratic public sphere," as Giroux (1988) said. As fewer corporations gain more control over publishing and the mass media, the sources of information become narrower, and the diversity and debate needed for democracy erode (Bagdikian 1987). Standardized testing and commercial textbooks have also limited diversity in the classroom. Teachers have to teach to the tests and to the bland, officially approved material in texts. The topical theme opposes these limits on thought, debate, and learning; it is a method that asserts democratic diversity in school and society against the narrowing of public discourse.

Topical themes thus ask students to step into territory ignored or covered uncritically by the standard curriculum and the mass media. They offer alternative contact with society and knowledge, a chance to push against the limits of knowledge in everyday life. Many students believe what they read and hear in school and in the media; others ignore both; some are suspicious of teachers, politicians, and news media but lack access to diverse points of view and information. The topical theme fills this void, as an original and critical conversation about social issues not yet being discussed in daily life, not being studied critically in the standard syllabus and not being reported meaningfully in the media. It serves a different empowerment function from the generative theme, which adds *critical* discussion about things students already know and talk about *uncritically* every day.

What students already know, do, experience, and say is the generative base for this critical pedagogy. But as Frankenstein and Powell (1991) said about student-based ideas in critical math, "We are not suggesting that the curriculum should be composed solely of those ideas. . . . Teachers can suggest new themes, ones they judge important, and be strong influences without being superiors constraining and controlling the learning environment (29–30). While we listen to students' themes, we organize them using our critical and theoretical frameworks, and we re-present them as problems challenging students' previous perceptions. We also suggest themes that may not occur to students" (48). Their students research how they use math in their daily lives but also examine topics about social inequality that the teachers choose.

A Basic Topical Theme: "The Anthropological Notion of Culture"

Even though Freire's literacy work was built around generative themes taken from the daily lives and words of students, in practice Freire's literacy teams began with an important topical theme: all people have knowledge and make culture. Freire called this theme "the anthropological notion of culture." It was not an idea students brought to class. It was not a situation they talked about in everyday life. It was, rather, a democratic principle and a scientific assertion structured into the curriculum by the educators.

Generatively, to teach writing and reading, Freirean literacy programs in Brazil analyzed polysyllabic Portuguese words rooted in the students' lives—*slum, brick, vote, factory,* and so on. These words animated discussion; they were broken up syllabically and then recombined to make other words. But *topically* the program began with pictured situations used for a long dialogue on the anthropological notion of culture. Before single generative words were taught through thematic pictures, the students and teachers had extended discussions on a topic chosen for its ability to empower the students' voices, intellectual curiosity, and hope. Freire explained the meaning of the anthropological approach to culture. "It is," he said, "the distinction between the world of nature and the world of culture; the active role of men *in* and *with* their reality . . . culture as the addition made by men to a world they did not make; culture as the result of men's labor, of their efforts to create and recreate . . . culture as a systematic acquisition of human experience (but as creative assimilation, not as information-storing); the democratization of culture; the learning of reading and writing as a key to the world of written communication" (1973, 46). This democratic theme was not part of everyday life; the illiterate students did not speak of themselves as makers of culture; they discovered that in the literacy class because of a topical theme introduced by the teachers. In this regard, Freire told the story of a woman in a literacy circle who responded to a drawing of flowers in a vase. She said that the flowers in the field are nature, but once in the vase, the flowers become decoration, or culture. And she now considered herself a culture maker because she knew how to arrange flowers in a vase. Others knew how to use tools to build things, which helped them to see their existing powers in everyday life and to define their activity as culture.

"The human power to make and remake culture" was an empowering topical theme when introduced in a problem-posing literacy class. If culture were defined only as what the elite speaks, makes, likes, or does, then the literacy class would be oppressive, not empowering. It would silence the language of daily life, as well as the creative actions, the constructive work, and even the sense of things held by ordinary people. The Brazilian peasants and workers in the literacy classes lacked political power, but unknown to themselves they had a complex culture and language. They were like the Creole college students in the Virgin Islands and Christensen's high school students in Oregon in that respect. Through a democratic literacy class, they gained a new awareness of culture, which Dewey defined as the ability to perceive meaning and to make meaning in society. These men and women in Brazil thought that their role was to follow orders and to be told by the teacher what things mean, not to make meaning and question society. To help transform this powerlessness, Freire introduced the anthropological concept of culture—that all people had culture, made culture, and had the power to *remake* the culture they already possessed and were continually re-producing. Such a literacy class is action for cultural democracy. Con-nected to the militant politics of Brazil in 1964, which mobilized people for social change, the literacy program was doubly transformative in its potential—to overcome the illiteracy and the economic subordination of its students. It was eliminated by the elite and the military in the April coup of that year.

Before the coup, the program presented students with drawings of human beings, objects, and animals in recognizable or typical situa-tions. Students discussed how they understood the pictures highlight-ing the differences between nature and culture. The human power to transform nature was called culture. The slides for this preliminary dia-logue on culture making showed people as hunters and ranchers and potters, and ended with a picture of the literacy class itself, the latest cultural act by some people to transform their conditions. After this starting point, the first slides for introducing polysyllabic generative words were presented.

This start to a basic literacy class, a long critical dialogue on culture making, began outside the generative themes of daily life, in the topical domain. The large issue of the human power to make culture was con-cretely related to student experience through reference to their daily actions, like flower arranging, house building, and learning to read and write. It is encouraging to see how an empowering topical theme brought in from the outside can inspire students in a pedagogy built essentially on generative themes.

From Generative to Topical: Inside Out and Outside In

Freire developed the problem-posing approach in nonformal, community-based adult literacy programs in a poor Third World coun-try, not in schools and colleges where academic subjects are required for each grade or level. In formal institutions and in the developed north-ern hemisphere, the pedagogy needs to be reinvented. The generative theme, most developed as a pedagogical approach, remains a primary democratic base for building student-centered programs in education systems now dominated by bureaucracy and teacher-centered classes. But the topical theme and the academic theme need equal develop-ment if critical-democratic learning and problem-posing are to benefit students and teachers across the curriculum and at different levels.

In adapting problem-posing in the States, at a predominantly white low-budget public college, I found that I could introduce topical themes without beginning with a general anthropological theme like nature versus culture. I could introduce in class specific social issues related to racism or sexism, for example, without a preliminary discussion of the human power to make and remake culture. What I did need in advance of introducing topical themes were generative themes suggested by the students. To encourage the students' participation in a topical theme, I found it useful to work first on generative issues drawn from their culture. The familiar quality of a generative theme enabled them to launch a discourse rooted in their thought and language. The generative start for problem-posing taught me to keep the student-centered base as the foundation for integrating themes less discussed in their experience. Beginning with student-based material, I started at the thematic level, not at the level of single words. I did not have to start with generative words to develop basic literacy because my students are already literate.

Further, because my college students in New York City live in a media-drenched urban center tattooed by lavish wealth and wretched poverty, I could count on some of them having crossed paths with larger social issues even though few had given critical thought to them. Those students who did refer to social problems would often repeat the quick messages they had learned in school or from the media, confirming the need for in-depth critical inquiry. Finally, these students could bypass a general discussion on the human power to make culture because they are already preoccupied with the question of power, although not in a critical or liberating way. They are not marginalized peasants from an underdeveloped nation; they are assertive, aspiring individualists seeking buying power in a runaway consumer society whose government and elite dominate world affairs—and them. They express a self-assertion that is in tune with the power, affluence, and aggression of the nation and economy they belong to. But despite their feistiness and their desire for the good life, they have absorbed a political disempowerment different from that learned by Freire's Brazilian students. My students learned that they should face their future and the dominant power in society alone, counting only on their personal power to make their way forward or to sink from bad breaks or their own fault. This sink-or-swim individualism helps disempower them while keeping power and wealth in the hands of those few who already have it. Self-reliance, which I will discuss below, is an extreme form of individualism common in everyday life and learning. It is an oppressive ideology that helps transfer blame for failure from the system to the individual. My students do not see it that way, however, which makes it good material for a topical theme.

From the Outside In: The Process of the Topical Theme

Up to now, I have discussed the topical theme as an issue at a distance from student speech. Presented by the teacher, it asks students to reflect on a social problem. Because it is largely outside student talk or reflection, the topical theme has to be offered with great respect and caution. Introducing a topical theme is a teacher's professional and moral right as long as it is appropriate for the subject matter of the class and for the age and level of the students, situated inside a participatory process, and not framed as a sermon or harangue. A teacher has a right to introduce topical themes because she or he is a thinking citizen, a professional educator, and a moral human being with freedom of speech to present important issues to others. Further, the teacher directs a serious learning process, and topical issues like apartheid or nuclear contamination or secret government wars are consequential, not frivolous. Because these issues are often ignored, underreported, or misrepresented in the traditional syllabus and in the media, it is the critical teacher's special responsibility to present them. Put simply, human beings in a democracy have the right to consider a far broader range of issues and questions than are delivered in the official syllabus or on the evening news. One of the critical teacher's responsibilities is to broaden these limits with topical themes. Cummins (1989) pointed to the absence of relevant social issues in the standard syllabus:

> The curriculum has been sanitized such that students rarely have the opportunity to discuss critically or write about issues that directly affect the society they will form. Issues such as racism, environmental pollution, U.S. policy in Central America, genetic engineering, global nuclear destruction, arms control, etc., are regarded as "too sensitive" for fragile and impressionable young minds. Instead, students are fed a neutralized diet of social studies, science, and language arts that is largely irrelevant to the enormous global problems that our generation is creating for our children's generation to resolve. (5–6)

Which topical theme to introduce is an in-process decision based on student learning as the problem-posing evolves.

For an example of a topical theme emerging in-process, I can report on a freshman writing class where the students chose personal growth as their primary generative theme. From their everyday ambitions, as well as from their guidance classes and freshman orientation, my students often adopt the phrase "personal growth" to name their aspirations. And fresh from their introductory psychology and sociology classes, some report coming across Maslow's hierarchy of needs, a model of human development built on a language of personal growth.

In the composition class, I asked students to write on three questions related to their self-selected generative theme: "What does "personal growth" mean to you? What helps personal growth? What are the obstacles to personal growth?"

In response to these questions, the students produced essays which I used as anonymous discussion texts and as material for exercises in usage and composing. I led class discussion about their ideas and used their papers to study skills like paragraphing and sentence boundaries. During these discussions, I wondered how to question their notions of success and failure. Students wrote that personal growth is a purely individual matter. Whether you succeed or fail in life depends solely on your individual qualities, your personal strengths. (I remember learning this message in my junior-high English class when we read Emerson's and Teddy Roosevelt's essays.) This self-reliant ideology hides the impact of such social factors as inequality and discrimination (based on race, sex, age, or class) and corporate domination of the economy. How could I pose the problem of the *social and economic system* affecting personal success? That the self was caught up in an unequal and undemocratic relationship with dominant groups in society?

Such discussion is made much easier if some students themselves express critical views. It is preferable to use students' essays to pose divergent points of view, if possible, to avoid the teacher's voice being the dominant questioning one. But in that class only one student mentioned racism as a factor in his personal growth, in a narrative of his life in a white high school, where he was treated as a stereotypical Hispanic. The other essays exhibited no divergent thinking and much emphasis on self-reliance. They did not perceive the school system or the economic system as problems, as systematic obstacles, as political factors functioning against certain groups and for others. Their education had denied them a critical appreciation of their society's power relations. It left them supposing that success in school and the job market were only private matters whose obstacles they had to face on their own. The best they could hope for was a lot of personal stamina, good breaks, and what they call pull or connections—having a friend or relative in a position to open a closed door. Why some won and many lost, students could explain only by the single great lesson: Win or lose, the individual is to blame. Each human being is a lone entrepreneur who succeeds or fails on the basis of her or his character, ingenuity, and talents. If you fail to pull yourself up by your own bootstraps, blame only yourself.

This version of self-reliance permeated the students in that composition class, and was common in my other classes also. It is prevalent enough to be a cliché of American culture. Yet each time I think about the bootstrap cliché, it strikes me as remarkably romantic, as heroic as it is false and oppressive. Imagine: the lone heroic individual versus society, the underdog against the big system, winner take all, sink or swim you are on your own. Hearing this ideology every year in class, I have always been impressed with the toughness and resilience of my nonelite students. They are substantial human beings, complex people who do not want or deserve pity. I have never felt sorry for them, even though I maintain they are manipulated and disempowered by the dominant culture. They meet life with brave resolve and without self-pity, but with few chances to critique and transform the ideology or the system that limits them.

To question the self-blaming, system-exonerating ideology of self-reliance, I intervened in that freshman comp class with a topical theme not generated by the students themselves but related to the theme they had chosen. To expand the generative theme of personal growth into the topical theme, "personal growth is affected by economic policy," I brought in readings about corporations fleeing our city for cheap labor areas and about city/state decisions to give various companies huge tax breaks to keep them in New York. I read these articles out loud with students, and then asked if this corporate/government economic policy would affect their taxes, their city services, and the education available to them. Would it impact their personal growth? Some students had heard that New York in particular and the United States in general were losing jobs to other places, but they had not reflected on this problem. They knew that their taxes were rising, their wages stagnating, and their city services declining. But, again, they did not have an explanation, except to point fingers at corrupt politicians or union featherbedding or welfare cheaters or recent immigrants. The readings I brought in for discussion suggested that corporate-government policies, not welfare recipients or city workers or immigrants or lone dirty politicians, were undermining their quality of life and blocking their desires for personal growth. These explanations for some of their problems ran counter to the lore of everyday life, which has a racist side that blames welfare and recent immigration for the economic decline of the country. But the news articles were situated in problems worrisome to students, so they took an interest in the material.

I was encouraged to lead an extended dialogue on the topic. In the course of it, students generally agreed that runaway plants and tax giveaways were bad, but a core of students defended the right of big business to gain these advantages and do what it pleased. I staked out a position for myself in this debate, but the discussion was a contentious draw, I would say. When the topical theme works democratically, the teacher who brings it to class with her or his authority is not guaranteed

an easy victory in the debate. At my college, the students are not push-
overs. They are smart, articulate, and committed to the ideologies they
bring to class. I argued for my point of view, but in that verbal bat-
tleground I had to fight my way into and out of the debate while some of
them tried to convince me and the other students that I was wrong—
which is the way it should be in democratic education.

To expand the topical theme from economic policy to other conditions influencing personal growth, I photocopied the essay written by
the Hispanic student who claimed that racism had been an obstacle to
his personal growth in the white high school he attended. White students there kept wanting him to talk jive like a ghetto Hispanic. He was
expected to be a party boy who liked to boogie and booze. He told me
privately that he had become an alcoholic in high school and was now
recovering. I was taken by the pathos and sincerity of his story, but that
is no guarantee that such a text will animate similar feelings in students.
An articulate and self-aware young man, he was agreeable to having his
essay read anonymously in class. With it before us, I posed the question
of racism being a limit on personal growth, and I invited reactions. The
discussion was disappointing. The white and minority students in class
responded minimally. I prodded students, asking if they had ever witnessed racial incidents in high school or on the job. Few wanted to answer. Thinking they might feel more comfortable writing privately
about this issue, I asked each person to write down a racist experience
she or he had had. Students did record some unpleasant and even har-
rowing encounters, a few of which I photocopied and read aloud with
them. Even so, the essays did not stir up class discussion. The students'
resistance was obvious. They withdrew from a tense topic in New York
life.

Student resistance had crippled the theme. After mulling over the
impasse, I decided to switch to another topic: sexism as an obstacle to
personal growth. I made the issue concrete by reading a news article
about young women in Ireland doing cheap clerical labor, under the
supervision of a young Irish male, for a runaway New York insurance
firm that had relocated its claims processing across the Atlantic. This
relocation was facilitated by the latest developments in computerized
clerical work. The high-tech revolution helped the company replace
American labor with cheaper workers in foreign countries; the runaway New York firm used satellite and cable contact to control a far-
flung computerized operation.

On the one hand, this story offered a chance to think critically about
the glamorized world of high tech. Were computers a good thing for
working people or for management? Is high tech a neutral, nonpolitical

force in society? The new computerized office starting up in Ireland had taken jobs away from New York, but had done more than open up clerical work in Ireland. Inequality takes many forms and crosses all borders. In this case, patriarchy over there and over here shaped the new operation. The Irish office immediately installed a male supervisor over a pool of low-paid women workers. A provocative photo accompanying the article showed a young male supervisor standing in front of the female office pool. That image helped spur dialogue. One woman in class announced with dismay that she worked for the New York company that was taking jobs to Ireland.

Opening up to the theme of sexual inequality, another woman told how she was driven out of an architecture firm because she was the only female apprentice and the men refused to share their trade secrets with her. The men would go to lunch without her, excluding her from their professional bonding. Office hours were lonely, threatening to retard her career. She quit. These personal experiences provoked lively and prolonged class discussion, which led finally from computers and runaway shops into writing essays on the question, "Are men and women equal in the United States?" The writing and discussion on this issue inspired probing debate. After the theme went through a process of writing, editing, revising, and class discussion, the time was ripe for a revision of their original essays on personal growth, to consolidate the critical dialogue.

I asked the students to rewrite their essays in a new format, with the paragraphing focused on separate issues, such as examining individual qualities that help or hinder growth as well as societal factors that serve as resources or obstacles to growth. The students rewrote their essays and attempted to integrate the topical issues into a new structure. Not surprisingly, some were better thought out than others. I photocopied several to use for class discussion, which opened up for this theme in ways it had not for the theme of racism.

I tested topical themes in this class, knowing that it is the teacher's right to use them while it is the students' right to reject them. I did not insist on the race issue when the students persistently refused to discuss it. Students cannot be thought of as a captive audience. If they don't want to discuss a topical theme, they must not be forced to do so. Forced discussion is wholly contradictory to critical-democratic education; it is just another version of the authoritarianism of the traditional school system. No ideals justify indoctrinating students. Their right of refusal must be equal to the teacher's right of presentation. That is what it means for authority to be democratic and mutual instead of authoritarian and unilateral. Further, the topical theme should be introduced as a participatory problem rather than as a lecture, so that the floor is always open for student voices to reflect and disagree. In the case of the example above—corporate policy and personal growth—a number of students defended tax breaks for giant companies as the only way to keep jobs in the city. Though they were not persuaded against tax abatements for big business, the issue became an open public debate, instead of being swept under the rug of self-reliant ideology.

Making the Topical Theme Work

I can report, too, on my use of such topical themes as the arms race and the Contra War in Nicaragua, in a nonfiction writing course for evening students.

For a student-centered start that also focused on the idea of transformation, I asked students to write about an incident in their lives that changed them and taught them something other people could learn from. Students wrote a rough draft, wrote a second draft, and then read their essays in peer groups for feedback on preparing a third draft. Following that, we discussed some of the essays in the class as a whole. They were largely narratives of family events, accidents, army stories, and so on, written as personally important but not socially relevant.

To connect personal experience with larger issues, I brought in readings about individuals whose transformation involved political change. One was the well-publicized story of Lois Gibbs, whose children were being poisoned by toxic wastes in the infamous Love Canal area in Buffalo, New York, until she and her neighbors organized. Gibbs later became a leader in campaigns against toxic dumping. Another article detailed a strike by women office workers against a bank in Minnesota, an event that changed the women's family lives, their social and work lives, and their political awareness. Each of the articles was an occasion to study writing techniques as well as the intersection of changes in self with change in society.

Our discussion of the content and the writing methods in both the students' stories and in the outside readings laid the groundwork for a topical theme some distance from personal experience. The good working relationships in the class encouraged me to introduce the difficult theme of the nuclear arms race, which was a current issue stirring much global concern, though little at my college. I decided to test a political issue not contained in their day-to-day conversation. Could a global problem cross paths meaningfully with their lives?

I wanted to introduce a global issue, hoping that they would do the same with their peers at work and in their neighborhoods. My interest was to situate a topical theme into their everyday lives, not only into a critical classroom. Was there open space in daily life not being used for critical discourse? Could a critical classroom reach out and fill some of that space with a topical theme?

To find out, I asked the students to interview their peers outside class about the arms race. But first, as an introduction to the theme, I asked them to write briefly about what the phrase "nuclear arms race" meant to them. We discussed their understandings. They spoke about the missiles accumulating here and in what was then the Soviet Union as if this was a dangerous but necessary way of life. I responded to their thoughts and read my own definition but did not deliver a lecture on the subject. Instead, I asked them to read selections from Helen Caldicott's *Nuclear Madness* and Jonathan Schell's *Fate of the Earth*, two texts widely discussed at that moment. I also brought in articles from the *New York Times* in which nuclear experts took opposing sides in the arms race. The students wrote reviews of these materials in addition to having class discussion of them. Then I asked each student to design a questionnaire about the arms race that he or she could administer to friends, family, and coworkers. We discussed different versions of the questionnaire, and I asked them to include some questions from me along with their own. Each would interview ten people and then write up a report that we would discuss in class.

The students accepted this project, and the results were often compelling. They and their peers outside class had some extraordinary conversations about an issue they had never before discussed seriously. One woman took over the conversation in her car pool for daily on-the-road discussions about the arms race. She was not at all reluctant to take advantage of a captive audience. As they drove to work, she said, each day her friends' resistance wore down, and they agreed to talk a little more about war and peace in the nuclear age. Another student, a man, took the questionnaire into his favorite bar, where he caught some hell—stronger resistance than did the woman in the car pool. Listening to their reports, I was taken by the students' intelligence and resourcefulness. I wondered to myself what the political impact would be if thousands of classes took critical discussion into everyday life to fill up the open space available for peer debate. Each of the twenty students in my class examined a global issue with ten peers. Multiply that by thousands of writing classes under way each term, and it is intriguing to imagine what a critical education system might add to public life if it replaced the traditional one we now have.

In another project, I compiled a packet of newspaper readings on the Contra War in Nicaragua. These reports were from mainstream media; some criticized the Sandinista government then in office in Nicaragua; some took a White House view of events; others criticized various aspects of America's role in the war. As before, I asked students to write what they knew about the Contra War, before they read anything and before I said anything, and we discussed their initial perceptions. In general, they had little information about the war and were not much concerned about it. Then I asked students to review the packet of readings, discuss the material in class, and design a questionnaire for their peers, once again to create some critical discussion in everyday life about a topical issue not in their daily conversation. We reviewed the various questionnaires students came up with, and again I asked them to include some of my questions with theirs.

Students held interviews and compared their own opinions with those of their subjects. They wrote up reports, comparing their own thoughts before and after reading the packet, in order to reflect on the state of their own learning. In class, we read selections from their surveys and their reviews of the packet, and discussed their changing perceptions about foreign policy, vis-à-vis Nicaragua.

This topical theme was illuminating and sobering for the students. They did not like to hear about this chapter in their nation's history. They had not known that their government was pursuing an illegal war, resulting in many civilian casualties. On the whole, they produced serious essays about Washington violating domestic and international law to make war on Nicaragua. They persisted in reading the materials and in interviewing people despite the difficulty of the topic and the resistance of their peers to discussing the issue. Like the topic of the arms race, students created a moment of political discourse in daily life around an issue that was not being discussed. From the bottom up, some small debate on foreign policy went on, unsupervised by authorities, in a corner of the city. At the end, I mentioned some activities under way to protest the Contra War, but these adult students appeared not ready to act on their knowledge.

Topical Themes at Other Levels

For another example of the topical theme, I can turn to a curriculum on apartheid developed by William Bigelow, a high-school teacher in Oregon, reported in *Strangers in Their Own Country* (1985) and in a guide, *Witness to Apartheid* (1987), to accompany a film by the same title.

To simulate apartheid, the teacher begins by dividing the classroom into two sections, one part 87 percent of the room (symbolizing the vast amount of South African land set aside for the 4.5 million whites) and the other 13 percent (the small amount left to the 22.5 million blacks). The class is then divided into two unequal groups, with five-sixths of the students being designated "black" and required to squeeze into the small 13 percent of the classroom, while the "white" minority of one-sixth roams the big space. The large black group cannot leave its corner without permission from the whites. This graphic introduction to life under apartheid teaches through participatory experience, not lecturing. To strengthen the effect, Bigelow asks the small group of whites to rule the majority by jailing troublemakers (in a special "prison" part of the room) and by handing out rewards, in this case chocolate candies.

This simulation is followed by films, discussion, readings, and some letter writing to students detained by the South African regime. The students read stories by South African students about their lives under apartheid, and then write letters in which they imagine themselves to be Blacks writing to antiapartheid supporters in North America.

The curriculum is well researched with student handouts on South Africa's economy and politics. But the purpose is not simply to transfer information. The students are asked to examine the reports on education, for example, and then decide how they would feel going to school under these conditions and what demands they would make to the authorities, to change these conditions. Bigelow's inventive curriculum encourages students to see knowledge as an active part of history. The students are not talking about apartheid when the class begins, so it is not a theme generated from their everyday lives. Bigelow's choice of apartheid as a topical theme shows how remote material can be made experiential and situated within a participatory curriculum.

Still, Bigelow and his co-teacher Christensen report that students can and do resist, especially when the teacher stakes out a position on topical material that is unfamiliar or contrary to everyday talk, the politics of the mainstream media, and the traditional syllabus. One way to ease student resistance to topical themes is to offer choices as well as the right of rejection. In class, I routinely ask students to suggest their own themes for discussion in addition to my choice of topical themes. When introducing a topical theme like tax breaks for corporations threatening to leave New York, I have other articles ready, to provide options should students reject discussion of a theme I offer.

Further, I count on a participatory beginning to help students feel they are codeveloping the study instead of merely listening to a teacher ride her or his thematic hobbyhorse. One interactive format I use is peer groups, which make collaborative reports on a topical theme, for class discussion. I do this by bringing in a reading or by posing a problem like "Why is there no Labor section in any major newspaper equal to every paper's Business pages?" I ask students to write their explanations, read to each other in groups, consult about their positions, and report as a group for whole-class debate. This cooperative learning format avoids having the teacher lecture students on a topical theme and then wait for them to respond verbally one at a time. It is difficult for many students to think on their feet in response to a teacher's lecture, question, or introduction of a topical theme. The writing and group consultation format allows them to think through their responses and to seek feedback from each other. In this format, they have the time and support to gain confidence and to develop a position collectively. By providing time and formats for students to develop their positions before the teacher comments on the issue, this cooperative approach to topical themes democratizes the teacher's authority. The topical issue enters the class process in a way that strengthens the students' ability to think it over and criticize it. In this way, there is less chance of students being silenced by the teacher's lecture or introduction of a theme. Substantial class time for students to think over their points of view before the teacher provides her or his opinions lessens the risk that the students' ideas will be overwhelmed by the teacher's. This approach maintains the teacher's authority to propose subject matter while also developing the students' authority to criticize it.

The process of *individual writing followed by small-group discussion leading to whole-class dialogue* insures that everyone spends time on the tasks—writing, reading to peers, debating the issue, and preparing to report. If the teacher only asks verbal questions for verbal responses, then the most assertive, most scholastic students will routinely dominate discussion, encouraging the others to fade out from the subject matter. By writing individually and consulting collaboratively before general discussion, more students use their minds and exercise their literacy on the topic.

Another way to increase student participation and to lower resistance to topical themes is to introduce them through personal narratives, like a doctor's touching report on the death of civilian families during the Contra War in Nicaragua, or another doctor's vision of the aftermath of a nuclear exchange between the superpowers, or an African-American's reflections on his early life in poverty and what it cost him to move up the ranks in a white-dominated society, or a woman scientist's account of sexist obstacles when she tried to enter a man's profession.

These approaches will make students less resistant to topical themes. Still, I expect some resistance, given their experience in traditional classrooms and their exposure to the official syllabus and the mass media. I don't give up after occasional moments of resistance in class. But in the face of persistent rejection I withdraw the theme and go on to new topics.

Some Origins of Student Resistance to Topical Themes

Part of the students' resistance to topical themes comes from their having internalized narrow perspectives in mass education and mass culture. They learn which topics, learning styles, and ways of seeing the world are normative. The normative views—like "You have to make it on your own" and "Columbus discovered America"—become habitual limits on public discourse and imagination. Such discourse in the United States occupies a narrow band on the political spectrum, from moderate liberal to conservative. Students come of age with little exposure to diverse points of view. With some exceptions, like the abortion debate in the United States in the 1980s and 1990s, they are not used to hearing divergent views on major issues. They are unaccustomed to engaging in critical dialogue and examining the merits of distinct alternatives. Lacking such experience in diverse critical discussion, many students facing topical discourse in class feel awkward and uncomfortable. It takes time for them to get used to a democratic atmosphere of debate, where it's okay to agree with or to criticize the teacher, other students, and the status quo.

More resistance to topical themes and critical learning stems from the students' rejection of challenging school work. Passivity is easier than participation. The critical classroom is more demanding than traditional ones, which expect minimal response. Year by year, many students lose their childhood curiosity; schooling wears down their intellectual interests. Because of this, they often resist the challenge of the topical theme, which is an energetic invitation to step into something new, to think about big questions related to everyday life.

Faced with a new, challenging discourse, students may also resist because they don't want to break ranks with their peers and appear to join forces with the teacher. Staying silent and withdrawn, not joining in discussion, is one way to display group solidarity. A student who joins in the discussion enthusiastically may be thought of as a teacher's pet, trying to overshadow the others. That student risks becoming an outcast, mocked by his peers.

From still another perspective on resistance, I would say that careerism makes many of my college students see knowledge *instrumentally*. How is this class an instrument to make money, the students may wonder. They have much less interest in gaining knowledge for social change and for intellectual and emotional development than for financial gain. In the conservative climate and hard times of the 1980s and early 1990s, students learned to see themselves as individual careerists, not as social beings and world citizens whose future depended on cooperation, peace, ecology, and equality.

Still more resistance may be generated by the student-centered process because traditional schooling has taught students that knowledge is serious only if it comes from the teacher or the textbook. If a democratic teacher begins the curriculum with the students' questions and understandings, then she or he may become the victim of the students' disregard for their own knowledge, learned from years of schooling that ignored what they know, say, and can do. The teacher who respects and uses what students know cannot take it for granted that students will react favorably. Many students will need successive experiences of themselves as knowledgeable, articulate beings before they value what they bring to class.

These various sources of resistance indicate that the road to intellectual empowerment in the classroom requires patience, experimentation, negotiation, and careful observation of student learning.

In sum, students are smart enough to recognize the empowering classroom in general and the topical theme in particular as appeals to think critically about self and society, to act with dynamic curiosity about life, to feel deeply and to deliberate publicly in a classroom involving harder work than the traditional ones, and to take active responsibility for their education and for their role as citizens. This is a daunting prospect to many students who have given up expecting much from school or public life. Still, others will welcome the invitation. While students in my classes may say to themselves that the teacher is a liberal, a social reformer, a radical, or even a communist, they may not let these negative characterizations block their participation in a topical theme. The way the topical theme is presented has an impact on their acceptance or resistance. If the teacher-student communication is mutual and respectful prior to introducing a topical theme, then the chance for acceptance is better. To present unorthodox themes in a participatory setting requires good democratic relations with the students and patient leadership by the teacher.

A Third Option: Teaching the Academic Theme

Another thematic option for the empowering teacher can be called the academic theme. The academic theme represents a scholastic, professional, or technical body of knowledge which the teacher wants to introduce or has to introduce as a requirement. Drawn from specific disciplines—history, nursing, computer science, accounting, biology, engineering, literature, physics—this academic material is not generated from student culture. Neither is it a political issue or topic in society. The academic theme is structured knowledge in a teacher's field.

Academic themes, like topical themes, can provoke student resistance because they are remote from the discourse and knowledge of daily life. Like social topics, academic subjects are unfamiliar and challenging. With their own jargon and structure, traditional academic fields use a scholastic discourse even more alien to everyday life than topical themes do. They tend to be abstract and formal, while everyday conversation is concrete and colloquial. And academic training orients those who possess it to lecture those who don't. Specialists in bodies of knowledge traditionally deliver packaged information to the inexpert, a didactic behavior which interferes with student participation.

Subject matter in career or professional classes, like memorizing muscle groups to become a physical therapist or blood components to become a lab technician or programming languages to become a computer technician, may meet less resistance than traditional physics or history or literature classes, because career skills are perceived by students as concrete and commercially useful. Career programs speak to real world activity, not to scientific abstractions or to remote times or to unfamiliar works of art. Further, career programs are perceived by students to have a dollar value in the job market. The actual record of job placement by career programs is weak (Pincus 1980), but students in such courses can at least recognize in them some relevance to earning a living. This does not mean that courses in accounting or computers or nursing inspire students more than do the liberal arts, but students more readily believe in their financial payoff, in contrast to courses in literature or history, which have no apparent relationship to getting ahead.

Still, even in dollar career courses, most students will have to struggle through transfer-of-information lectures. Pouring information into students is an alienating method. It makes students resentful, and it silences them. There is a segment of the student population, perhaps 20 percent, to whom a teacher can lecture bodies of knowledge with hope of the material sinking in. I will have more to say about this group in the next chapter, which contrasts critical dialogue with teacher-talk. For now, I want to observe that most students are too alienated by lectures to absorb the dense transfer of information. For them, academic lectures are words in a foreign language. This nonelite majority can think critically about many things, but not through teacherly lectures. They bring to class many ideas about academic subjects like math, science, and history, but they have not learned to call what they know "knowledge." Teachers, they think, have the knowledge that counts in school, while students have the know-how that counts for living.

Teachers are college graduates filled with academic knowledge from professors who lectured them in the university. Teachers generally teach what they were taught and how they were taught. They tend to copy the subject mater and the teaching methods they observed. Routinely, they lecture students on material defined by departmental divisions. Each department, each profession, each career specialty occupies a balkanized corner of education. It is embarrassing to say again that these academic divisions have produced much narrowness in learning. This is an old issue that doesn't go away. Writing some decades back about the problem of specialization, Kohl (1969) said that the teacher "has been hired to teach a specific subject and, because of that fact, is restricted in her own freedom" (43). Opposing the existing limits in English education, Judy (1980) suggested that "English teachers should see their subject as inter-disciplinary. English is not just literature and grammar; it is history, anthropology, psychology, biology, chemistry, physics, home economics, shop, humanities, and art" (99). Judy proposed interdisciplinary teaching for a subject that many educators think is more open than "hard" academic subjects like economics, engineering, or chemistry. But Kohl insisted that student-centered learning can be attempted in academic fields more restricted by bodies of knowledge than are language arts classes:

English is not the only subject that can be presented in an open classroom. I have seen history, science, math, and physical education classes based on non-authoritarian principles. In each case the teachers introduce the students to the possibilities for learning in their subjects and then step back and let the students discover what they care to learn. . . . In history there are central themes such as war, exploitation, love, and power that can be explored. It is surprising how naturally students respond to being presented with choices in any subject (1969, 43–44).

Judy also urged thematic approaches to humanities classes, while Knoblauch and Brannon (1984) argued for using writing for the making of meaning in all parts of the liberal arts curriculum. The idea of interdisciplinary themes—like studying math and physics in a cross-department course in "light" or "sound" (a program at the Central Park East schools in New York)—needs broad application to science and technical programs as well. Teachers working with academic themes can benefit from the choice and exploration Kohl emphasized, even in courses with special skills or bodies of knowledge to teach. If students are offered choices for study they will feel more ownership in the process.

The Problem Is the Solution: Posing Academic Themes

The teacher can help students own an academic theme by posing the subject matter itself as the first problem, as in my writing class which began with the question "What is good writing?" In a math class, the question asked might be "What is mathematics?" followed by "What are addition, subtraction, division, multiplication? Can you define them in your own words and experience?" Frankenstein and Powell (1991) and others in the ethnomathmatics field emphasize student writing about their use of math in their everyday lives. Questions to draw out this awareness of math in daily experience could be "Can you give examples of people you know who use math? What math do you see at work, at home, on TV, or in the newspaper?" To take the academic theme one step beyond student experience, the teacher could ask "Who uses math in our society for what purpose?" Math is one of the most abstract and specialized academic subjects, so it is a good place for problem-posing to show critical, student-centered approaches.

For academic themes in history classes, the problem-posing teacher could ask "What is history?" This initial question could be followed by "What history is most important to you? What do you want to know? Do you have a history? How would you find out about your history? Is your history different from your parents' or grandparents' history? Is history changing over the years, getting better or worse than it was in the past? Does history affect your daily life?" After these problems have been posed, written about, and discussed in sequence, history could be made intimate by reading first-person accounts from a period, to give living experience to the distant era. After reading these accounts, students could discuss them in groups, to develop their understanding of the age and the person they had just encountered, to share thoughts on how the story in the text applies to their own lives, after which the whole class might discuss the material. Further, as Kohl suggested above, the major themes to be studied from any era—migration, industrialization, colonization, democracy, revolution, injustice, and so on—can be presented to students for discussion prior to encountering them in texts. To do this, the teacher could put on the board such words as *frontier, industrialization, revolution, inequality,* and ask students to write what these words mean to them, followed by small-group discussion and then whole-class dialogue on what the students think, until the students have elaborated a discourse in their own idiom about these concepts, into which any text or lecture will be situated. By elaborating their discourse prior to receiving commentary from the teacher, the students will have a chance to develop the material in their own terms, making it less likely they will be silenced by the teacher's authority or by textbooks in the study of an academic theme. Still another critical and student-centered way to pose history as a problem was offered by Giroux (1978) in a social studies curriculum. Giroux asked students to read primary materials and then write history themselves from these documents, to practice being historians who came up with competing interpretations of events that had to be thought through and debated in class. This is a creative way to merge student-centered pedagogy with academic material.

Transforming Academic Expertise into Academic Themes

Participatory problem-posing can transform remote academic knowledge into themes accessible to students. It involves a two-way transformation of subject matter and discourse. On the one hand, the subject matter, a body of knowledge, is introduced by the teacher as a problem for students to reflect on in their own language. On the other hand, the students who come to class with their own universe of words, themes, and experiences are challenged to go beyond themselves, into a new territory not generated from their backgrounds. This dual transformation of subject knowledge and student knowledge is also a transformation of the teacher's role and classroom discourse, from one-way delivery of information to democratic problem-posing. The two separate universes of academic discourse and student speech end their isolation and reinvent a new "third" discourse that I will elaborate on later.

Can such a mutual process work in all subject areas, not only in the "soft" disciplines of the humanities? Subjects like language arts, literature, and social studies have some historical roots in the scrutiny of self and society. On the other hand, the natural sciences, technologies, business courses, and professional programs tend toward information-centered instruction, driving social criticism and self-examination off the map. Critical teachers in any subject can correct this imbalance. Freire (1973) proposed that "everything can be presented problematically" (125). Academic or technical experts, he said, can carry on a dialogue with students because dialogue does not depend on the course content:

Dialogue in any situation (whether it involves scientific and technical knowledge, or experiential knowledge) demands the problematic confrontation of that very knowledge in its unquestionable relationship with the concrete reality in which it is engendered. . . . In a table to be learned by heart, 4 × 4 is one thing; 4 × 4 translated into concrete experience is another; e.g., making four bricks four times. Instead of mechanically memorizing 4 × 4, the pupil ought to discover its relation to something in human life. . . . It could be said that the task of the history teacher is to situate isolated historical facts in their totality, to "explain" history. For me, the task is different: it is to present the material in such a way as to encourage students to think critically so that they might give their own interpretations to the data. (124)

This experiential and critical approach to academic study could be posed as a series of questions: What context did this subject matter come out of? What historical conditions does it reflect? What is its relation to the students' context? For example, how can biology connect personal health to industrial practices and to diet in this age of explosive cancer rates?

In critical architecture, students might discuss the construction dominating their environs. What are the buildings like in their neighborhood, school, or college? Do they think any are beautiful or ugly? What new sites are under construction? For what purpose? In the brave new world of the late twentieth century, architecture is dominated by dense condo complexes in crowded cities and in rural areas once green, by sprawling indoor suburban shopping malls, by spindly urban needle towers rising tall and thin on narrow lots (blocking out sun and air), by massive office buildings pushing out housing in city centers, by expanded prisons as an answer to crime (incarcerating more of the poor), by wasteful nuclear home ports for naval battle groups, by teeming multiplex movie houses instead of neighborhood theaters, and by theme parks instead of public parks. If such developments were posed to architecture students as a problem, what could they conclude about their society's priorities and the ethics of their future work? In cities like New York, roads, subways, and bridges are crumbling; housing, hospitals, and schools are inadequate. If architecture students were asked what should be built to make life humane and wholesome, what priorities would they come up with?

In elementary or secondary science classes and in college-level introductory science courses, the problem-posing teacher could begin by asking students to define their understanding of the word "science." The discussion could lead into students researching how they already have biology or chemistry in their daily lives. From their points of view, what science do they see or do every day? At home, cooking? Fixing cars? Using computers? The teacher could go on to ask the students what questions about science they want to work on, as the starting point for mutually constructing the curriculum. To contextualize science into student experience, the teacher could bring questions to class, appropriate for the age level of the students, questions like, Why is apple cider bubbly and apple juice not? How does aspartame in beverages fool the tongue into tasting sweetness when it isn't sugar? Why does bread rise? What do antibiotics do in the body? How does a broken arm heal? These kinds of issues can teach science through everyday experiences.

In class, the critical science teacher would emphasize hands-on experiments to make the curriculum active. To include students in decision making, the science teacher could also present them with a choice of laboratory experiments demonstrating a material, a reaction, an element, or a process. Working on different experiments, the students would report their findings to the class as a whole. Science should be an adventurous field project, especially for younger students, taking trips, exploring the environment, observing weather and stars, growing plants, grains, and flowers. Such projects would require visits to gardening stores as well as reading about what to grow. Each of these activities could be written up in a science journal, so that writing became a method for learning.

Academic Problem-Posing: Media Studies and a Critical Literature Class

As a participatory way to teach academic subject matter, I offer my journalism and media classes a structured exercise that follows a long discussion of their opening questions and definitions of news and mass media. This exercise involves a paradigm for media in society. I put three boxes on the board and ask students to draw them in their notebooks (fig. 1). The paradigm poses the media as a social system of interactive fields. Field A is comprised of major news organizations where information is processed, packaged, and distributed. Field B is the world of newsworthy events that are covered by news organizations. Field C is the consumer audience that receives or buys news products or reports from media outlets. For the model to be interactive, the fields must exchange things and influences. I draw arrows to indicate connections and ask students to write on each arrow what the fields exchange. The students do this individually at their seats, compare their answers in groups of two, and report their conclusions for whole-class discussion. At the board, I write their suggestions on each arrow, question them about their choices, and lead discussion on their agreements and differences.

At this point, I expand the paradigm to include two more fields, government and business (fig. 2). These additions complicate the model, especially the dual business section, Field E, which I divide into major corporations that own the media and those that are mass advertisers on

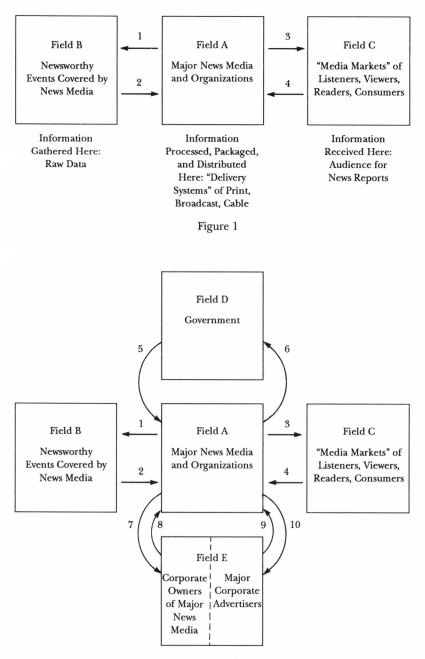

Figure 1

Figure 2

which the media depend for most of their revenue. Again I ask students to define the exchanges represented by the arrows, discuss their answers with partners, and report for class discussion.

This paradigm is a participatory academic problem that challenges the students' intelligence and ingenuity. In using it, they have asked what happens when the same corporation that owns media outlets is a big advertiser in the media, further complicating Field E. They have asked about the role of noncommercial operations like the Public Broadcasting System, and about the Associated Press, an organization that sells news to other media outlets, not to average citizens. They have wanted to know how advertising agencies that prepare commercials for the media fit into this model. Further, they ask what happens when business or government are newsworthy events covered in Field B. How do the media treat them, given the other connections they have? The problem of business and government influence on the media is built into the paradigm. If the issue does not come out of their questions, I draw it into discussion by asking, "In a democracy, what should be the relationship of government or business to the news media?"

This student-centered exercise asks them to develop in their own words a systematic vision of the news media in their lives. After they explain and discuss their perceptions of the arrows and their sense of the business-government-media linkage, I offer my comments, to include my knowledge and analysis in the exercise. This academic activity involves critical thinking and cooperative learning. It is followed up by a course text on the impact of mass advertising and monopoly ownership on democracy and the media (Bagdikian 1987).

In terms of teaching academic material like literature in a student-centered way, I might begin a literature class in New York by asking high school or college students, "Is street violence a problem in your lives?" I would ask them to write about and discuss this question. Further, I would suggest they ask family members' opinions on the issue, transcribe what they say, and bring that material in for class discussion. This would extend the inquiry into everyday life and make the theme a family experience, not merely a classroom-bound exercise.

In class, I would use an extended writing process for their compositions. After students had thought about the theme of violence for a few minutes, I would ask them to jot down their ideas, expand their notes, and choose the order for the points they wanted to make in their essay. After twenty to thirty minutes of writing first drafts, I would ask them to read over their papers to themselves, then read them to each other in small groups to gain feedback from peers, and finally to produce a revised draft from the group input. Following this writing process, we would read our compositions and use them as texts for examining good writing and for discussing the problem of violence.

Next, I would want to stimulate their imagination in rethinking this social problem. I might ask them to produce fiction: "Please write a story where someone tries to stop violence in your neighborhood." After some editing and revising of their stories, we would do class reading and discussion. I would ask them to read their stories to their families for their reaction before doing a final draft. I would publish these final drafts in booklets for the school and neighborhood, seeking out audiences to read the students' stories to encourage their self-image as writers.

I would then ask the class to study how violence has appeared in different texts through the ages—the official literature published in books compared to their unofficial self-created texts. I would ask them to read texts dealing with violence in society: fiction, nonfiction narratives, sociological essays. The class could move backward in time, to examine other moments of violence, like the slave revolt of Spartacus or accounts of Wat Tyler and the peasant revolts of the Middle Ages or *Romeo and Juliet* or *Henry IV* or the Puritan Army debates of the 1640s or chronicles of Columbus pillaging the Native American societies that he found or narratives of slave life and rebellion in the Old South. We could also read novels of civil wars like Scott's *Waverley* or Hemingway's *For Whom the Bell Tolls* or Malraux's *Man's Fate,* or accounts of industrial turmoil like Dickens's *Hard Times* or of urban life like Piri Thomas's *Down These Mean Streets* or of rural violence as in Alice Walker's *The Color Purple* or of political rebellion in Marge Piercy's *Vida.* I would ask them to read aloud at home one piece of literature, record their family's responses, and compare them to their own: "Did the literary text make sense to your family? How did they understand it? Did they think this was a good book? What did they say about it?" The family response would be discussed in class as another perception to be analyzed.

Lastly, I would ask students to write their responses to these questions: "What changes are needed to reduce violence? What should the mayor do to make your neighborhood safe? What should the police do? What should neighbors themselves do?" With the students' permission, I might send these essays to the mayor, the police chief, to local papers, and to community organizations for their reply. The final activity could be to invite community groups to class or to make voluntary visits to those groups' offices for a discussion on how to act on the problem. All in all, structuring literature into experience in a course like this would require extended critical activity, not an accelerated race to cover the syllabus, followed by a short-answer exam. The goal is to avoid a mere transfer of information, which is the passive method of traditional class-rooms. Students are *oversaturated* with fragmented academic informa-tion, not underexposed to content. They are underexposed to the passion of knowing themselves and their society. They are starved for meaningful contexts, for intellectual and emotional pleasure in the life of the mind, for holistic learning that feeds their understanding. Schooling teaches many students that education is a pointless ritual wrapped in meaningless words.

Meaningful Words: Problem-Posing Instead of Lectures

Academic subjects offer chances for participatory problem-posing, but unfortunately, specialized knowledge is most often delivered to stu-dents as inert information to memorize. Yet many teachers do not want students to merely swallow facts. Often they race through lectures be-cause they are required to cover large amounts of academic material. Their freedom to deviate depends on how closely they are policed by administrators and how cleverly they maneuver around the official syl-labus. Teachers are sometimes forced to abandon lecturing by the stu-dents, whose resistance to passive learning disrupts class until they are given something active to engage them.

Though faced by student resistance and a narrow official curricu-lum, many teachers want desperately to share their love for learning. They find history appealing, for example, because of the dramatic con-flicts of the past which changed society and passed down their effects to the present. Tracing contemporary life back to its origins is one way to experientialize the past for students. Physics and astronomy are excit-ing because of their reach beyond what we know about the universe. Many teachers have deep feeling for such knowledge and want to share it with students. Thus, lecturing on special knowledge sometimes starts from the best of intentions.

Empowering education does not reject a teacher's passion for knowl-edge or desire to pass on expertise. The critical pedagogy I describe in this book includes a role for the academic theme and even for a lecture situated in critical class dialogue, which I will explain later in the model for problem-posing. The academic and the topical themes take problem-posing farther into formal and advanced learning than do generative themes based in student culture. If the topical theme illumi-nates the social world of events mystified by the mass media and by the official syllabus, then the academic theme makes accessible the remote world of specialized knowledge.

The problem is how to present academic knowledge so that it does not silence students or sedate them. Dewey confronted the problem when he asked, "What is the place and meaning of subject-matter and of organization *within* experience? How does subject-matter function?" (1963, 20). His answer for the "new" progressive educators of his time was that "the newer education contrasts sharply with procedures which start with facts and truths that are outside the range of the experience of those taught, and which, therefore, have the problem of discovering ways and means of bringing them within experience. . . . But finding the material for learning within experience is only the first step. The next step is the progressive development of what is already experienced into a fuller and richer and also more organized form" (Dewey 1963, 73–74). The goal is structured, critical knowledge, but that cannot be the starting point. Student experience and understanding are the foundations into which academic material and structured knowledge are situated.

Situating Academic Knowledge

Just imagine how much curiosity and intelligence young people bring to life and how quickly they lose their enthusiasm for learning in passive schooling. Problem-posing through academic themes attempts to recover that eagerness to learn. Expert knowledge and structured subject matter can become fertile arenas for student development. But bodies of knowledge alienate students in classrooms organized as academic delivery systems. Academic language and bodies of knowledge need a multicultural compromise with the students' everyday language and experience. The academic world of knowledge is awesome, but unfortunately it was built without the participation of ordinary people and without respect for cultural diversity. It lives in a discourse and in places which exclude the nonelite. Everyday life is lived far from the benefit of academic study. By situating academic themes in problem-posing and in the students' understanding, the critical teacher tries to bring the two together.

Thus, problem-posing does not set itself against subject matter, scholarly knowledge, or intellectual passion. It seeks empowering formats for the study of any theme. Critical-democratic pedagogy can land on the doorstep of every subject, not merely in the form of the generative theme and not only in the form of the topical theme. Academic themes need a participatory process. In that process, the role of *dialogue* is crucial. I want now to consider the *dialogic* value in the agenda for this pedagogy, the making of democratic discourse in the classroom.

Critical Dialogue versus Teacher-Talk
Classroom Discourse and Social Inequality

4

Talking With: Dialogic Education and Empowerment

The first five values—participatory, affective, situated, multicultural, and problem-posing pedagogy—define some differences between traditional education and the program described in this book. An empowering teacher does not talk knowledge *at* students but talks *with* them. In a critical classroom, the teacher does not fill students unilaterally with information but rather encourages them to reflect mutually on the meaning of any subject matter before them. Such a classroom integrates structured knowledge into the students' speech and understandings by posing generative, topical, or academic themes. Hopefully, students will experience education as something *they* do rather than as something done to them. Further, students who make their education with the teacher have a chance to develop the critical thinking and democratic habits needed for active citizenship in society.

For critical and active learning, a sixth concept is central to problem-posing: dialogue. In this section, I will survey educational dialogue as a student-centered, teacher-directed process to develop critical thought and democratic participation. In doing this, I will contrast dialogue to teacher-talk, the one-way discourse of traditional classrooms that, I argue, alienates students, depresses their achievement, and supports inequality in school and society.

Empowering education as I present it here is a dialogic pedagogy. Mutual discussion is the heart of the method. Dialogue is simultaneously structured and creative. It is initiated and directed by a critical teacher but is democratically open to student intervention. Codeveloped by the teacher and the students, dialogue is neither a freewheeling conversation nor a teacher-dominated exchange. Balancing the teacher's authority and the students' input is the key to making the process both critical and democratic. Dialogic teachers offer students an open structure in which to develop. This openness includes their right to question the content and the process of dialogue, and even to reject them.

Critical Dialogue: The Roots in Human Development

As Freire discussed it, dialogue is an instructional method, a theory about discourse and learning, and a politics for cultural democracy. Its techniques and ideas extend beyond teaching and communication into human and social development. To him, dialogue

> must be understood as something taking part in the very historical nature of human beings. It is part of our historical process in becoming human beings . . . to the extent that humans have become more and more critically communicative beings. Dialogue is a moment where humans meet to reflect on their reality as they make and remake it. Something else: To the extent that we . . . communicate to each other as we become more able to transform our reality, we are able to *know that we know*, which is something *more* than just knowing. . . . We human beings know also that *we don't know.* Through dialogue, reflecting together on what we know and don't know, we can then act critically to transform reality. (Shor and Freire 1987, 98–99)

According to Freire, human beings are naturally inquisitive and communicative. By nature, he wrote, people are curious about their environment and conditions. They can learn what they know and don't know, and then use their knowledge to learn more as well as to solve problems they observe. Dialogue is a capacity and inclination of human beings to reflect together on the meaning of their experience and their knowledge.

Dialogue, then, can be thought of as the threads of communication that bind people together and prepare them for reflective action. Dialogue links people together through discourse and links their moments of reflection to their moments of action.

The politics of dialogue especially preoccupied Freire. He defined dialogue education as a "horizontal" relationship where people talk mutually, instead of the teacher talking at students or down to them. In this democratic discourse, the lecturing voice of the teacher is kept in check. According to Freire (1970, 1973), didactic lecturing, at the heart of traditional classrooms, is antidialogical, a vertical relationship between unequals, with authority on top and the students below, the authority speaking and the students being filled with official content.

Freire invested horizontal dialogue with a number of emotional values. One value was student-teacher camaraderie, which challenges the alienation that develops in traditional classrooms. Other values defined dialogue as "loving, humble, hopeful, trusting" (1973, 45). In another passage Freire was emphatic about what dialogue is *not:*

This dialogue cannot be reduced to the act of one person's "depositing" ideas in another, nor can it become a simple exchange of ideas to be "consumed" by the discussants. Nor yet is it a hostile, polemical argument between men who are committed neither to the naming of the world, nor to the search for truth. . . . It is an act of creation; it must not serve as a crafty instrument for the domination of one man by another. (1970, 77)

Student-teacher mutuality is the affective center of the method. The teacher leads the dialogic curriculum with the students' participation. This kind of teacher balances leading with listening to students, in a form of authority Freire called "radical democratic directiveness" (Shor and Freire 1987, 171).

Directive and Democratic: Teacher Authority and Dialogue

Dialogue is a democratic, directed, and critical discourse different from teacher-student exchanges in traditional classrooms. For one thing, it becomes a meeting ground to reconcile students and teachers separated by the unilateral authority of the teacher in traditional education. Secondly, dialogue is a mutually created discourse which questions existing canons of knowledge and challenges power relations in the classroom and in society.

To summarize some qualities of classroom dialogue, I can offer the following outline:

- a formal learning group directed by a critical teacher who has leadership responsibilities but who codevelops the class, negotiates the curriculum, and shares decision making with the students, using her or his authority in a cooperative manner;
- a process whose participants are responsible for evaluating the learning in progress, with qualitative methods for feedback and assessment, on an individual and group basis;
- critical consciousness of self, received knowledge, and society is a goal, in a learning experience which questions the status quo;
- an interactive, mutual discourse considering action outcomes beyond the classroom;
- time-limited, with a known start and end for each session and for the term, inside a structured program, formal school or college, or in a nonformal unit of education in a church, union hall, or community center;
- at times can be an educational part of a political group or voluntary association;
- for democratic change and cultural diversity in school and society; against regressive ideologies like racism and sexism, which are challenged in ways appropriate to the age of the students, the subject

matter, and the political climate at the institution and in the community;

• situated in the conditions and cultures of the students so that their language, themes, understandings, levels of development, and needs are the starting points;

• frontloads student expression and backloads teacher expertise and bodies of knowledge.

As I have said, dialogue in my freshman composition class often begins with students writing on the question "What is good writing?" I use my authority to lead the class, but I begin by posing a problem through which the students launch the discourse. I backload my comments following their remarks. My teacher's authority would have been traditionally authoritarian if I had posed the question and answered it myself, in a unilateral construction of the classroom discourse. Students would then have to adapt their thought and language to the words I establish as the foundation for studying the subject. Rather than beginning with a didactic, one-way lecture on the subject matter, I routinely pose a problem for dialogue as a participatory opening, thus inviting students to assume authority in making the curriculum with me from the beginning. The discourse starts with their responses, out of which come the issues and questions for further dialogue.

After they respond to my initial problem-posing, I respond to their statements. As they speak and write, I ask questions and make probing comments to draw out more responses. I learn from students the centrality of certain themes in their lives, and re-present them as problems for reflecting on the ordinary in an extraordinary way. I take a theme suggested by the writings, comments, or reading matter that students bring to class, and turn it back to them in problem form: "Should abortion remain a legal choice for women or should it be banned?" or "Should higher education be free and open to all who want it?" or "Should there be tuition and entry requirements?" or "Should there be required courses in college, or should students only take classes related to their majors?" In regard to topical themes, if no students suggest a key social issue in our opening dialogues, I often introduce one topically after their themes have helped us develop a working relationship.

Presenting a theme to students is not the same as lecturing on it. I present questions and issues inside a problem-posing dialogue. As the dialogue proceeds, I integrate and contextualize the material evolving in class. I offer comments, questions, and resource material. For example, if the class discussion on racism or sexism idealizes a peaceful golden age of American life, before affirmative action, feminism, or recent lawsuits and campaigns against sexual harassment, racial violence, and segregation, I bring in readings that provide historical and socio-logical background on the long-term battles in the United States over inequality, with a view to challenging myths of a prefeminist, pre–civil rights paradise in the past.

In a dialogic study of an academic theme like the mass media, I begin with a question for writing: "What do the words 'mass media' mean to you?" Students then write their definitions of "mass media." I invite them also to write down the questions they have about mass media. I do not start with a lecture. Instead, I join the class in writing a definition that I will read only after a dialogue on theirs is under way. This dialogic study of a specific subject matter—mass media—starts with the students' self-defined understandings and their questions. From this exercise, they learn that they already have knowledge and ideas that they can articulate in writing and in speech. They also learn that the teacher in this course asks a lot of questions and listens carefully to their answers, which are re-presented to them for close scrutiny. The teacher does not launch into a monologue. Communication is not one-way. Students' remarks do not get lost in the teacher's "talking over" their comments. I draw on my academic knowledge, whether in literature, mass media, or writing, only after students have established a foundation in their own words. I adjust my expertise to fit the shape of a dialogue they evolve in responding to problem-themes and my questions. These dialogic habits of the teacher communicate respect for the students. Their thoughts and feelings matter.

To vary the form of dialogue, from whole-group to small-group discussion, I ask students to consult with one or several neighbors sitting nearby, as a cooperative exercise, before reporting to the reconvened class. As each group reports definitions and questions, about "mass media," for example, I listen, take notes, and respond briefly. My responses do not correct each student as he or she reports; that would turn the class into a teacher-centered oral examination for students. Instead, I ask questions so that they will extend their remarks, providing more of their own words as the foundation of dialogue, but also giving me contact with the way they think and use language. At the end of their reporting, I read back to the class their own words and ask them to reflect on their definitions, asking, for example, "Do any of the definitions of 'mass media' contradict each other?" and "Are there common words, phrases, and ideas running through these definitions?" This encourages them to conceptualize their own work, which is an important critical habit of mind. Then I read my definition, asking students how it compares with their own.

In my definition, I offer structured subject matter. In the case of media study, I focus on delivery systems and scale of organization, contrasting high-tech, corporate mass media with community-based, alternate, small-scale, or noncommercial media. This gives students an academic framework for distinguishing corporate communications from low-tech media. It also reveals alternative information sources previously unknown to them and the huge inequality between the power of mass media and alternative ones. I also bring in copies of alternative publications unavailable at their newsstands.

Then I read aloud their questions about mass media and ask them to choose the common threads to launch our dialogue. I lead discussion on the key questions emerging from their own thinking. The words and thoughts of students are again the starting points, the base for codeveloping a dialogue in class about the systemic relations of business and government to the mass media and their audiences.

Codevelopment of Curriculum through Dialogue: Shared Authority

Dialogue transforms the teacher's unilateral authority by putting limits on his or her dominating voice and calling on the students to codevelop a joint learning process. The teacher opens the process to greater student participation, less student resistance, and more fertile contact with student thought and experience. Student participation feeds the teacher's research on how students think and learn. Such knowledge is the foundation on which dialogic teachers build successively deeper levels of thematic inquiry.

As one method of exploring the students' language and thinking and of developing their capacity for self-scrutiny, I ask students to do a self-study in writing. In the media class, the self-study is about their daily newspaper; in freshman composition, it is about their writing habits and their previous writing classes. The questions in the media self-study ask: "What newspaper do you read every day? Why do you read it? When did you start? How does it compare with other newspapers in the city? How often do you read the paper? How do you read it—page by page, article by article, headlines only, back to front or vice versa? What kind of events are covered most fully by your newspaper and what kind of stories appear least often? What are the politics of your daily paper? How can you tell? What do you like best about your newspaper? What changes in the paper should the editors and owners make? Why?" Teachers in other disciplines might begin with a biology self-study or an economics self-study, and so on, to find out what students already know of the subject and how they experience it every day. This activity would serve jointly as the students' self-analysis and a teacher's classroom research.

In media classes, the self-study tells me which dailies they read and how they read them. Knowing this, I can orient media references to their papers and bring them into class, to ground academic analysis in materials they know. The self-study also informs me initially about their cognitive and political development. And the quality of their writing tells me what usage exercises would be appropriate to develop their already existing literacy.

Further, from the self-studies I learn about their political understanding or lack of it. Not surprisingly, most students cannot define the politics of their newspapers. In their self-studies, most leave blank the question that asks them to describe their newspapers' politics. A few take a stab at it, either saying that their newspaper has no politics or characterizing it as liberal or conservative. Most lack a framework through which to name or perceive politics in the media, a significant part of their social lives. From a Deweyan point of view, they need a democratic education enabling them to perceive meaning in their culture and experience. From a Freirean perspective, they need a critical education so that they can read politics in their society when they read the printed word.

Mystified by both politics and the printed word, students in my classes have trouble understanding the world reported in their daily papers. They do notice that one or another paper supports this or that politician, but they may not know if that person is a Democrat or a Republican, conservative or liberal. The students are not sure what politics the paper is endorsing when it chooses a candidate. I don't give them quick answers in a lecture but try to develop their understanding through dialogue.

To begin a dialogue on politics in the media, I ask students to define two political words some have already used and which are often used around them—"liberal" and "conservative." I put these words on the board and ask students to write their definitions. Next, they read their definitions in peer groups to consult with each other and then report serially to the class as a whole. I take notes as each student or each delegate from a peer group reads her or his definitions. I ask questions along the way to clarify, connect, differentiate, and draw out what students are reading. From my notes, I read back to them what they have written, re-presenting their material for dialogue, so that they can identify common ideas as well as disagreements in their responses. Through this dialogic format, we generate some consensual and some competing definitions, which will be tested in the next phase by applying them to events reported in the media.

I write my own definitions of "liberal" and "conservative" but hold them until after the students have read and discussed theirs. When I read mine, I ask students to compare them to the ones they wrote, to make *their* discourse the starting point into which my academic thought enters.

After this exercise I ask the class to study articles, columns, and editorials and to decide whether the kind of politics displayed in each is liberal or conservative. I also ask the class to identify stands taken by various papers on topical issues like abortion or sex education in schools. I ask them further to read their newspapers at home and bring in two articles, one they would label liberal and one conservative, with reasons why they chose each—in writing. Their selections become part of the ongoing dialogue.

It is a challenge for my students to develop political definitions and then apply them to familiar and unfamiliar media material. This is not a simple exercise. At one level of abstraction, politics can be defined by generic labels such as "liberal" or "conservative," but students don't have one way of understanding these words among themselves, and they don't possess my definitions for these labels, so a dialogue is needed to clarify what they mean.

At another level, politics can be specified by reference to single issues. We can say, for example, that a newspaper is pro-choice or anti-abortion. If students notice such single-issue stands taken by the media, the next step is to abstract those specific items into general categories and to understand these positions ideologically, deciding whether such a stand is liberal or conservative. This abstracting of political concepts in relation to single issues can help students develop the ability to see general meanings in their immediate experience.

To go beyond liberal or conservative ideas to radical criticism, I have asked students to do the media project I mentioned before, to analyze why major media outlets have business sections but not labor ones and to construct a model Working Day section for a newspaper. This exercise reveals some hidden politics in the media that extend beyond the limits of liberalism and conservatism.

After our dialogue has worked through their self-studies, their definitions of liberal and conservative, and their self-selected articles, I provide packets of news reports for a study of journalistic vocabulary. This vocabulary offers structured knowledge in the field, which conceptualizes the meaning of events. I choose articles that include one or more of the following words: whitewash, smokescreen, stonewalling, trial balloon, jawboning, leak, unnamed source, atmospherics, tilt, waffling, and spin. To define these concepts here would be too long a digression. In class, I draw attention to these words and other news concepts, like puff piece and fluff, and ask students if they know what they mean. Some students know some of them and a few are willing to guess, but most are unfamiliar, which makes a good occasion for the teacher's expertise. I provide definitions after students have had a chance to speak and then ask them to discuss the situation reported by each article, to grasp what kind of situation is being characterized by each term. Students read other articles I provide to determine on their own which categories are applicable. They do this work first individually and then consult in groups before discussion by the whole class. Next, I ask students to read their newspapers at home and bring in their own examples. With their own choices in hand, they discuss their readings of the media from a new conceptual framework. This dialogic course's interest in subject matter also includes studying an academic text analyzing ownership of information sources, *The Media Monopoly* (1987) by Bagdikian. In this way, the dialogue is student-centered as well as critical and academic.

Limits on Critical Dialogue: Teacher-Talk and Student Silence

In the classroom, the transfer of subject matter from teacher to students limits dialogue and active questioning. In such a unilateral syllabus, the students are told what to do and what things mean. Through this passive, authoritarian discourse, students gradually lose their childhood joy of learning. They also lose confidence in their thoughts and language, making them defensively silent in the presence of a teacher who apparently has the answers worked out already. Their ideas seem to matter little in transfer classrooms, so why should they participate? Unfortunately, the effects of nondialogic classrooms spill over into participatory ones. Even when students trust the good intentions of a dialogic teacher who listens to them, many have already learned in traditional classes that a good student keeps quiet and agrees with the teacher.

Mass schooling conditions students and teachers to think that education is rigorous only if the teacher does most of the talking. If a critical-democratic teacher listens to students and encourages them to express themselves, students may question the validity of this dialogic education, precisely because it begins with their speech and respects their diversity and knowledge. This is one of the saddest consequences of the classroom discourse I refer to as teacher-talk.

Now, teachers say many things during class, and not all their utter-

ances are negative or silencing. Some matters of classroom management, like assigning projects and organizing peer groups, require
teachers to talk at length. There is also the need for teachers to explain
or summarize things at appropriate moments. As authorities in the
classroom, teachers display a variety of distinctive contents and styles in
their talk (Barnes 1976; Heath 1983; Cazden 1988).

That authoritative voice can function democratically or undemo-
cratically. To clarify how the teacher's voice becomes an undemocratic
instrument of teacher-talk that silences students and critical thought, I
can first summarize some of the contents of teacherly utterances as
• lectures and summaries on subject matter;
• narrative demonstrations of technical procedures;
• explanations of charts, equipment, and materials;
• instructions for doing homework, seat work, group work, and taking
  tests;
• reports of test results;
• direct questions to students on subject matter;
• verbal evaluation of student responses;
• comments and questions to students to clarify their spoken or written
  remarks;
• coaching advice to students during an exercise;
• comments and criticisms to discipline students;
• exhortations to perform better;
• announcements of upcoming events;
• taking attendance;
• teachers' reminiscences and comic asides.

Taken one by one, in a dialogic classroom, some of these utterances
can have a useful role in classrooms. Taken as a whole, inside a teacher-
centered curriculum that transfers knowledge to students, this agenda
of utterances functions to limit participation and silence students.

The styles of teacher-talk that make it a silencing, undemocratic discourse could be listed as follows:
• doing analysis ahead of and without the students;
• speaking quickly and too long in academic or technical jargon;
• talking over the students: interrupting them before they finish speaking; behaving impatiently when they speak, as if their remarks are un-
  important or as if the answer to the teacher's question is so easy the
  students should be ashamed of not knowing it quickly;
• asking questions requiring only brief or one-word answers the teacher
  already knows;
• answering their own questions when students cannot respond to the

material or to the discourse established unilaterally by the teacher;
- summarizing the class hour as a ritual to end a lesson instead of inviting students to share in making the summary;
- restricting time for the students' responses and questions;
- giving safe, traditional answers to students' questions or remarks instead of critical responses;
- restricting discussion of the students' experiences;
- limiting discussion and writing to required or teacher-selected themes and readings;
- discouraging students from responding to each other's remarks;
- not offering choices of themes and readings for discussion and study;
- discounting the students' reaction to the material when it strays from the ideal answer in the teacher's mind;
- correcting student speech to insist on standard usage; rejecting the students' speech (community idiom) as a vehicle for class discussion and writing; sending messages to students that they speak "bad" or "broken" English;
- responding to male students more often and more seriously than to female students; catering to the impulsive and instant responses of men while not structuring the class to meet the female students' needs for deliberation; allowing male students to interrupt female students and dominate discussion;
- asking complex, important questions of male students and simpler ones of female students;
- making no special efforts to include minority students in the discourse and multicultural themes in the readings and syllabus;
- lecturing uncritically from the official syllabus or the required textbook instead of questioning the nature of the course content; communicating to students that the subject matter is fixed and cannot be challenged, as if competing or alternative perspectives do not exist.

These antidialogic styles create the discourse of teacher-talk, which silences students. They establish a teacher-centered idiom for the classroom. Confronting teacher-talk is a first step in transforming unilateral discourse into democratic dialogue.

Because dialogue is the democratic negation, or opposite, of teacher-talk, a counter-agenda for dialogic styles could be made by restating the above list in opposite terms. In the classroom, a dialogic teacher would
- do analysis with the students' participation;
- avoid jargon or obscure allusions that intimidate students into silence;
- pose thought-provoking, open-ended problems to students so that they feel challenged in thinking them through;

- avoid short-answer questions, which make students feel like robots calling out the one right answer; encourage students themselves to come up with thought-provoking questions for discussion;
- be patient in listening to students and in giving them time to think on their feet, to think in groups, to write, and to read with understanding;
- invite students to speak from experience, integrating that material into social issues and academic themes;
- invite students to suggest themes for study and ask them to select reading matter;
- draw students out with questions after each one speaks and encourage them to respond to each other, instead of the teacher making the first and only response after a student speaks;
- respect non-standard student speech as a legitimate, rule-governed dialect for the classroom, parallel to Standard English, which also should be used and studied;
- ask students to summarize what the class hour accomplished and failed to do; join the students in making the summary rather than letting one party monopolize it;
- respond thoughtfully to female students' remarks; acknowledge women's issues in the classroom; treat unequal gender relations in class with seriousness, such as the impulsive hand raising by males and the more deliberate style of response by females; when men interrupt women, present such behavior as a problem that the students should reflect on and resolve with the teacher;
- seek equal participation for minority students; ask for their comments during the dialogue, consult with them to urge their involvement, include culturally diverse material in the curriculum;
- pose critical interpretations of the course subject matter and invite students to discuss alternative ways of understanding the course content.

This counter-agenda for dialogic discourse avoids habits that silence students, including the central style of teacher-talk, the transfer-of-information lecture.

Transfer Lectures and the Entrenched Position of Teacher-Talk

The transfer lecture on course content is the most common instructional method. It transmits information through the narrating voice of the teacher. Sometimes it is called frontal pedagogy because the teacher speaks from the front of the room to students sitting in rows; sometimes it is known as direct instruction because the teacher specifies exactly what the students should memorize. This traditional method of teaching, entrenched after generations of practice in schools and colleges, dominates our classrooms.

The dominance of teacher-talk, or "telling," in the classroom troubled one of the most thoughtful observers of American education, John Goodlad, architect of an eight-year study of schooling completed in the 1980s. Goodlad reported that

> No matter how we approach the classroom in an effort to understand what goes on, the teacher comes through as coach, quarterback, referee, and even rule-maker. But there the analogy must stop because there is no team. . . . On one hand, many teachers verbalize the importance of students increasingly becoming independent learners; on the other, most view themselves as needing to be in control of the decision-making process. The classroom is a constrained and constraining environment. The prospect of this setting slipping from their control is frightening for many teachers, not surprisingly. (1984, 108–9)

Goodlad's research into teacher-talk in traditional classrooms revealed minimal student participation:

> We observed that, on the average, about 75% of class time was spent on instruction and that nearly 70% of this was "talk"—usually teacher to students. Teachers out-talked the entire class of students by a ratio of three to one. . . . These findings are so consistent in the schools of our sample that I have difficulty assuming that things are much different in schools elsewhere. Clearly, the bulk of this teacher-talk was instructing in the sense of telling. Barely 5% of this instructional time was designed to create students' anticipation of needing to respond. Not even 1% required some kind of open response involving reasoning or perhaps an opinion from students. (1984, 229)

The degree of teacher-talk and student silence reported here is staggering. Less than 1 percent of the teacher-talk called for some open response from students. This is the stubborn reality faced by students and by dialogic teachers when they attempt to conduct a participatory classroom. The sad absence of dialogue that Goodlad found in the 1980s confirmed the results of his earlier survey of some 260 classrooms in the 1960s, from which he concluded that "Teaching was predominantly telling and questioning by the teacher, with children responding one by one or occasionally in chorus" (quoted in Silberman 1970, 159).

In another report on American schools, Sizer (1984) saw the same absence of dialogue:

> Save in extracurricular or coaching situations, such as athletics, drama, or shop classes, there is little opportunity for sustained conversation between student and teacher. The mode is a one-sentence or two-sentence exchange. . . . Dia-

logue is strikingly absent, and as a result the opportunity of teachers to challenge students' ideas in a systematic and logical way is limited. . . . One must infer that careful probing of students' thinking is not a high priority. (82)

This chronic problem of teacher-talk and student silence had come earlier to the attention of Silberman (1970):

Most teachers dominate the classroom, giving students no option except that of passivity. Exhaustive studies of classroom language in almost every part of the country, and in almost every kind of school, reveal a pattern that is striking in its uniformity: teachers do almost all the talking, accounting, on average, for two-thirds to three-quarters of all classroom communication. There are differences, of course, from teacher to teacher, but the differences are surprisingly small. (148)

Silberman cited research demonstrating that the most child-centered teacher initiated talk some 55.2 percent of the time and the most subject-centered teacher, 80.7 percent. Further, when students spoke, they responded minimally to the teacher's questions.

Those minimal responses are not the result of student mediocrity but are imposed by the discourse in the classroom, according to studies of language in school by Heath (1978, 1982), Sola and Bennett (1985), and Fine (1987). Fine, for example, wrote that teacher-talk and the official curriculum "obscure the very social, economic, and therefore experiential conditions of students' daily lives . . . and expel critical 'talk' about these conditions" (157). Heath (1978) found that teacher-talk in the classroom relied on a few restrictive patterns, such as "question-response-evaluation," where teachers ask short-answer "what-questions," students respond briefly, and the teacher evaluates their responses. This dominant pattern trains students to be passive respondents to official talk. Further, in studies of community versus school literacy, Heath (1983) showed how school language favored the literacy habits of middle-class children while denying the communication patterns of working-class pupils.

The inhibiting of the students' voices is an embarrassingly old outcome of teacher-talk. Dewey commented on the language problems of students in traditional classrooms:

Think of the absurdity of having to teach language as a thing by itself. If there is anything the child will do before he goes to school, it is to talk of the things that interest him. But when there are no vital interests appealed to in the school, when language is used simply for the repetition of lessons, it is not surprising that one of the chief difficulties of school work has come to be instruction in the mother-tongue. Since the language taught is unnatural, not growing out of the real desire to communicate vital impressions and convictions, the freedom of children in its use gradually disappears, until finally the high school teacher has to invent all kinds of devices to assist in getting any spontaneous and full use of speech. (1971, 55–56)

Dewey's reference to "vital issues" being absent from the curriculum anticipated Freire's turn toward generative themes taken from the problematic conditions of student life. This reference to vitality also points to the value of the topical theme in bringing the dramatic issues of society into the classroom. Unfortunately, the language problems Dewey observed a century ago in high school are still there and have infected college classrooms as well. With the expansion of mass higher education after 1950 in the United States, new community colleges adopted the old pedagogy (Cross 1971; Cohen and Brawer 1982). Teacher-talk still dominates mass education at all levels, undermining the democratic potential of expanded access.

Teacher Resistance to Dialogue: Persistent Habits

The problem of moving teachers away from teacher-talk and toward dialogue has preoccupied a number of empowering educators. Freire reported on his experience in organizing literacy projects in Brazil:

A major problem in setting up the program is instructing the teams of coordinators. Teaching the purely technical aspects of the procedure is not difficult. The difficulty lies rather in the creation of a new attitude—that of dialogue, so absent in our upbringing and education. The coordinators must be converted to dialogue in order to carry out education rather than domestication. Dialogue is an I-Thou relationship, and thus necessarily a relationship between two subjects. Each time the "Thou" is changed into an object, an "It," dialogue is subverted and education is changed to deformation. (1973, 52)

"Domestication" means making students passive receptacles for official knowledge. Domesticated students are no threat to inequality; they tolerate or celebrate the status quo. To be active, cognitive, and critical meant to Freire being a "subject," a person who has conscious goals and seeks methods to reach them, someone who takes her or his place in the world as a thinking citizen, a codeveloper of her or his education, and a re-maker of society who questions the unequal order of things. To promote this kind of democratic development in students, teachers have to first develop it in themselves.

Freire's complaint about teachers' resistance to dialogue kept recurring. When members of the elite decide to work for popular empowerment, he said, they show "a lack of confidence in the people's ability to think, to want, and to know. . . . They talk about the people, but they do not trust them." (1970, 46) Teachers from elite backgrounds were disposed to tell the peasants what to think, instead of engaging in dialogue with them. Freire's concern appeared again in his report of his literacy work with the new government in Guinea-Bissau: "In the last analysis, I am convinced that it is easier to create a new type of intellectual—forged in the unity between theory, manual labor, and intellectual work—than to reeducate an elitist intellectual. When I say this, I do not discount the validity of such reeducation when it does occur" (1978, 104). Still later, in regard to Guinea-Bissau and the problem of elitism among educators, Freire repeated his complaint with some irony:

One of the obstacles we sometimes come up against, standing in the way of this essential participation by the popular classes in the creation of the new education, is the old authoritarian inflexibility, which . . . is always liable to be reactivated, and, in its view, reorganizing education in favor of the popular classes is a task to be carried out by "experts" who know very well what must be done for the people. . . . (1989, 77)

For the literacy programs of newly freed Guinea-Bissau, I mentioned that Freire advised against using Portuguese as the base language, urging Creole instead. But the Guinean political cadres opted for the high-status language of the former masters (Freire and Macedo 1987, 160–69).

The difficulty of transforming the traditional habits of educators has been reported in other empowering projects. The problem came to the attention of Hope and Timmel, two community educators who worked long-term in East Africa. From their rich experience, they wrote an instructive three-volume guide, in which they noted "major problems with supervision and encouragement of animators [problem-posing, community-based, dialogic educators]. . . . The training of animators needs to become deeper, especially to help teachers understand the problems of the participants. Help is needed for animators not to slip back into using old methods" (1984, 1:119). The old authoritarian methods of academic experts lecturing non-academic students also appeared in the Adult Learning Project in Edinburgh. This program used outside consultants at times in its learning sessions but found that "some of the experts were unused to building interdisciplinary programmes and working dialogically. . . . Several resource people found it hard to dialogue with participants, and tended to hog the airwaves" (Kirkwood and Kirkwood 1989, 13, 68).

In another part of the world, the Nicaraguan Literacy Crusade (1980) also had problems implementing dialogic methods. Freire consulted with the Crusade organizers in 1979, and the campaign won the

UNESCO First Prize (Hirshon 1983). But weaknesses limited the impact of the young literacy volunteers. In a thoughtful study of the Crusade, Miller (1985) wrote:

The dialogue process was one of the weakest areas of the method, but it was still a significant advance over the rote memorization methods that had previously been used in the Nicaraguan educational system. . . . The process itself suffered from one major flaw. It did not include a step specifically designed to elicit discussion about the learners' individual personal relationships to the situation being analyzed. As a consequence the participants' sense of identification with the problem under discussion and feelings of responsibility for its solution were lessened. (220)

The lesser role for the students' voices decreased their participation in the classes. Without a moment for them to make their own meaning about the problem posed, mutual dialogue turned into teacherly monologue and student silence. This frustrated the young teachers, according to Miller, who fell back on the teacher-talk of the old education they themselves went through: "When large numbers of volunteers found that they could get people to discuss a photograph only superficially, some began to add speeches and lectures to the process. This spontaneous addition undermined the method" (220).

These reports on teacher resistance to dialogue suggest the prolonged transformation teachers need to change the habit of teacher-talk. One teacher who changed over a lifetime as she taught Maori schoolchildren, Ashton-Warner (1963), wrote that good teaching was the ability to engage students in meaningful discussion. She listened to the words of her pupils and used their themes for constructing "organic" readers reflecting their words and lives, instead of imposing Eurocentric basals with frontal grammar lessons.

Some Origins of Teacher Resistance to Dialogic Education

Future teachers have their craft modeled for them in the traditional schools and colleges they attend. They usually take formal teacher education programs that certify them. But in reality, all of their schooling is preparation for teaching because it socializes them year after year into the old norms of instruction. The socialization of teachers into traditional methods was a point Goodlad began with in his study of American teacher education:

What future teachers experience in schools and classrooms during their years as students profoundly shapes their later beliefs and practices. As teachers they follow closely the models they have observed. Mental stereotypes developed over years of observing their own teachers are not challenged or fundamentally

changed, apparently, by their experiences in formal teacher preparation programs. . . . Current practice exerts virtual tyrannical control over neophyte
teachers, and, consequently, considerable influence over their teaching performance later in their careers, as well. (1990, xiii, xv)

Students who become teachers learn the unilateral style of teacher authority. They observe that the normative discourse for the classroom is
one-way teacher-talk. Education is experienced as a delivery system,
with the teacher as a deliverer of skills and information to student receivers. This means lecturing students, transmitting official facts and
ideas to them, drilling them in standard usage, keeping them busy with
worksheets when they refuse to sit quietly for lectures, and eliciting
short verbal responses to factual questions. Education is something
done to students by teachers who dominate the classroom. Education is
serious when the teacher talks and students listen. With few dialogic
models to learn from, teachers tend to follow professional traditions.

On the job, urban and rural teachers are especially burdened by the
size of their classes, the number of classes they are assigned, the short
class hour, the many academic and personal needs of the students, the
oppressive paperwork and bureaucracy, the absence of resources and
support services, and the restrictions of required tests, texts, and syllabi.
Teachers themselves lack power in their institutions, which are run
from the top down. These institutions generally discourage experimenting and even punish teachers who rock the boat. Teacher-talk can
be a path of least resistance to the existing regime, or in everyday par-
lance, going along to get along.

Some teachers lecture because it makes them feel more secure, in
control of classes that intimidate them. It can be unsettling to teach unfamiliar students every year, especially in poorly run and badly funded
schools. Teachers often work in poor areas where the well-being of students and families has been virtually abandoned by society. But teachers in wealthier districts can also feel intimidated by the daily demand to
teach in front of alienated classes and by the emotional problems of students from affluent homes. Some teachers lack the experience, maturity, or support to allow their students freedom. They relieve their
insecurity by imposing stern discipline and a rigid curriculum on students. By transferring an approved syllabus, the teacher has a ready-
made means for asserting her or his authority. This frees the anxious
teacher from having to meet the students on their own terms, in their
own culture and language, and from inventing a critical and democratic
education with them. Lecturing is a safer, more reassuring way to teach
because teachers can establish a position that keeps students at a distance. It is far more challenging for the teacher to bring out students'

thought as the raw material for inventing the curriculum. It is also more challenging to share authority. Codeveloping a syllabus with students takes some experimental courage on the part of teachers.

Thus, some teachers who lecture or use worksheets to control the class do so to gain a protective distance from the students. This is especially true when teachers are put off by class or racial differences between them and their students. Teacher-talk is one way to deny the diversity of the students, because the differences of the students are bewildering, threatening, or demanding. Instead of facing up to the bewilderment, some educators hide from the problem by portraying students as uncultured, undisciplined, mediocre people, which justifies authoritarian structure to teach them what they don't know, for their own good.

To challenge this teacher alienation from students, we need multicultural, classroom-oriented, and student-centered programs of teacher education. We need, too, school and community support groups for teachers. It is hard for isolated teachers to relax in class and to experiment without support from other teachers, from administrators, and from parents.

Resistance to Teaching Subject Matter Dialogically

Still other teachers choose frontal lecturing over dialogue because they think subject matter cannot be taught dialogically. They honestly wonder how basic information can be developed in students if the class is participatory. Because the knowledge and skills they want to teach don't come from students, can a student-centered class teach anything significant? Problem-posing teachers ask questions for mutual dialogue, but traditional teachers do not see course content as a question; it is for them an established body of knowledge possessed by the teacher, not by the students. Concerned with transmitting skills or bodies of knowledge, many teachers think that little will get learned unless they lecture. Put simply, they have the knowledge, skills, and correct usage students lack, the information and language students need to succeed in school and do well in the business world. Many teachers with good intentions want to deliver that knowledge to students as efficiently as possible, which explains the appeal of didactic lecturing to them, as a fast funnel of information. Some think that minority students especially have been shortchanged by not getting the information or skills possessed by white students and the elite. They think it is time for teachers to give it to them directly.

It is, however, a mistake to see dialogic pedagogy as an approach that leaves out structured knowledge and literacy skills, just as it is a mistake to think that direct instruction is a fast way to teach information and correct usage. I have been arguing with examples that student-centered critical teaching balances the authority and expertise of the teacher with the culture and language of the students. To develop critical thought in students, the dialogic teacher integrates formal knowledge and literacy skills into a cooperative learning process so that students participate actively in their education. Passive, direct instruction puts their learning habits to sleep. It has already been tried for over a century and has failed as a means to educate masses of students. The passive curriculum of teacher-talk has dominated mass schooling since its inception, producing high dropout rates, underachievement, weak literacy, and undeveloped critical thought. Simply telling students what they must know cannot guarantee that they will listen, will learn it, will remember it, and will be rewarded for it in the job market. Without active student participation in the making of knowledge, the classroom will remain a boring place of undemocratic transfers of information, which alienates most students from serious study, thus turning them away from the very knowledge and skills the teacher hopes to pass on.

From another point of view, I would say that it is a mistake to pose traditional education as a means to overcome inequality in society. Mass schooling is not set up to transform an unequal society. On the one hand, mass education helps confirm inequality in society, through unequal funding of public school districts and higher education and through discriminatory tracking of pupils into different curricula. On the other hand, deficits of skills, language, and knowledge do not hold the disadvantaged down. Whites do not earn more than minorities, and men more than women, because their speech, skills, and knowledge are superior. Rather, the skin color, gender, English dialect, and job connections of some groups have been historically privileged over those of others. If education is posed as the answer to inequality, it is risky to assume that teachers who transfer bodies of knowledge and skills to disadvantaged students will be giving those groups what they need to become equal. On the one hand, teacher-centered classes will cheat the disadvantaged of the chance to develop independent critical thought, democratic habits, and cooperative learning skills. On the other hand, the problem would be falsely posed as educational deficits in the poor, in females, and in minorities rather than as class, gender, and race inequalities in school and society. Here again, the traditional approach blames the victim and protects the system. The deficient individual is set up as the problem and the traditional curriculum as the solution— another version of the myth of education as "the great equalizer," propagated by Horace Mann in the nineteenth century. For education to equalize society, according to this view, it has to fill the defective disadvantaged with the cultivation they lack for success, justifying again the one-way transfer of knowledge, skills, and correct usage.

In 1987, Hirsch became a celebrated spokesperson for the myth of education as the great equalizer, in terms of personal deficits and the disadvantaged. He itemized a Eurocentric "national literate culture" covering some sixty-four pages, which he said every American needs to know, especially the disadvantaged, who could use this knowledge to improve their condition. He argued that traditional knowledge was a key to success: "Cultural literacy constitutes the only sure avenue of opportunity for disadvantaged children, the only reliable way of combating the social determinism that now condemns them to remain in the same social and educational condition as their parents. . . . It should energize people to learn that only a few hundred pages of information stand between the literate and the illiterate, between dependence and autonomy" (1987, xiii, 143). Hirsch was entirely serious about the few hundred pages standing between the disadvantaged and their success in society. He provided those pages in two dictionaries, a large one for adults (1988, 546 pages) and a smaller one for children (1989, 248 pages), followed by a series of elementary curriculum guides appearing in the early 1990s.

Hirsch took progressive education to task because it rejects transmitting specific subject matter and correct usage to students, misled, he claimed, by its romantic desire to follow the students' interests and speech. He repeated traditional claims against student-centered pedagogy, namely, that it lacks structure, content, and high standards for language and achievement. On the other hand, he offered no critique of the long-term, pervasive inequality in pupil funding, in discriminatory school tracking, or in culturally biased standardized testing, nor did he explore the historical, racial, sexual, and class biases in society that influence educational and economic policies. His "cultural literacy" dictionaries gave teacher-talk two authoritative volumes of information to deliver to students, along with a scholar's rationale to continue the transfer style of teaching dominant in schools and colleges.

Can Traditional Teaching Empower the Disadvantaged?
Is Education a Great Equalizer?

It is worth looking closely to see if education, dominated by teacher-talk and Eurocentric culture, has been a great equalizer. Has society been made more equal by providing more traditional schooling? The record is not encouraging, especially if we focus on race. In recent decades, minorities dramatically narrowed the gap between themselves and whites in terms of high school graduation. For example, nonwhites from 25 to 29 years old have made impressive educational gains. Some 82 percent of them had gone through at least high school by 1986, up from 12.1 percent in 1940, almost equal to the 86.6 percent of whites their same age who also finished secondary education (Digest of Education Statistics 1989). In addition, Mortenson and Wu (1990) found that from 1972 to 1989 African-Americans from 18 to 24 years old had improved their high school graduation rate from 64.2 percent to 72.6 percent, while the white rate had only inched up from 83.3 percent to 83.8 percent. As more African-Americans were finishing high school, more were also taking the Scholastic Aptitude Test (SAT) for college entry. Despite an *increasing* number of African-Americans taking the SAT, which tends to depress overall scores, these minority students managed to *raise* their composite SAT scores 64 points by 1991, narrowing the historic 258-point gap between them and their white counterparts, as white students' scores stagnated from the 1970s on (College Board, 1991). But despite an increasing high-school graduation rate and higher scores on the SAT, the National Assessment of Education Progress, and the American College Testing Program, African-American high-school seniors had less access to college and less change of staying in college and graduating than whites. In a study of this racial inequity, Mortenson (1991) observed:

The college access rates for black high school graduates declined sharply between 1978 and 1983, the same period that white college access rates were increasing. . . . Baccalaureate degree attainment rates for white high school graduates have increased slightly during the 1980s, while the rate for blacks has dropped sharply. The failure of the black experience in higher education is all the more striking given the substantial improvement in preparation for college by blacks in elementary and secondary education. (vi)

Given the higher graduation rates and test scores of African-Americans and the flattened rates and scores for whites, Mortenson concluded that the increased access of whites and decreased access of African-Americans to college degrees was "the sharpest imaginable contrast." Greater achievement did not produce greater equality in higher education for this disadvantaged group.

Compounding racial inequality, lower family income also works against the collegiate aspirations of nonelite students. Schmitt (1989) found that only 6.8 percent of poorer high-school seniors from the 1980 class had graduated from college six years later. Mortenson and Wu (1990) further reported:

In 1989 a student from the bottom quartile of the family income distribution . . . had a 6 percent chance of graduating from high school, enrolling in college, and graduating by age 24. If the student came from the second family income quartile . . . his or her chances doubled to about 12 percent. At the next income quartile . . . the student's chances doubled again to about 27 percent. And between the third and top family income quartile . . . the student's chances redoubled again to about 55 percent. (124)

In community colleges enrolling five million students in the United States, where poorer groups and minorities are overrepresented, less than 500,000 two-year degrees are awarded each year, suggesting that fewer than 20 percent of these collegians graduate within four semesters (American Council on Education 1990). According to Goodlad (1990), 55 percent of African-Americans and 51 percent of Latinos who enter college do not have a degree twelve years later, while the same figure for whites is 33 percent. As of 1988, 16.8 percent of whites from 25 to 29 years old had completed four years of college compared to 9.4 percent of African-Americans and 8.1 percent for Hispanics (*Digest of Education Statistics*, 1989).

Unequal access to college degrees means unequal access to the best-paying jobs, which require college credentials. But even college graduation cannot guarantee income equity. Meisenheimer (1990) reported that in 1979 the median income of African-American male college graduates was 84 percent of the white male incomes in the 25 to 64 age group; ten years later the income differential had slipped to 76 percent. For younger men, 25 to 34, the ten-year decline was a little steeper, from 89 percent of the whites' income to 79 percent, but younger African-American women in this age group were able to improve their income position vis-à-vis younger white women, from 76 percent to 89 percent in the ten-year period. Equally striking is the report that in 1987 the median income of African-American males over 25 who had graduated from college was about the same as whites who had only graduated from high school, approximately $26,550 (U.S. Census Bureau 1989).

To see educational gains failing to translate into economic gains for discriminated groups, another place to look is the comparative unemployment rates of whites and minorities. Here, too, the evidence is not encouraging in terms of education being a great equalizer. The overall minority unemployment rate from the 1950s through the 1980s stayed virtually the same, in good times and bad, at about *twice* the unemployment rate of whites, despite the long-term advance in minority educational achievement (*Monthly Labor Review* 1989).

If education is a strong equalizer, we could at least expect some employment equity over the decades, just as we could expect rising high-school achievement to produce higher rates of African-American college success. Some explanations for this declining college success rate could be found in government economic policy in the 1980s, which produced an increasing number of people below the poverty line, weakening the financial floor under people of color, who are disproportionately represented in lower income groups. Further, higher college costs, more restrictive entry exams, lower federal aid to schools and colleges, loan programs replacing grants and scholarships, more required remediation, and increasing racist incidents on campus in the 1980s are among the other factors that may have discouraged students of color from attending college or completing their course of study.

The rising educational achievement of African-Americans in particular and their failure to achieve equality of employment, income, and access to college degrees suggest that the causes of inequality are rooted in the system, not in personal or group deficits. Discriminated groups have been demonstrating higher educational achievement in school and on standardized tests, but society is not rewarding these gains. Educational gains apparently cannot wipe out economic and social inequality, though some determined individuals from discriminated groups can move up through the system. Schooling can at best offer personal success stories for some students who start out at the bottom, but it cannot by itself equalize society.

Personal Success and Systemic Failures

Despite the weakness of education in reducing inequality, some disadvantaged students do use schooling to move up. The standard syllabus works for them. Teacher-talk in traditional education can be thought of as a cultural donation that a few can use to personal advantage, but not something that whole groups can employ to improve their unequal position in school and society.

Academic knowledge, correct usage, and work discipline cannot be drilled into the *bulk* of students to make them academic achievers and job-market successes. Only some students from poor, minority, or working-class homes can break the standard language and knowledge codes. This is not because only some are intelligent. They all possess intelligence. But only a fraction experience a peculiar blend of circumstances that makes them the academic cream of the crop, positioned for upward mobility. The peculiar blend of conditions that siphons off some for upward mobility includes access to the limited amount of excellent instruction available in poorly funded schools, a stable home that maintains a floor of support under a child selected for success, some extra resources or attention directed at the child's development, and a disposition in the child toward print materials and language learning, so that the child from a home where nonstandard English is spoken is oriented towards breaking the usage code and behavior rules favored by teacher-talk. (There are also exceptional children who will rise no matter how much *bad* is done *to* them or how little *good* is done *for* them.)

Individuals from minority groups and the lower classes who use teacher-talk and Eurocentric culture to climb up need bulldog stamina to tolerate the tedium of passive schooling, the indignity of surrendering their speaking idiom for an elite one, and the long delay in rewards from the job market. About this prolonged self-denial, McLaren (1989) wrote that "For many economically disadvantaged students, success in school means a type of forced cultural suicide, and in the case of minority youth, racial suicide" (215). He referred to anthropologist John Ogbu, who examined the plight of minority students trying to use school for upward mobility. Ogbu found that

blacks and similar minorities (e.g. American Indians) believe that for a minority person to succeed in school academically, he or she must learn to think and act white. Furthermore, in order to think and act white enough to be rewarded by whites or white institutions like the schools, a minority person must give up his or her own minority-group attitudes, ways of thinking, and behaving. . . . That is, striving for success is a subtractive process: the individual black student following school standard practices that lead to academic success is perceived as adopting a white cultural frame of reference . . . as acting white. (Quoted in McLaren 1989, 212)

Students from minority, female, and working-class groups face special challenges and sacrifices when trying to "make it" through education. Many face the painful choice between allegiance to their roots or to success.

Upwardly mobile individuals make headway partly because of their tolerance for teacher-talk and their patience in awaiting future payoffs, and partly because the huge numbers of peers left behind *do not rise with them*, and thus do not overtax the limited rewards in the job market. The successful lower-class student partly owes her or his success to the many who drop out of high school or don't go on to graduate from college—which is the vast majority.

Limited upward mobility helps maintain an unequal society. For the status quo to remain what it is, the economic system needs a *high* dropout rate and a flow of *some* lower-class climbers up the ranks. If the situation were reversed, an unequal society like that of the United States would face a crisis. That is, a *low* dropout rate and a *high* graduation rate would create serious pressures. If masses of students succeeded in school and college, the economic system could not possibly meet their expectations. On the one hand, wealth is not distributed equitably to those who work for it. Only some college graduates enter professions with good starting salaries (engineers, lawyers, doctors). On the other hand, even in the best of times there are not enough good-paying jobs to reward a mass of high achievers. The traditional curriculum of one-way teacher-talk, pervasive tracking, standardized tests, basic skills drills, memorized information, standard usage, and dull commercial textbooks is a program structured to produce the high degree of failure that relieves the unequal economic system of the need to reward a mass of high-achieving graduates.

To maintain inequality, then, the system needs a limited number of individuals who climb up and are certified for success, along with a mass of people certified as mediocre and blaming themselves for their own failures. Low scores on literacy and placement tests, and D's in English, provide apparently nonpolitical, scientific means for sorting out the gifted few (Clark 1960; Owen 1985; Meier 1989). Teacher-talk, a frontal pedagogy that denies student culture, contributes to depressing the achievement and aspirations of nonelite students.

Critical dialogue opposes all mechanisms for sustaining inequality. Dialogue has a *majoritarian* interest in the rights, voices, and potential of nonelite groups, not a philanthropic interest in the rise of a few individuals. It is a critical thinking curriculum for the majority who lack power, in a project oriented to questioning inequality in school and society.

Teaching for the Majority: Dialogue against Inequality

Inequality has been an unstable arrangement throughout history, but some periods are more stable than others. The political fit of teacher-talk with regenerating inequality in each new generation can produce stability only as long as failing students tolerate lesser schooling, lesser jobs, and political disempowerment. The dilemma since the youth rebellion of the 1960s has been the refusal of many students to accept their own subordination. Some of their resistance to authority has included self-destructive drug and alcohol addictions, sexual license and teenage pregnancy, violence and reckless behavior, sabotage of teacher-talk and the official syllabus, defiant anti-intellectualism, and work alienation on the job. The disaffection of the young means that the high failure rate of education adds to social instability. But the contradiction is that the economic system requires a high failure rate to maintain inequality, making educational and social life unstable. Inequality in the economic system would have to be transformed to reward higher achievement in schools and colleges.

Teacher-talk cannot solve these problems. It creates problems. Teacher-talk generates underachievement and alienation. It will continue to do so until teachers and students develop mutual dialogue. By itself, dialogic education cannot change inequality in society or guarantee success in the job market. But it can change the students' experience of learning, encouraging them to learn more and to develop the intellectual and affective powers to think about transforming society. The power to think critically and to act constructively; the power to study in depth, to understand school, society, work, politics, and our lives; and the power to feel hopeful about an equitable future—these are some of the goals embraced by dialogue when teachers and students accept the invitation.

Rethinking Knowledge and Society
"Desocialization" and "Critical Consciousness"

5

Democratic Authority and Intellectual Life

Classrooms thrive on democratic dialogue where learning is an open debate. Students need vigorous discussion in class for education to be active and challenging. On the other hand, teacher-talk depresses students. Teacherly monologue limits their speech and development. Feeling limited, they will turn away from intellectual life as an uninspiring experience.

While depressing the thought and action of students, teacher-talk classrooms also invite teacher depression. Teachers thrive on responses to their labors, and silent classes weaken their morale. Without lively student participation, they risk declining into burnout year by year.

To lead dynamic dialogue, teachers can develop some resources: their conceptual habits of mind, their capacity to do classroom research, their ability to listen carefully to students and to include them in reflecting on the dialogue underway, their skill in group dynamics, and their verbal creativity in posing problems for discussion. Teachers also need a commitment to democracy, which includes sharing authority with students. Allowing students' themes, understandings, and cultural diversity to codevelop the curriculum is one democratic goal of dialogue. But sharing power and integrating multicultural material are not easy, given the unilateral authority and monocultural traditions modeled for teachers in their own education.

The depth of the teacher's democratic habits influences student participation and learning. Cummins (1989), for example, concluded from his classroom research that "bilingual programs would be expected to have varied effects depending upon the extent to which they explicitly attempt to reverse the pattern of dominant-dominated power relations in the society at large" (38). The more egalitarian the relationship between teacher and students in the classroom, and the more the curriculum was built around the culture of the students, he found, the more chance it had to lower student resistance and to engage student participation. The development of the teacher as a democratic authority is thus a priority. The teacher's commitment to democratizing school and society gives her or him long-term goals, which help a teacher stick with experimental methods until some answers emerge. Transforming traditional education to dialogic problem-posing is an extended project rich in ups and downs.

Conceptual Resources: Developing Analytic Powers

As one resource for dialogue, a conceptual habit of mind is worthy of special attention. It enables the teacher and students to focus issues and to frame questions while dialogue is in progress. The teacher who leads and models dialogue is primarily responsible for synthesizing the students' remarks into questions and statements which re-present that material as a focused problem for further reflection. The teacher uses her or his authority and training to model reflection on the discussion, so that students themselves can see and practice it. This may be the most challenging moment for a dialogic teacher—to synthesize student responses while class is in progress.

In synthesizing class dialogue, the teacher has a limited time in class to devise a question or statement that pulls the process forward to the next phase of inquiry. If the synthesis of the dialogue is weak or inauthentic, then students are likely to resist responding, or they will respond in ways that lead the discussion astray. The refusal or inability of students to respond to syntheses posed by the teacher is an in-progress check on the problem-posing process, requiring an alternative synthesis to make the discourse flow again.

At times my students and I are not able to synthesize the dialogue well, because too much is happening at once, because our concentration wanders, because we follow a private thought that misses the heart of the issue, or because we are speaking too many steps ahead of the discussion. At those moments, I or others pose a question which students resist or which they seize on and take off into digressions. I notice the loss of direction and try to refocus the issue if time allows. I also ask students to attempt a new synthesis. Because few teachers have had this synthesizing experience in dialogue, they need to practice it often with a teacher who models verbal reflection on reflection.

In participatory classes where their remarks are taken seriously, students may begin speaking with a rush of voices. When students accept critical dialogue, a group that starts out unwilling to say anything can become a group where everyone wants to talk at once. This can be dizzying, exhilarating, and difficult for the teacher, stretching her or his group leadership to the limit. The dialogic teacher has to be fast in mind and speech, to structure the discussion so that people take turns and respond to each other. At this point, a teacher's democratic confidence in his or her students' intelligence supports the willingness to let the dialogue follow their remarks and their attempts at a synthesis.

Forward Development: Dialogue and Desocialization

Because critical-democratic dialogue questions traditional classroom relations, teacher-talk, unilateral authority, and the official syllabus, it can be thought of as *desocialization,* the seventh value on the agenda for empowering education. Desocialization refers to questioning the social behaviors and experiences in school and daily life that make us into the people we are. It involves critically examining learned behavior, received values, familiar language, habitual perceptions, existing knowledge and power relations, and traditional discourse in class and out. I will discuss two areas of desocialization in this chapter: (1) Desocialization from traditional school conditioning that interferes with critical thought, from the routine script of teacher-talk and student passivity, from the alienating roles teachers and students learn in mass education; and (2) Desocialization from mass culture, from regressive values absorbed from mass media and daily life, such as racism, sexism, class prejudice, homophobia, self-reliant individualism, excessive consumerism, authority-dependence, celebrations of militarism, and so on. Obviously, there is overlap between school behavior and school knowledge with the values learned outside of school, but in order to look at the situation systematically, it is useful to separate the two domains.

Socialization is the long process by which newborn individuals become adult members of their society. Socialization happens to everyone who grows up in a society, but people do not get the same input into their development. Social experience can vary greatly, depending on an individual's class, race, sex, region, physical ability, religion, ethnicity, and decade of birth (in terms of changing political, economic, and moral climates). People are socialized in the subcultures and economic levels of their families, which have unequal resources, opportunities, and power at their disposal. For example, many white families can afford private daycare and can hire women of color to tend their young children, who also benefit from having more toys and books bought for them, so that these children get extra attention to and care for their early development, while poor children get less. Further, public schools attended by poor and lower-income students differ from the well-funded schools offered to children of the elite. Moreover, the experiences of students in the academic tracks differ greatly from those of students tracked into remedial and vocational classes, and attending an elite private university is a different socialization into life and learning than attending a community college. Females get different and unequal socialization than males in school, in college, on the job, in the street, and at home. People of color develop in social conditions far more restrictive than those of whites. In sum, these unequal social experiences produce groups with different characters, abilities, and relationships to power in society. Diverse groups can have things in common—for example, baseball, cars, rock music, and fast foods are cultural phenomena in the United States that cut across class lines. Still, the stratified groups differ in many key respects, like dialect, dress, income, aspirations, and political participation. Basically, the privileged groups—the elite, whites, males—have more power, resources, and choices available for their development. Their privileged positions include the power to lead and maintain the status quo and to dominate the socialization of other groups.

Socialization includes compulsory mass education, which helps reproduce existing inequalities (Bowles and Gintis 1976; Oakes 1985). Working people did not create for themselves overcrowded and underfunded schools, subordinate tracks in education, and vocationalized community colleges. These lesser experiences were invented for them by elite policymakers. No one volunteers to become a third-class citizen. Average people don't go out looking for bad education, low-paying jobs, crowded neighborhoods, and less political influence in society; they want for themselves and their children the resources and choices available in the best schools, residential areas, and jobs. But schoolchildren from poor and working homes receive the limited learning and shabby treatment which confirm their lower status. Unequal funding, inadequate staffing and facilities, and weak curricula—all decisions made from above—dominate the socializing experiences of students from below.

Outside education, socialization is also dominated from above. The mass media exert a powerful influence on society and on everyday life. Control of the media is in the hands of a few giant conglomerates. These organizations produce few critical documentaries about themselves, the media, their power over politicians, or the extent to which the economic system is implicated in the critical problems of daily living. Instead, film and TV are devoted to sensational scandals, managed news, sex, horror stories and the supernatural, narratives about the police and the mafia, and romanticized family sitcoms. The case of some media politics in New York can illustrate how socializing culture is created from above by an elite for average people. The ailing *New York Post* was bought in 1988 by Peter Kalikow, a Manhattan real estate magnate reportedly worth $450 million. (He filed for bankruptcy in 1991.) Kalikow purchased the paper from Rupert Murdoch, an Australian press lord with an international media empire. Kalikow hired Peter Price as his publisher to continue producing the *Post* as a politically conservative, sensationalized tabloid for a mass audience. At that moment, Price was also publishing the elite *Avenue* magazine for rich residents in Manhattan. In this domain of culture production, the elite publish for the elite and for the nonelite as well, determining the style and politics of the media available at all levels. Working people do not publish their own daily newspapers or books just as they do not set up their own public schools, colleges, TV stations, or film studios; their influential school and media experiences are produced for them by an elite. If the elite did not dominate the schooling, media, and socialization of everyone, then it would be in a weak position to maintain the status quo and its privileged position. It could not readily persuade people to tolerate or celebrate the system as it is, socially unequal and environmentally destructive. To dominate socialization means to influence dramatically how people see the world and act in it.

But to dominate socialization is not the same as controlling totally how people develop, think, or live. The influence of the elite is not complete, even though it has been effective in sustaining an unequal status quo. Domination contradicts the democratic ideals espoused by Western societies. However, the level of resistance at work, in political life, and in schools is high. There is a culture of resistance in everyday life through which students and workers undermine authority, stymie the boss, cover for each other, develop their own communications, and negotiate for their needs; there is a culture of feminism spreading in society through which women negotiate individually and politically for their needs despite male dominance in daily life and in society at large; there is also a drive for multiculturalism led by people of color.

At the level of organization, a large number of dissident groups and alternative media exist. Autonomous politics and media at this level are small-scale and low-budget, but they are widespread in American life. A number of public and private schools are democratically co-governed by parents and teachers, while critical and creative educators in many traditional schools and colleges teach against the standard curriculum and organize for democratic change. Grass roots culture also includes handicrafts like weaving, woodwork, and quilting, as well as street performances. This indigenous culture is a counter to the dominant commercial marketplace. The commercial market coexists with it and occasionally distributes grass roots products for profit, as in the case of break-dancing films and some rap records. Because the political system has democratic traditions and is not a monolith and because the economic system can profit from marketing some autonomous culture, a few products critical of society make it to a mass audience, as in the case of Chapman's militant songs in the late 1980s and *Boyz N the Hood*, Singleton's extraordinary rendition of Los Angles ghetto life in 1991. But for the most part, opposition culture survives in radical small presses, newsweeklies, and magazines, in handmade film, video, and audio tape, in listener-supported radio and noncommercial cable TV, in dissident gallery exhibits, in alternate conferences and organizations, and in modest music cafés. These forms develop their own audiences, production facilities, and publicity networks.

On the whole, the vast inequality between mass media and alternate media, between corporate power and citizen power, and between traditional schooling and the number of critical classrooms or cooperatively run schools, interferes enormously with the growth of democracy. People come of age in a political and economic system dominated by elite products, language, perceptions, and policies. Students develop in a mass culture and traditional curriculum delivered to them, not created with them. We are inundated with messages and models for human behavior, such as that real men are tough and self-reliant, or that deep down in our hearts we all want to be rich and number one, or that the poor are lazy and get what they deserve, or that space shuttles are a great advance for humankind, or that women belong in the kitchen, or that we have to choose between keeping jobs or ending pollution, or that happiness is a new car, or that the Gulf War was a heroic victory for all Americans to celebrate. Specifically, students learn that education is something done to them, not something they do. A good student answers questions but doesn't question answers. Knowledge and authority are fixed and unilateral. To get a good grade, agree with the teacher, compete with other students, and memorize as much as you can. A serious classroom is one where the teacher does most of the talking and gives lots of tests. These patterns of socialization are not permanent or invulnerable, but they predominate, setting the tone for how people grow up dependent on the status quo.

When educators offer problem-posing, democratic dialogue in the classroom, they challenge socialization into the myths, values, and relations of the dominant culture. They also challenge the structure of authority in school and society, against unilateral power and for shared responsibility. In doing this, teachers offer a critical rethinking of existing socialization, which is the process I call desocialization. Critical teachers provide a social experience in education that questions previous experiences in school and society and that models new values, relationships, discourse, knowledge, and versions of authority. One new behavior pattern is participation. Another desocializing experience is student codevelopment of the curriculum. Still another is cooperative learning. A fourth occurs when students ask what is left out of the official syllabus and the commercial text, instead of memorizing their contents without question; a fifth when they reflect on how knowledge relates to action; a sixth when they study without the need for punitive tests to motivate interest; a seventh when they listen carefully to each other and respond without the need for teacherly intervention; an eighth when they write and read with authentic interest and speak with confidence, curiosity, and a passion for knowing.

Another value worthy of desocialization is competitive self-reliance. The self-reliance commonly absorbed by students develops them as isolated beings dissociated from public life and from cooperative relations with others. Of course people need to develop as self-starting, responsible, and aspiring individuals. But competitive self-reliance teaches people that win or lose we have to make it on our own. We are encouraged to build solitary careers where only our ambitions, incomes, buying power, and immediate family count. Public life, social justice, community, world peace, and the environment disappear as serious concerns. Success here is the power to make lots of money so that we can buy more than we need. This extreme individualism encourages us to blame ourselves should we fail to strike it rich by our lone efforts. It orients us to see personal initiative as the only resource people have. We do not learn that the system has been transformed in the past by organized efforts and can be changed again. The life laid out for us is to fit in one by one as winners or losers in a status quo presented as permanent and as the best of all systems.

Socialized into self-reliant individualism, we face society on our own, lone figures versus an economic leviathan. Such disempowerment is helped along by grading practices which evaluate pupils separately, one by one, and by that practice in teacher-talk where teachers question students verbally in class one by one. Teacher-talk helps socialize students into competing units relating individually to the teacher's interrogating voice. Against this disabling isolation, dialogue offers cooperative values and critical rethinking of knowledge and society.

Educational Counterculture: Desocializing Classrooms

One example of a desocializing course is a high-school class in history and English co-taught by Bigelow and Christensen. As reported by Bigelow (1989), they chose the theme "Columbus discovered America," a legend long fixed in American life. Hirsch (1989) thought the Columbus story so important for young students that he included in his children's dictionary of cultural literacy a romantic illustration of Columbus presenting Indians to the noble court in Spain. While Hirsch promoted a Eurocentric view of Columbus discovering America, Bigelow and Christensen sought to desocialize themselves and the students from this myth.

In taking on the Columbus myth, Bigelow (1989) found the admiral's exploits already embedded in the students' thinking:

> As the year opens, my students may not know when the Civil War was fought, what James Madison or Frederick Douglass did or where the Underground Railroad went, but they do know that a brave fellow named Christopher Columbus discovered America . . . Indeed, this bit of historical lore may be the only knowledge class members share in common. (635)

Bigelow and Christensen took student knowledge as the base for questioning received wisdom:

> Some students learned that Columbus sailed on three ships and that his sailors worried whether they would ever see land again. Others know from readings and teachers that when the admiral landed he was greeted by naked reddish-skinned people whom he called Indians. And still others may know Columbus gave these people little trinkets and returned to Spain with a few of the Indians to show King Ferdinand and Queen Isabella. (635)

The thoughts of students on the subject are the point at which critical dialogue begins. Those thoughts are social outcomes learned in mass culture and the traditional curriculum, two socializing agencies. In a desocializing class, existing knowledge is examined with the goal of gaining critical distance on what has been absorbed uncritically in school and everyday life.

Desocialization does more than question existing knowledge. It recognizes that socialization and curriculum are political processes of inclusion and exclusion; that is, what people learn to believe, say, want, and do presupposes other knowledge and choices left out of their development. Students in my media class discovered that business news is included in every daily paper while labor news is routinely missing; until then, the news had given them an unbalanced and unexamined socialization into seeing their society. In the traditional curriculum, the dominance of male, Eurocentric culture in the syllabus has meant the exclusion of multicultural material related to women, minorities, labor, and non-Western societies. Specifically, in regard to the Columbus myth, Bigelow pointed out that "What students don't know is that year after year their textbooks, by omission or otherwise, have been lying to them on a grand scale" (635). His course took on the task of integrating what was left out:

What is also true is that Columbus took hundreds of Indians slaves and sent them back to Spain where most of them were sold and subsequently died. What is also true is that in his quest for gold Columbus had the hands cut off any Indian who did not return with his or her three-month quota. And what is also true is that on one island alone, Hispaniola, an entire race of people were wiped off the face of the earth in a mere forty years of Spanish administration. (635)

Though Bigelow and Christensen possessed historical facts that challenged the myths of the official culture, they did not lecture students with an alternate body of knowledge. Their expertise did not take the form of a passive transfer of their perspective to students. Instead, they chose a problem-posing process.

As an experiential way to pose Columbus as a problem, Bigelow started the term by stealing a student's purse in front of the other students. Through this stratagem, he hoped to pose the problem of what it means to discover and possess something that belongs to someone else. Native Americans had been in the Western Hemisphere for thousands of years before the Europeans arrived. Their territory was not an uninhabited place discovered by white newcomers.

To make the stolen purse analogy work, Bigelow had secretly arranged with a female student before class to let him steal her purse. That done, he announced in class that the purse was indeed his (even though the students had seen him take it). The students objected to this chutzpah, but to prove it was his, Bigelow opened the purse and claimed all the possessions inside, including the hairbrush and lipstick. He reported that the students were "mildly outraged that I would pry into someone's possessions with such utter disregard for her privacy" (636).

After the students refused to agree that the purse was his, Bigelow then posed the second phase of the problem by asking "What if I said I *discovered* this purse, then would it be mine?" This decision still went against Bigelow, the students insisting it was not his purse even if he had discovered it somewhere, because it belonged to the student who owned it. Bigelow moved to the third phase of the problem-posing, where he contextualized it historically: "Why do we say that Columbus discovered America? . . . . Were there people on the land before Columbus arrived? Who had been on the land longer, Columbus or the Indians? Who knew the land better? Who had put their labor into making the land produce?" (636). Class dialogue on these issues moved forward from Bigelow's questions to a critical discussion of the verb *discover*. The investigation of key words is often central to problem-posing. Extraordinary attention to ordinary language in a critical context can encourage desocialization from received wisdom, which is often expressed in phrases and clichés long taken for granted. Bigelow and Christensen asked students to generate other words besides *discovered*, which textbooks could use to describe more accurately what Columbus did to the New World. The students offered such substitutes as "stole" it, "took" it, "ripped it off," "invaded it," and "conquered it." They renamed and reperceived an important moment of history in their own words, in an exercise where language skills, academic knowledge, and social awareness mutually evolved.

This problem-posing around language and history included reading historical accounts of Columbus. With a participatory and critical opening, the co-teachers brought in readings that narrated Columbus's rampage through native American society. The assignment was for students to compare this account of Columbus with the stories told in their school texts. They foraged in the library and in their old elementary and middle-school books, to find out what image of Columbus had been offered to them and to compare that image with the one in texts offered by the co-teachers. With a diversity of perspectives, they were asked which explanation made most sense to them. Texts in this curriculum are not the last word on the subject but rather become an area of competing interpretations. Transforming the students' experience of texts from bland official consensus to lively political contention is one desocializing goal of democratic dialogue.

Students read the differing accounts and then wrote comparisons of the critical and the official texts. To help structure their academic thinking, the teachers provided some guidelines in preparing reports: compare the accounts for factual differences and accuracy, for material omitted which is needed for a full understanding, for the motives ascribed to Columbus, for the person or persons you end up rooting for, and for the function of pictures in the books as aids in communicating messages about Columbus. The guidelines ended with two thinking questions:

In your opinion, *why* does the book portray the Columbus/Indian encounter in the way it does? Can you think of any groups in our society who might have an interest in people having an inaccurate view of history? (Bigelow 1989, 639)

Regarding the last question, on desocialization from received knowledge, Bigelow commented that it is important for students to think about whose interest is served by promoting a limited or false understanding of history. This in turn encourages them to question why something is written as it is, to argue with the text, to get into the habit of making meaning instead of waiting to be told what things mean. Bigelow suggested that thinking about whose interest is served by lying about Columbus may desocialize students from the values such myths encourage, like feeling that white Europeans should dominate minorities or other countries because might makes right, or because they are more "civilized."

As Bigelow put it: "We want to equip students to build a truly democratic society . . . We hope that if a student is able to maintain a critical distance from the written word, then it's possible to maintain that same distance from one's society; to stand back, look hard and ask, 'Why is it like this? How can I make it better?'" (643).

In another project in this class, Bigelow and Christensen took a less familiar incident in American history for academic study and desocialization: the Cherokee Removal of 1832. They studied the forced relocation of the Cherokee Nation from its ancestral homeland in the Southeast to west of the Mississippi, during the Jackson presidency, when native American lands were seized to develop plantations. Against their will, at the point of bayonets, the Cherokees were forced out of their homes by the United States government and put on a long march westward (the infamous "Trail of Tears"). By introducing this event, Bigelow and Christensen transformed the syllabus from a celebration of the status quo and a massage of the past into a critical examination of power and justice in American history. But again, they didn't lecture students; they read about and discussed the Removal with the students and then asked them to role-play the various forces involved: Cherokees, plantation owners, bankers, and members of the Jackson administration.

Next, the teachers asked students to write about a time in their own lives when they had their rights violated and what, if anything, they did about the injustice. This integrated the historical theme into student autobiography, rooting academic material in experience, combining generative and academic themes.

When Bigelow and Christensen asked students to read their stories, they suggested that they listen to each others' accounts for a new knowledge created in critical discourse—what they call the collective text. Such a text is a group portrait assembled from the various reports. It is a composite account of the group's experiences and understandings told in the group's own words, through which students do what I call "extraordinarily reexperiencing the ordinary," gaining critical knowledge of their unexamined experience. The collective text can build peer relations and desocialize students from authority-dependence, that is, from waiting for the teacher to say what things mean and what to do next. Students address each other and have a chance to identify with each other's lives. After hearing what rights students felt they possessed and their responses when those rights were violated, the students synthesized a conceptual whole from the contributing parts, seeking a collective text that allowed them to summarize the meaning of their experiences, including whether and how they resisted unjust authority.

As it turned out, minority students in that class wrote accounts of racist experiences that surprised the whites, who had been sheltered from knowing the day-to-day reality of people of color in America. The white students also reported problems with injustice, but these involved clashes with authoritarian teachers and administrators over rules and behavior, not over race. From this cross-cultural education in racial experiences, the Cherokee Removal curriculum led to a dialogue on what it means to accept or to act against injustice. This is a creative and critical way to connect history to personal experience, to connect white and minority experiences, under a theme of rights violation, and to desocialize students from uncritical appreciation of their nation's past and current racial problems.

Critical Re-perception of Past and Present

In terms of desocialization from a regressive ideology like racism, I reported earlier on a freshman composition class where students rejected a theme of racism that I offered and compelled me to seek a different topic. In another class I taught, the Columbus myth led to a productive exploration of racism. This second class, an evening session for working adults, was a second-level literature/humanities course titled "Utopia." In that class, students had been redesigning the college's curriculum, governance, and physical layout, in an exercise called "Utopia College," which invited them to imagine the kind of institution they wished they were attending, based on their critique of the existing college. I decided to integrate Columbus as an academic theme for the new curriculum they were working on.

I asked them to write down and discuss what they knew about Columbus. They gave traditional responses similar to those in Bigelow's class. Next, I told them that a scholar had published two dictionaries of cultural literacy that told Americans what they ought to know about Columbus and other things. Before offering them this official material, I asked them to refine what they had written on Columbus into two separate long paragraphs, one that could go into a dictionary for adults and the other for children. They edited and revised their passages and came up with their choices, which I asked them to read in groups of four, discuss, and then fashion into a group statement for each of the proposed volumes. We heard each group report and discussed the similarities and differences in their passages, which were mostly renditions of the official myth. I then brought in Hirsch's two dictionaries for cultural literacy and read aloud the passages on Columbus to the students, asking students to compare their choices for adults and for children with Hirsch's. This interesting exercise clarified the roots of their own knowledge in official history: what they had written was remarkably close to Hirsch.

To question their socialization into the Columbus myth, I then asked them to read a chapter from Zinn's *People's History of the United States* (1980), which offered a critical account of Columbus very different from the official story. The students were shocked to hear what went on in the years after 1492. The room was dead silent as I read excerpts from the chapter detailing the brutality of Columbus and his men against the natives. Some demanded to know why they hadn't been told these things in school. Instead of responding to that crucial question, I posed it back to them for dialogue. They reflected on their own question about what was excluded from their education, what they weren't told. After some discussion, they concluded that the truth might have made them question other myths and values being fed them by authorities as they grew up. I asked them if children should be told the real story or only a mythic version of events. They argued it out and agreed that school should tell the real story, not the "pretty" story, adding that it shouldn't be told to kids in a horrifying way. I next asked them to rewrite their original passages and come up with new paragraphs for an adult dictionary and a children's dictionary, the rewrite to include the new material they had learned about Columbus. They now had to synthesize their learning into their own language in economical and effective passages for two separate audiences, a not-so-simple task of critical literacy. They wrote, edited, revised, discussed their work in peer groups, reported to the whole class, and came up with new selections which integrated knowledge they lacked when they wrote their original paragraphs before. Though the new passages described Columbus's treatment of the people he encountered, the students avoided lurid language. They were rewriting their history texts and rereading their society. To test if this group's development included a desire to act on their knowledge, I mentioned that a group was meeting at the Graduate Center to plan alternative activities related to the upcoming Columbus quincentenary. But, at that moment, no one took me up on my invitation.

To point the way to another kind of action, I asked if they thought a special course on racism would be of value at our college, as an addition to the curriculum they had already been reinventing. I wanted to reconnect the Columbus exercise to the project of imagining a new college curriculum. I had been thinking about such a course on racism, given the racial conditions in the area and the city. To get this dialogue under way, I asked each student to write her or his responses to a few questions: "What is racism? Is racism a problem in our society? What causes racism?" The students wrote their answers, read and worked in peer groups, and presented group statements aloud for whole-class dialogue. I wrote my answers also, and read them during the dialogue. The discussion fascinated me. Students generally agreed that racism is a problem but could not agree on causes. Some blamed racist white parents, some blamed hostile or unambitious African-Americans, some blamed "forced busing" and the integration imposed on the schools, some denounced welfare and affirmative action for giving minorities special privileges, some white students denounced the blatant racism they had witnessed in their white neighborhoods, some blamed the media for inflaming prejudice by the loud coverage of racist attacks, some blamed the schools for not teaching tolerance.

To deepen the discussion on racism, to give it an academic dimension, I read with the class another chapter from Zinn, on the period of slavery in the United States. This section covered the deliberate and cruel separation of the races, the subordination of Africans, and the development of legal and cultural foundations for white supremacy. Next, we read a revealing piece from Gould (1981) on the racist use of pseudoscientific measurement in the 1800s to prove that African-Americans were inferior to whites. This historical background had as sobering an effect on the class as the earlier chapter on Columbus. They had never been told about the systematic oppression of Africans in the United States and were not aware of early solidarity between poor indentured whites and African slaves. From here, the class broke into project groups to plan a new course on racism, designing and debating everything from the title of the course to the readings, number of students, and class format. The students also debated whether the course should be required or an elective. Some asked whether it's fair to require people to study something they don't want to. Others said it was too important to leave out of a student's education. Still others said that if it was voluntary, the people who took it would need it the least, because the worst racists would avoid the course if they could. The longer we discussed this theme, the more support there developed for a course on racism at the college, which helped me decide to teach it in the fall of 1991 as one small way to help students develop some critical thinking on an issue bedeviling New York and the entire country.

I remember that one group in that Utopia class included two African-born students, who added a unique perspective to the dialogue. They suggested naming the proposed course "Apartheid in America" to indicate how bad racism is here. The room was quiet when they reported. The mostly white class was attentive and sobered by the perspective of the two Africans. The whites here, like those in Bigelow and Christensen's class, were unaware of the bigotry faced daily by people of color in the United States. Because students themselves were engaged in critical thinking and were addressing each other, they relieved me of the sole responsibility of desocializing perception on this theme. I could lecture less, dialogue more, and let the mutual process itself challenge socialization.

A Model for Desocialized Thinking: Critical Consciousness

Desocializing dialogue tries to develop *critical consciousness*. Freire (1973) developed a three-step model of development leading to critical consciousness. The three levels, intransitive, semi-transitive, and critical-transitive thought, sometimes exist in a pure state but can overlap.

Intransitive consciousness denies the power of human beings to change their lives or society. It is a static condition of fatalism which rejects human agency, denying that people can transform their conditions. Intransitive thinking is often magical and mystical, nonhistorical and prescientific. The intransitive person thinks that what happens in society and life is controlled by inscrutable or divine forces, by an all-powerful elite, or by dumb luck and accidents. These explanations for history and everyday events lead to a disempowering conclusion: ordinary human beings cannot control, understand, or change the way things are. Life is the way it has to be. The system is permanent and invulnerable. Things will either work out or they won't, no matter what you do. The powerful forces in life and society will do whatever they want, no matter what you think or say. You cannot act in society to change it, but you can pray for divine help, rub a rabbit's foot, buy a lottery ticket, or spend a lot of time in wishful thinking. The intransitive individual accepts or celebrates the status quo, has the most closed mind, and lives in political disempowerment, even though he or she may be hardworking, satisfied, and rich in personal relationships.

At the next level, a person with semi-transitive consciousness believes in cause and effect and in the human power to learn and to change things. But the world, nearby and far away, is thought of in isolated pieces, as if life and society existed in unrelated parts. The semi-transitive individual seeks to change things one at a time. She or he does not connect the pieces of reality into meaningful wholes but rather acts on parts in a disconnected way. This unintegrated view of the world does not perceive how separate parts of society condition each other or how a whole social system is implicated in producing single effects in any one part.

Semi-transitive thought is partially empowered because it accepts human agency in the making of personal and social change. This kind of thinking can take many concrete shapes that lead to partial or contradictory changes. For example, policymakers can raise requirements for high-school graduation without funding the new demands and without coming to grips with inequality in school and society, conditions that lead to student resistance to the official curriculum and eventually to dropping out. Educators concerned about the literacy crisis can emphasize grammar skills as the students' problem, without holistically considering the language students bring to class and the role of participation in helping students learn. Unruly students can be forced out of school to make halls and classrooms safer, only to make streets and playgrounds less safe. Similarly, city councils can pass laws forbidding homeless people to cluster in train stations, to make those spaces less crowded, but if the authorities don't provide housing for the displaced homeless, they just transfer the indoor problem into an outdoor one. Philanthropic groups may set up soup kitchens for the hungry without asking why so many people are hungry in the first place, in a wealthy country with an agricultural surplus each year. Urban planners may burn garbage or bury it to get it out of sight, without considering the resulting air and ground pollution, the root causes of an unmanageable waste stream, or the need to set up a vigorous recycling industry. Reformers in or out of government can propose health care plans without asking why so many people are getting sick. Politicians build more jails to cope with the exploding prison population in America without confronting poverty as a fundamental cause of crime and without facing the racial inequities of punishment. Thus, semi-transitive consciousness is one-dimensional, short-term thinking that leads to acting on an isolated problem, ignoring root causes and long-term solutions, and often creating other problems because the social system underlying a problem is not addressed.

Finally, critical consciousness, or critical transitivity, allows people to make broad connections between individual experience and social issues, between single problems and the larger social system. The critically conscious individual connects personal and social domains when studying or acting on any problem or subject matter. In education, critically conscious teachers and students synthesize personal and social meanings with a specific theme, text, or issue. The problem of literacy, for example, is addressed in a context related to the everyday life and language of students. History and literature are studied in relation to student autobiography. Science is contextualized inside student experience and in relation to power and problems in society. A class for critical consciousness explores the historical context out of which knowledge has emerged and its relation to the current social context. It suggests that people can learn what they need to know to act transformatively on the conditions they discover in school and society.

With critical consciousness, students are better able to see any subject as a thing in itself whose parts influence each other, as something related to and conditioned by other dimensions in the curriculum and society, as something with a historical context, and as something related to the students' personal context. Any subject matter examined in a critical classroom belongs to a larger context of history and society and has a relationship to the students' context. It developed somewhere for a reason, and it is still changing now. These are the dynamic qualities of critical consciousness which make it the intellectual centerpiece of a desocializing program.

To a critically conscious person, society is a human creation, which we can know and transform, not a mysterious whirl of events beyond understanding or intervention. The various parts of society affect each other, even though not all people have the same power to make laws, policies, trends, mass media, and income. Elite groups wield dominant power and wealth, but nonelite sectors can organize to change power relations. Knowing who the elite is, how it got there, how it operates in the economic system, and how its power can be democratized requires critical consciousness.

One example I mentioned earlier shows what it means to practice critical consciousness in class: the mass media's lavish coverage of business news and its inattention to labor reporting. The news rarely covers trade unions, organizing drives, boycotts, and labor disputes. When it does, the emphasis is often on violence during a strike, or on public inconvenience caused by striking workers, or on how new labor settlements will raise the cost of living or taxes for everyone else (Parenti 1988). Negative reports on labor can discourage public support for unions and strikers while helping the public tolerate strike-breaking. When labor news is covered, readers often see unions as violent, mafia-dominated, self-serving, or otherwise opposed to the public good. People learn little about the benefits, history, or methods of labor organization, in contrast to the in-depth education in commerce offered by the media's business analyses, background reports, personality profiles, corporate takeover dramas, and charts. A class project to criticize this inequity helps desocialize students from some media manipulation. When students in my media class produced their versions of a labor news section, they were practicing critical consciousness. The curriculum invited them to critically re-perceive a part of their unexamined social experience.

In sum, the desocialized thinking called critical consciousness refers to the way we see ourselves in relation to knowledge and power in society, to the way we use and study language, and to the way we act in school and daily life to reproduce or to transform our conditions. This consciousness can be summarized as four qualities:

1. *Power Awareness:* **Knowing that society and history are made by contending forces and interests, that human action makes society, and that society is unfinished and can be transformed;** discovering how power and policy-making interact in society, with some groups holding dominant control; how history and social policy can be changed by organized action from the bottom up; how ordinary people already make everyday life and the larger society by their work, play, family life, voting, purchasing; how economic policy affects daily life; how one can insert oneself into cooperative action to make change.

2. *Critical Literacy:* **Habits of thought, reading, writing, and speaking which go beneath surface meaning, first impressions, dominant myths, official pronouncements, traditional clichés, received wisdom, and mere opinions, to understand the deep meaning, root causes, social context, ideology, and personal consequences of any action, event, object, process, organization, experience, text, subject matter, policy, mass media, or discourse;** thinking in-depth about books, statements, print and broadcast media, traditional sayings, official policies, public speeches, commercial messages, political propaganda, familiar ideas, required syllabi; questioning official knowledge, existing authority, traditional relationships, and ways of speaking; exercising a curiosity to understand the root causes of events; using language so that words reveal the deep meaning of anything under discussion; applying that meaning to your own context and imagining how to act on that meaning to change the conditions it reflects.

3. *Permanent Desocialization:* **Understanding and challenging artificial, political limits on human development; questioning power and inequality in the status quo; examining socialized values in consciousness and in society which hold back democratic change in individuals and in the larger culture; seeing self and social transformation as a**

joint process; acknowledging and rejecting regressive values, actions, speech, and institutional practices reflecting racism, sexism, class hierarchy, homophobia, militarism, excessive consumerism, self-reliant individualism, environmental waste, the elite monopoly on the mass media, the bureaucratic control of institutions like schools and colleges, and the fascination with the rich and powerful cultivated by the dominant media; nurturing a passion for justice and a concern for the environment, for the community and for public life.

4. *Self-education/Organization:* **Self-organized transformative education to develop critical thought and cooperative action;** knowing how to study critically in groups or individually, how to find out about an issue or subject, how to get academic help; taking the initiative to transform the classroom into a critical student-teacher dialogue; building peer-organized learning networks; seeking affective learning for the rich development of human feeling; acknowledging the value of humor, passion, curiosity, intuition, and outrage as emotional dimensions of knowledge; developing educational projects coordinated with political groups, voluntary associations, or social movements; using critical reflection as a basis for cooperative action in society.

Situated Goals: The Real Possibilities for Change

Critical consciousness is a goal of desocializing dialogue, but the transformation possible in any class varies from situation to situation. How a class desocializes, through what means and in what direction, depends on specific circumstances. The age, race, sex, and career goals of students influence the outcomes, among other variables. What is appropriate for older students may not be for younger ones; the curriculum that works for African-American students may not be useful for white students; the critical curriculum that interests technology students may differ from one that appeals to English majors. Other situated factors include the school or college's physical and social conditions that affect teacher-student morale and concentration. Still other conditions affecting desocialization in critical classrooms are the openness of students to democratic dialogue, the level of the course and the nature of the subject matter, the quality of the students' emotional and intellectual lives at home and in the streets, the size of classes, and administrative interference with or tolerance of experimentation.

Desocialization should fit the students as well as the subject matter and the political climate surrounding the classroom. The students' diverse cultures, speech, and thoughts make up the ground on which a desocializing curriculum first plants its feet. Some students are more open than others to transformative learning, due to their age or political maturity or to the permissiveness of the local authorities. Dialogic teachers need to research their students, institutions, and communities to discover how much open space exists for desocializing education. The empowering program described in this book presupposes enough open space for critical teachers to experiment in their classrooms. If the school or college has a rigidly policed curriculum with mandated texts or frequent standardized testing, then the space for empowering education will be restricted. Critical teachers in these circumstances find ways to create space by teaching around the restrictions and by organizing with colleagues or parents or both for curricular changes. In restrictive settings, finding allies with whom to launch campaigns for school democracy can open up the space needed for empowering programs. That space cannot be taken for granted in the traditional institutions most teachers work in. It has to be discovered and broadened with like-minded allies.

One less apparent obstacle to desocialization is the degree of "accelerated" perception students display. Students exposed to mass culture develop speeded-up habits of thinking, looking, and speaking, which I described earlier (Shor 1987). Accelerated perception weakens the students' ability to examine ideas, texts, and events. Students are uncomfortable with the slow pace of reading and critical dialogue, which are deliberate, not fast like everyday conversation. The phenomenon of acceleration occurs from a variety of speeded-up experiences in everyday life, from television to rock videos to electronic games to instant video replays to fast cars to escalators to answering machines to word processors to microwave ovens to automated banking machines to the universal product code at supermarket checkout counters. Acceleration also results from the hectic pace of life in urban and suburban areas, where the speed of movement and media interfere with thoughtful scrutiny.

To counter this acceleration of speech and perception, the desocializing class can provide exercises for deceleration. Some practical ways to decelerate perception include

• self-reflective journal keeping;
• cooperative group work in class;
• reading out loud printed texts for class discussion to grasp their meaning and not just say the words;
• process methods for writing that include adequate time for successive thinking, composing, and rewriting;
• extended peer discussion of problems posed in class;
• long-term active research projects that evolve phase by phase;

• narrative grading rather than only number or letter grades, to encourage serious dialogue between student and teacher about the quality of the work;
• and self-editing and peer-editing methods to focus unhurried attention on the students' own texts.

Besides the speeded pace of perception which limits critical learning, there are other conditioned classroom behaviors standing in the way of critical learning. I mean such teacher-student interactions as playing dumb, getting by, reading the riot act, and having the final word. Playing dumb and getting by are habits developed in students already alienated by authoritarian classrooms. They are ways students learn to defend themselves against unilateral authority in school. By playing dumb, they distract the teacher and slow down the class, thus getting by with the least work possible. The second pair of classroom habits— reading the riot act and having the final word—are ways some teachers assert their authority and knowledge while unfortunately silencing students: they start class by setting down rigid rules and end class by giving a ritual summary. Later, I will suggest how a desocializing classroom can address these destructive habits.

Given the varying situation of each classroom, the limits on empowering education, and the multiple influences on students and teachers, there can be *general* paradigms of critical consciousness and *general* models for problem-posing, but not a fixed curriculum for how classes should operate from day to day or where they must end up. When it comes to desocialization, there is not one model against which any classroom can be measured. The development of any group is best measured internally, by assessing where the students began and where they have moved to. Each group will have its own evolving process. The best way for teachers to know what is being learned and not learned is by observing student activity and expression.

Sensible programs are those situated in the real limits and possibilities of the people and the places where the programs operate. Instead of one formula, I want to suggest a range of goals for desocialized behavior and thought in the classroom.

On the one hand, critical consciousness represents desocialization from some regressive values routinely absorbed in school and everyday life. To one degree or another, average students are silenced in teacher-centered classrooms. Held back from natural curiosity and dialogue, they grow up with underdeveloped academic interests. In class, they display depressed performance levels, having learned that education is something done to them, not something they do. Further, in daily life as well as in mass education, they are exposed variously to racism, sexism, homophobia, fascination with the rich and powerful, excessive consumerism, the generation gap, heroic militarism, self-reliant individualism, and a dependent relationship to authority. In this totality of socializing experiences, students are developed into passive learners, uninvolved citizens, and underperforming workers urged to buy things they don't need. Desocialization succeeds when it challenges anti-intellectualism, underperformance, nonparticipation, regressive social values, and apathy toward public life. Clearly, critical dialogue cannot challenge all these things at once, and it does not have to.

The question is where to begin in challenging the socialization students bring to class. Of the many values and behaviors expressed by students, which offers the proper starting point? The whole picture of student socialization presents too many values to tackle in a single classroom. It is wise to begin a desocializing curriculum with a key theme or value. Which to focus on is always a situated decision, determined by the concrete situation of the classroom, school, community, and age of students. By studying the students' use of language, by learning about their community life, and by discovering their interests, the empowering educator learns the key words through which to enter their existing universe for an exercise in desocialization. The empowering educator is also prepared to back off and change the subject if students exercise their democratic right to reject the themes under study.

Questioning socialized values in dialogue means expelling thought and language from their unexamined nests in consciousness, placing them on the table for critical scrutiny. With some critical distance on material not yet examined, people have a chance to see the matter in a new light, from a fresh perspective that enables them to choose the old or invent the new. This process gives students a chance to exercise informed choice, which is a foundation of democracy.

To define the kind of society modeled by dialogue and desocialization, I will go on in the next chapter to the eighth value on the agenda of empowering education: democracy. The goal of dialogic education is egalitarian democracy in class, in school, and in society. This democracy means an equal investment in the development of people from all cultures and both sexes. It also means equal access by the diverse cultures in society to political power, economic well-being, media production and distribution, and the school curriculum.

Democracy should offer teachers and students freedom to question their socialization, to rethink the status quo, and to act effectively on their critical knowledge. Traditional schools are not now enabling students or teachers to behave as reflective citizens in a multicultural democracy. Experiencing weak democracy in school, students respond with much resistance. Student resistance encourages teacher burnout among other sorry effects. Democratic, desocializing classes can reduce student alienation and foster critical learning, opening doors to the exercise of their many latent gifts.

Democratic Authority
Resistance, Subject Matter, and the Learning Process

6

Weak Democracy, Strong Resistance:
Why Some Students Play Dumb

Few things frustrate teachers more than students playing dumb. It is sad and exasperating. But playing dumb is produced by schooling itself, not invented whimsically by students who are stupid. They are, in fact, smart enough to twist their behavior into fake dumbness. If they are not dumb, what do they gain from pretending to be?

I referred before to playing dumb and to another student strategy called getting by, as well as to teacherly behaviors I call reading the riot act and having the last word. I will now discuss these habits as windows into democracy, the next item in this framework for empowering education. I have been suggesting that democratic authority is basic to empowerment and the dialogic process. In this chapter, I will focus the discussion of democracy on the problems of student resistance and on teaching subject matter democratically.

To begin with student resistance, I would say that playing dumb is a response to a school culture that offers on the whole a negative experience of education. Generally speaking, mass education presents students with undemocratic authority, passive learning and teacher-talk, depressant tracking, dull texts and standardizing testing, bland curricula, and shabby facilities in many districts. By themselves, these experiences can make intellectual life unappealing, but the turn away from academic life is often compounded by conditions outside school. The decline of social services and civic life in some communities has affected the families and streets where children grow up, undermining the support many need to perform at their best in the classroom. Conditions in and out of school thus provoke many kinds of student behavior, including a desire to play dumb in class. I will focus here on education as a generator of negative behavior.

To understand how undemocratic education generates resistance

135

like playing dumb, it is useful to remind ourselves of some of Dewey's ideas. For Dewey, human beings do not invent their behavior in a vacuum or in a laboratory. Behavior develops from experience and experience is social. Education is a developmental social experience which can produce one or another outcome in student behavior and learning. That outcome is influenced by the values and practices of the curriculum. Democratic education seeks to maximize participation in the curriculum, so that students develop intellectual curiosity, scientific thinking, cooperative relations, social habits, and self-discipline. Unfortunately, this is not happening in mass education. It is still structured as a pouring of knowledge into students, Dewey's own metaphor for passive teaching methods.

Dewey defined democracy as "more than a form of government; it is primarily a mode of associated living, of conjoint communicated experience" (1966, 87). Democracy, he insisted, is a process of open communication and mutual governance in a community of shared power, where all members have a chance to express ideas, to frame purposes, and to act on intentions. Unilateral power destroys democracy, in Dewey's conception, because a few monopolize authority to give orders and to define purposes, limiting the experience of others. As long as some wield dominating power and others take orders, as long as unequal wealth and power shape the education offered students, Dewey doubted that democracy or learning could flourish:

It is not enough to see to it that education is not actively used as an instrument to make easier the exploitation of one class by another. School facilities must be secured of such amplitude and efficiency as will in fact and not simply in name discount the effects of economic inequalities, and secure to all the wards of the nation equality of equipment for their future careers. (1966, 98)

A curriculum that is not "an instrument to make easier the exploitation of one class by another" emerges when students codevelop the syllabus and practice critical thought on knowledge and society. Another of Dewey's suggestions, to "discount the effects of economic inequalities" would require that poor and working students receive an extra investment in their schooling to compensate for the long-term unequal funding which we inherit.

Extra funding of poorer districts and nonelite colleges would be a great aid to democratic education, but students from nonelite families will also require a transformed curriculum. Dewey set the tone for connecting curricular reform to funding if the end result was to be a democratic school and society:

This end demands not only adequate administrative provision of school facilities, and such supplementation of family resources as will enable youth to take advantage of them, but also such modification of traditional ideals of culture, traditional subjects of study and traditional methods of teaching and discipline as will retain all the youth under educational influence until they are equipped to be masters of their own economic and social careers. (1966, 98)

Deweyan democracy means more than just free access to public schooling. It means enabling students to stay in school and to use it both as a personal developmental experience and as a force for cultural democracy.

Cultural and curricular democracy met for Dewey in his mutual definition of culture and education as active ways of learning and doing, not as fixed bodies of knowledge established and transmitted by authority. Culture, to Dewey, meant the ability to perceive meaning in experience and to act on that meaning. The purpose of democratic education, then, was to increase the students' abilities to make meaning from their experience and to act on it. Education succeeded when it increased the students' ability to learn, to act on learning, and to want more learning. Culture was the outcome of educated action and active education. He did not define culture as cultivation, that is, as a prepackaged list of facts, rules of usage, and Great Books.

Dewey's democratic agenda was advanced for his time and remains unfulfilled in ours. Given his early definition of education as a place where students should actively gain culture, make culture, and become active democratic citizens, it is sad to discuss now, decades later, students' resistance to learning, especially their talent for playing dumb in the classroom.

Resistance to Authority

Students who play dumb have learned in traditional classrooms that their role is to answer questions, not to question answers. Unable to perceive purpose or community in the curriculum, they grow up unequipped to analyze and transform their world.

Facing unilateral teacher-talk and authority in school, many reject intellectual life in the name of their autonomy. In class, this rejection takes many forms, and is a complex way of sabotaging oneself and authority at the same time, as Willis (1981) revealed in his study of anti-intellectual schoolboys in Britain. Strategies for denying school authority become strategies for denying one's own intellectual development, to keep invasive authority at bay. Among those strategies of resistance are playing dumb and getting by.

By playing dumb, students sabotage teacher-talk. They resist the teacherly authority that is imposing an alien culture on them. They reject the official syllabus that ignores their language, interests, conditions, and participation. Because the standard curriculum makes their subjectivity invisible, they are provoked to act out their vanished identity in ways that undermine the syllabus. Teacher-centered curricula define and create students as subordinates and deficits. To resist this unhappy designation, students disrupt the process by pretending to be dumb. Their fake dumbness takes a variety of shapes. They ask the same questions again and again; they ask for instructions to be repeated; they miss assignments and deadlines; they do the second thing first and the first thing second, like reading next week's chapter this week; they sit in the wrong seat or go to the wrong room. Fake dumbness originates as a way to keep the teacher and domination at bay, to prevent authority from invading their cultural space or erasing their identity.

Playing dumb wastes class time and the teacher's energy. As a strategy to undermine authority, it can limit the demands of a dominating curriculum. It undermines the lesson plan. Instead of going ahead with the prearranged plan, the teacher has to cope with a roadblock of fake noncomprehension. Here the students exercise a negative power. They can do this without understanding their behavior as I have defined it in this section. Some of what they do is conscious and some is a reflexive resistance to authority.

The second negative strategy of resistance, getting by, is just as clever as playing dumb. To get by, students manipulate the teacher for a grade while doing the least work possible. They do the minimum needed to pass or to get a *C* or low *B*. Or they sleep through the first half of the term, close to a *C, D,* or *F,* and then come on furiously in the later part, raising their grades on average to a *D, C,* or *B.* Generous teachers who like to grade students on their best work can often be manipulated to count the end more than the beginning. This variety of getting by is only one of the ways students manipulate teachers. It can remind us that students are not helpless people vulnerable to any scheme invented by the teacher. In getting by and in playing dumb, they show themselves resourceful and resilient, even if it's for negative or defensive purposes.

When getting by, students pay attention to the teacher's words, not because the content is inspiring but because they want to see what the limits and rules are and to pick up on the teacher's values. If they can mimic the teacher's words and values in discussion, on a paper, or on an exam, then it is easier to get a good grade. Speaking and writing like teacher-talk is the easiest way to get by. Students learn this trick early when answering direct questions and when taking exams. They get few responses to their own words or interests in traditional classes, but they do see how the teacher has answers already worked out in her or his own idiom. So they mimic the teacher's words to get by with the least effort and the highest grade. (Some of my students joke that A stands for agreeing with the teacher and D stands for disagreeing.) Students cleverly adapt to the undemocratic discourse of mass education. They are psyching out the teacher to see what her or his key values and words are.

Habits of resistance are learned early and well by many students in traditional schools. Unfortunately, these habits are carried into democratic and critical classrooms. Having internalized resistance to authority in schooling, students take their sabotaging skills wherever they go. Because of this, empowering educators face traditional student resistance as well as resistance coming from the invitation to empowerment itself.

Student resistance matches the resistance of the school to the students' diverse culture and interests. Students who come to school speaking community dialects quickly discover that traditional classrooms operate in an English idiom foreign to most of them. The discourse needed to do well is standard usage, the dialect of the elite. A fraction of students from nonelite homes can adapt to standard usage as their second dialect. Of the majority who don't, some retreat into silence, some into the fake voices of playing dumb and getting by, and some into disruptive behavior or dropping out of school altogether. Many students who copy teacher-talk and mimic teacherly values appear to do what's expected of them while actually memorizing the least necessary information, using it in the least demanding way, and forgetting it soon. In the culture war of the classroom, getting by and playing dumb express the students' contempt for a learning process which treats them with contempt.

Pretending to be dumb also establishes peer group identity. The dumb pretender gets recognized by other students as someone who acts up against the system, and he or she enjoys the prestige of the rebel. But rebellion is prestigious only when the existing powers are seen as oppressive. Rebellion may be common to the young, but it is not inevitable. Authority provokes resistance when it unilaterally makes rules and imposes an alien culture.

Enabling Some, Disabling the Rest: Undemocratic Tracking

Dewey suggested that education should increase the student's ability to learn more and to have more meaningful experiences. For some students, schooling does this. But the majority of students in the U.S. spend their school lives in the middle and low tracks of the system. A democratic program for education should be concerned first with this majority.

The tracking system may be the most undemocratic mechanism of mass education. In an analysis of tracking drawn from an eight-year study of schooling, Oakes (1985) observed: "Students seen as different are separated into different classes and then provided with vastly different kinds of knowledge and with markedly different opportunities to learn. It is in these ways that schools exacerbate the differences among the students who attend them" (111-12). Bennett (1991) reported similar findings and reached similar conclusions in a case study of first grade in an urban Appalachian school:

In this classroom, a mandated system of ability grouping in which at least one-third of each class was identified as "slow" learners determined the pace and type of instruction students experienced in the classroom and consequently limited their movement into higher-level groups. The school and social identities of these students were reinforced in classroom activities based on this ability-grouped reading program. . . . Students belonging to the lowest reading groups were provided with the most repetitive instructional practices. They were continually told through classroom practices that they were the less capable, "slower" students. (46)

One democratic alternative to tracking is cooperative learning through mixed-ability groups, as Schniedewind and Davidson (1983, 1987) and Slavin (1987, 1988) discussed it for the elementary grades. Another approach is the Accelerated Schools program designed by Levin (1987, 1988, 1990), which provides active, high-achieving, cooperative learning for at-risk students, who are offered challenging lessons once thought appropriate only for the gifted. In addition, Levin proposed taking a "whole-school" reform approach, where parents, teachers, administrators, staff, and students jointly participate in school management and planning.

Despite the advances made in cooperative learning, in "whole language" instruction based in meaningful texts and student expression, and in critical teaching; and despite the advances made in Levin's model for Accelerated Schools, in the Essential Schools developed by Sizer (1984), and in those schools following the integrated community-school approach of Comer (1980), tracking still predominates in mass education. Oakes (1985) observed that tracking in education did not invent social inequality but helped confirm it. Her findings questioned the meritocratic and democratic claims of education:

Everywhere we turn we see the likelihood of in-school barriers to upward mobility for capable poor and minority students. The measures of talent seem clearly to work against them, resulting in their placement in groups identified as slow. Once there, their achievement seems to be further inhibited by the type of knowledge they are exposed to and the quality of learning opportunities they are afforded. . . . Those least likely to do well were given the least in the three areas of school experience we studied (classroom climate, distribution of knowledge, opportunities to learn). Those most likely to do well were given the best. (134–35)

The neediest received the least and the most successful got the most, an upside-down formula appropriate only in a system based in inequality.

Oakes also found, interestingly, that students in all tracks, high to low, were offered passive, teacher-talk education. Most teachers were still pouring knowledge into students at all levels. High-track students did not have a participatory, student-centered curriculum in the schools she observed, but in the higher tracks, where white kids were overrepresented, students were exposed to academic, challenging material to stimulate their intellects and aspirations. Perhaps most important, in terms of affective development, upper-track kids were bathed in encouraging feedback, given many positive signals that they were the current and future elite. In contrast, lower-track kids experienced punitive and disapproving attitudes from teachers. In the lower tracks, Oakes observed the same depressant socialization witnessed by Bennett, with kids subjected to stern discipline, rote drills, and shallow subject matter. They were already being treated as the underclass of society.

Thousands of classroom hours socialize students in these ways until the new generation fits the existing inequalities of the system. As I mentioned earlier, Bowles and Gintis (1976) called this school-society link "the correspondence principle," where schooling corresponds to and helps reproduce class divisions. Oakes, impressed by the unscientific basis and unequal results of tracking, suggested that Bowles and Gintis should be taken seriously for their critique of capitalism as the economic source of inequality in schooling. The insights of Oakes, Bowles, and Gintis need one addition here, namely the insistence by Giroux (1983) on human agency, that is, on the ways students and teachers resist inequality and subordination.

Subordination and Getting By: Resistance as Low Performance

Downward tracking into dull, punitive classes encourages nonelite students to develop low expectations. Many come to expect less from society, from their intelligence, and from the job market. But the contradiction here is, How do you get high performance from people tracked toward low wages?

Low performance and student resistance to schooling in the United States came to the attention of Sizer in his study of high schools (1984). He observed a number of burned-out teachers defeated by students' rejection of academic work. In those classrooms, teachers and students had an unspoken arrangement that Sizer called a Conspiracy for the Least. In this getting-by accord, students agreed to behave well as long as teachers required very little from them. Because teachers and administrators prize orderly classrooms, students could use the threat of disruption to limit the demands of the standard curriculum on them. From the traditional classrooms he observed, Sizer concluded that in one sense "kids run schools," with their decision to cooperate, disrupt, or withdraw. Despite the nominal authority of teachers and administrators, apparently subordinate students actually have the power to determine the classroom's demeanor and outcome. In a power struggle such as this, however, student control is defensive and even self-destructive.

The students' defensive maneuvers allow them to assert themselves against the authority of the teacher. Students may not co-govern or codevelop the curriculum, but they know how to sabotage any regime that subordinates them and can also carry over sabotage into democratic classes intent on empowering them. This negative student power is totally different from transforming the curriculum positively into one for self and social change. Their sabotage is not a negotiation for an empowering curriculum but rather a reactive assault on the existing one.

Teachers who wonder whether critical classrooms manipulate students can recognize here the clever defenses students develop in school. They are the products of a domineering system that leads them to develop their own protections. School, like every institution in society, needs mass cooperation to work. Popular resistance undermines authority, whether through mass organization or through what I have called an unorganized performance strike. In undemocratic institutions (school or work), authority (teachers or bosses) and students (or workers) become hostages to each other. Their undemocratic relationship deforms both sides and cripples their potential productivity. The practice of democratic authority in the classroom is an attempt to end this standoff, so that purposes can be cooperatively developed with less conflict.

Conflict or Cooperation in the Classroom

In resisting undemocratic education, many mainstream students over-learn the performance strike. Their resistance is so well practiced that they can resist even empowering classrooms. In democratic classes, there is no open road to critical study or cooperation. It's important to reiterate that problem-posing teachers also face habits of resistance developed in the regular curriculum, even if they practice democratic authority. Teacher-centered pedagogy provokes student resistance, which spreads out from the official syllabus, infecting all corners of education.

Critical-democratic teachers hope to lower student resistance by drawing on the students' interests and by basing the curriculum in their language and understandings. About the empowering potential of learning, Dewey said that "knowledge is humanistic in quality not because it is about human products of the past, but because of what it does in liberating human intelligence and human sympathy" (1966, 230). To Dewey, it was "illiberal and immoral" to train students to join an undemocratic work world restricted by undemocratic authority. Education for democracy would encourage students to develop as *change agents* in school and society.

To enable democratic change, education needs, among other things, independence from business goals. Education should not be preoccupied with training for narrow job skills or with promoting the image of private enterprise. Students need a general, critical education that teaches them to learn how to learn, to question, to do research, to work alone and in groups, and to act from reflective knowledge. Job training should be extracurricular or postgraduate, or even the responsibility of employers themselves. Curriculum should not be driven by business needs because business policy is not made democratically at the workplace or in society. Business, industry, and the job market are not democratic or public institutions. They are operated hierarchically and privately from the top down. Why should education in a democracy subordinate itself to an undemocratic sector of society? Further, the labor needs of business change too often to warrant developing long-term curricula around them. The job market and the economy are not stable. Without warning, jobs appear and disappear. Without consulting employees, management can decide to close shop or to relocate plants and offices or to lay off workers. Education cannot be democratic if it is at the service of these forces.

Finally, for democratic education, teachers and students need freedom from standardized tests, commercial textbooks, basal readers, and required syllabi. These traditional practices restrict student-centered, dialogic, and participatory education. Freedom for teachers and students to invent methods and materials is crucial for democracy in education. There should be frequent and rigorous assessments of student learning. There need to be high standards for student development. But the instruments used to test and measure students should be based in a student-centered, cooperative curriculum. This means emphasizing narrative grading, portfolio assessments, group projects and performances, individual exhibitions, and essay examinations that promote critical thinking instead of standardized or short-answer tests. Because so much of traditional schooling is now organized around commercial texts, standardized tests, letter grades, and individual grading, it will not be easy to make this transformation, especially when large class size encourages teachers to give short-answer examinations that are easy for them to grade. Change will require an inside/outside strategy: empowering curriculum inside the classroom; democratic coalitions of teachers, students, and parents outside.

Monday Morning Agenda: Democratic Process and Content

For day-to-day lessons, my earlier discussion of how to teach dialogically anticipated the question of how to teach democratically. Dialogue is a student-centered, cooperative form of learning. A dialogic, problem-posing class evolves mutually from the knowledge of teacher and students. The teacher directs the process but not as a unilateral authority. The themes, thoughts, and diverse cultures of students come first; into this material the teacher integrates expert knowledge and social issues.

As I discussed earlier, many teachers have doubts about developing the curriculum from student input. If the teacher is the expert in a body of knowledge, how can she or he expect students to codevelop the course? How can uninformed students learn biology democratically? What will get learned in a history class codeveloped by students? Some would argue that democracy ends where ignorance begins. But critical-democratic educators do not define learning as the one-way transmission of existing knowledge. That would simply reinforce the status quo in school and society. Empowering education, in the framework of this book, is the exploration of subject matter in its social context with critical themes and bodies of knowledge integrated into student language and experience. The dialogic teacher cannot abandon structured content, the empowering class must have expert knowledge, and the democratic curriculum must be a rigorous process; but problem-posing changes all three elements.

As Dewey posed the issue for student-centered programs, academic expertise is structured *into* student experience, not set ahead of experience or separate from it. "The first approach to any subject in school," he wrote, "if thought is to be aroused and not words acquired, should be as unscholastic as possible. . . . (1966, 154) Isolation of subject matter from a social context is the chief obstruction in current practice to securing a general training of mind. Literature, art, religion, when thus dissociated, are just as narrowing as the technical things which the professional upholders of general education strenuously oppose" (1966, 67). Dewey emphasized the need for the teacher to discover the structures of student experience and learning so that academic knowledge could be integrated into them.

Democratic teachers of content areas, such as biology, history, literature, or nursing, could start by discussing how students see the course matter, what questions they have about it, and how the subject area relates to their experience. This situates dialogue in student subjectivity—their language, thought, aspiration, and memory. Then the problem-posing expands, moving outward to critical exploration of social conditions and academic materials. There are several intersecting contexts here: the student context as the starting point, the social context of the larger culture, and the academic context (a body of knowledge from a subject area).

In merging student context with academic context, the syllabus of a course should not be built around the encyclopedic information of a discipline. For a general and critical introduction to a field, students do not need blackboards full of data, lectures transferring information, or textbook chapters full of charts, equations, and terms. Such detailed bodies of knowledge are inappropriate for the general education most students need. Encyclopedic subject matter is appropriate only for upper-level collegiate majors and for graduate students in a field. For general education, students should experience relevance, subjectivity, and provocative debates in an area, not orthodoxies of information. In general science classes, they can study the chemicals, preservatives, and dyes added to their food and beverages. What are these substances? Why are they used? When did they enter the food chain, and why? What are the effects on the body? Which groups and individuals defend them? Which argue against them? Biology, chemistry, earth science, or health science classes could ask, How many acres and resources are used nationally to brew beer, ferment wine, and distill liquor? How many people could be fed if this acreage was devoted to food production? What would students say is the best use of these resources? How are alcoholic beverages made? Have the processes changed over history? What is each, as a chemical substance? Why do grapes and grains contain the potential for wine, beer, and whiskey? What is the state of being drunk? How does it happen physiologically? What long-term effects on the body does alcohol have (or sugar or caffeine or salt)? How much of these substances are in the students' diets and in the school cafeteria menu? Earlier I suggested that science classes could situate their bodies of knowledge in the local environment of the students' school and community. This would mean studying plants and trees in the vicinity or the quality of the local air or the indoor air of the school or college building or the water students drink from school fountains. Analyzing the air in urban classrooms could be especially revealing, to discover the chemical residues from vehicle emissions, home chimneys, and industrial smokestacks. This scientific study could be integrated with social science classes looking at environmental policy, especially in regard to the emissions standards debated at various levels of government. Studying air, food, and water could point to action campaigns against major polluters nearby. Examining the nutritional value of school lunches could lead to organizing for a healthier menu. To integrate literacy development into the study, these science classes could write reports to other students, teachers, parents, and administrators about the school air or the menu. Inspired by the relevance of science, some students will decide to major in it, at which point their own career choice justifies the transition from general education to confronting the encyclopedic canons in the field.

Avoiding passive transfers of information, the critical-democratic class can begin by exploring student knowledge or by posing the subject matter itself as a problem, through such questions as "What is good writing?" or "What does 'mass media' mean to you?" or "What is chemistry?" or "What makes a building architecturally good?" Opening with a problem invites a student-centered dialogue to begin. This establishes student perception as the foundation. As students share their perceptions, democratic teachers use them as the material into which successive problems and bodies of knowledge are structured.

Students need to be well informed if they are to act democratically in school and society. But masses of information are not needed to practice critical thought and democratic participation. Critical thinking is an analytic and imaginative habit of mind, which reflects on material in a meaningful context; it is not a warehouse of data (Brookfield 1987, 3–34). As Booth (1987) wrote, "The last thing American education needs is one more collection of inert information, a nostrum to be poured raw into minds not actively engaged in reading, thinking, writing, and talking. . . . Abstracted lists of terms would not motivate our students to become spontaneous learners. . . . They would increase the tendency of too many of our schools to kill whatever spontaneity the children bring when they enter school" (viii–ix).

Thus, democratic education opposes fact-saturation and skills-drilling. It asserts the difference between general education and education for majors in a field. Posing academic bodies of knowledge for students to memorize is destructive and inappropriate for most of the time spent by most students in school. Through problem-posing dialogue, students can gain skills and information, but in meaningful contexts, as part of a critical inquiry, in a program centered in the students' language and learning. How to do this practically in the classroom is worthy of detailed examples.

Democratic Curriculum: Transforming Subject Matter

To bring out the students' critical habits of mind, dialogic teachers employ a problem-posing method that frontloads student thought and backloads teacher commentary. Without a dialogic process, classrooms will be dominated by teacher-talk. Without critical inquiry into knowledge and society, they will be cultural transmissions supporting the status quo.

To begin critical-democratic classes, I ask questions like these: "What is news?" "What does 'mass media' mean?" "What is good writing?" and "What is 'the American Dream'?" Students provide the opening texts and questions for dialogue. Other critical-democratic methods have been developed by Frankenstein (1989), a pioneering educator who is part of a critical math and ethnomathematics movement. To begin critical math, Frankenstein asks students to write and reflect on their math experiences in school and daily life. From this student-centered opening, the teacher learns about the anxiety, anger, and misperceptions students bring to class, as well as their state of knowledge about math. Frankenstein then poses problems re-presenting the students' experiences, taken from their statements about mathematics:

"I'm the only one who didn't learn elementary school math when I should have."

"I'll never be able to learn math."

"Smart people do math fast, in their heads, and in one sitting."

"I'm stupid if I make a mistake or ask a question in class."

"There is only one correct answer to each math problem."

"There is only one correct way of solving each math problem" (Frankenstein 1989, 18–20).

These statements speak to the disabling consciousness students bring to class, the interferences to learning. Frankenstein offers them as generative themes for discussion. Through reflection, students gain some distance from the perceptions disabling their development. This starting point treats students as capable beings who can face and overcome obstacles, not as cultural deficits to be filled with knowledge. Their doubts are brought under control even as they are being brought out in the open. Students become part of a learning community where problems are social and soluble, not mysterious or permanent personal failures.

Frankenstein also provides autobiographical stories about people who felt anxiety about mathematics and then overcame it. This is material she integrates into the student-centered opening of the class. In addition, she poses some small math problems to demonstrate that the students already know some math. They do initial computation to achieve much the same goals I set for my students' early compositions in a writing class—to open with active learning where students experience and display what they already know and can do.

Frankenstein underlines how essential it is to teach an academic subject dialogically and democratically:

Knowledge of basic mathematics and statistics is an important part of gaining real popular, democratic control over the economic, political, and social structures of our society. . . . When we develop specific strategies for an emancipatory education, it is vital that we include such mathematical literacy. (Frankenstein, 1987, 180)

In math literacy courses for college adults, Frankenstein also advises a student-centered beginning: "Teachers can ask students about the issues that concern them at work, about the nonwork activities that interest them, about topics they would like to know in more depth. . . . These discussions can indicate the starting point for the curriculum" (196).

In these courses, Frankenstein integrated critical themes like racial and sexual inequality, monopoly control of the economy, the military budget, and tax loopholes for the rich. Through these themes, she sought democratic content to go along with the democratic process. Her goal as a critical teacher, in one exercise, was to reveal how the federal government hides the true size of the military budget by including military costs in non-defense categories. Military spending is not easy to measure because the published military budget is only part of the cost. It is made to appear smaller than it is, for example, by charging the production of nuclear warheads to the Department of Energy. Another cloaking device is the practice of counting the Social Security trust fund as part of federal spending so that the enormous military budget can be made to appear as a smaller percentage of total federal outlays. Citizens are kept from knowing the true costs of militarism; democratic math undertakes to reveal what is hidden.

One exercise asks students to compute the real cost of the military budget by collecting all military-related expenses from such categories as research and development, veterans' expenses, and space shuttle programs. Students are provided figures for the total federal budget as well as a breakdown of individual categories, from which they can discover the actual outlays for militarism and what percentages they are of the federal budget. The students in collaborative groups also have to decide how to present their research findings, whether as raw data, as percentages, or in graphs. Each group makes a research report to the class. When the real price of past, present, and future wars turns out to be twice the published figure of the military budget, students may understand why their taxes are high and their social services poor.

Taxes are the theme of a second critical math exercise suggested by Frankenstein. "A mathematically illiterate population can be convinced," she said, "that social welfare programs are responsible for their declining standard of living" (1987, 193). Uninformed people can have racist feelings provoked by thinking that their taxes are high to support minority families on welfare, this despite the fact that poor white families outnumber poor minority families. Frankenstein offers exercises relating to tax subsidies for the rich, which dwarf payments to the poor. For example, from her original course, developed in the 1970s, she provided students with statistics revealing that the richest 160,000 taxpayers received $7.2 billion worth of loopholes in 1975, while the maximum payment to a welfare family of four was $5,000. Students gain experience in dealing with large numbers through this exercise, as well as in division, when they divide the number of wealthy taxpayers into the aggregate loophole sum, to come out with an average subsidy of $45,000 to each person in this upper-class group—about nine times the amount awarded to a family of four on welfare that year. These figures are not the material for a lecture on inequality. Rather, Frankenstein uses them to construct problems where the subject matter and computation themselves raise democratic issues.

As a further example of critical math raising democratic issues, percentages in her class are learned with material showing the high rate of monopoly control in the food industry. Students are presented the following problem:

Fifty out of the 32,000 U.S. food manufacturing firms make 75% of the net profits. Of these top fifty corporations, thirty-one bought 63% of the national media advertising, or roughly $5 billion in 1977. Of the top twenty-five advertisers from all industries, eighteen were food companies. What percent of the U.S. food manufacturing firms make 75% of the net profits? (1987, 206)

Frankenstein comments that this problem can lead to a discussion of agribusiness and corporate monopoly of economic power, as well as to food advertising on TV, which promotes low-nutrient, high-calorie foods. After providing the above example, Frankenstein asks student to invent their own math problems involving a solution in percentages. This is a practical way to encourage their codevelopment of the curriculum. Another exercise teaches percentages and chart reading through analysis of the racial composition of American professional basketball teams, comparing them for the ratio of white to African-American players on each team in relation to the populations of the cities they play in. As it turns out, the racial composition of professional teams mirrors the racial composition of their home cities.

According to Frankenstein, "Traditional teaching methods convince students that they are stupid and inferior because they can't do arithmetic, that they have no knowledge to share with others, and that they are cheating if they do their schoolwork with others. Such methods effectively prepare students to compete for work at boring jobs over which they have no control" (1987, 207). To help reverse this disempowerment, Frankenstein teaches students to teach each other. She has them lead class discussion on math problems while modeling to them the difference between telling and teaching. Further, her students work out problems in groups to reverse their sense of isolation and their competitiveness. These groups discuss which homework problem was the hardest and the easiest, and they invent math problems for quizzes. Students keep journals to reflect on their work and on the class process. Lastly, Frankenstein makes error itself a theme of study in class, by asking students to figure out the logic of errors they or others make, to see themselves as thinking beings even when they don't get the answer right.

These democratic approaches integrate the students' context and thought with a critical appreciation of mathematics and society. They use math to discover such things as the large subsidies given to the nuclear power industry and how much more nuclear-generated electricity would cost if those companies had to foot their own bills instead of using tax funds. Such academic work develops math and cooperative relations in students while also orienting attention to undemocratic conditions in society.

Frankenstein's work was invented at the college level, but much of it appears adaptable to high school.

Elementary Democracy: Young Critical Math

For critical and democratic methods evolved especially for elementary grades, the work of Schniedewind and Davidson (1983, 1987), Ada and de Olave (1986), and Ada (1988) are rich resources. Ada and de Olave creatively adapt Freirean methods to bilingual education, offering Hispanic elementary students critical literacy in their home language and in English. Since their readers and essays have been reported on in detail by Cummins (1989), I will limit my discussion to Schniedewind and Davidson (1987), who describe classes in which math is a subject useful for democratic student development.

To raise elementary students' awareness of discrimination, they ask children to examine immediate parts of their experience: their textbooks, the personnel in school, the bulletin boards on the school's walls, and their favorite TV programs. For each context, students tabulate the sex, race, class, and age groups of the people they see. For example, when they examine bulletin boards at school or illustrations in a textbook or programs on TV, how many men, women, whites, minorities, old people, young people appear? What are they doing? When students tabulate the personnel at school, how many men, women, whites, minorities, old and young people, are employed here? What kinds of jobs does each group have? Students do this research in groups and report to the class. Their research can be expressed in percentages or graphs, to encourage them to develop math skills. Those skills reveal inequality in their immediate environments, which becomes a social theme for discussion in class.

In researching their environments, students not only count, categorize, and present the different numbers of human beings they encounter but also what each is doing, as a way to discover that certain groups will appear most frequently as the leaders and high-achievers (predominantly white men) while others will be more often be represented in subordinate roles (women, minorities, working people, older people). Further, students are asked to count the examples of people working cooperatively with those working individually. These problems raise the issues of inequality and competitive individualism in their surroundings, which become the subjects of class dialogue.

In another cooperative learning exercise for elementary and middle-school students, Schniedewind and Davidson ask the students to break into groups and write learning materials for the class itself. The students codevelop the curriculum here by breaking into groups to write their own math textbook. To guide their work, the teachers propose a sample problem to orient the students to cooperative learning:

Clorae and Jason's class has decided to have a communal pencil and pen supply bought by money the class has earned collectively so that all children can have equal access to these. Pencils were on sale at the drugstore. Clorae buys 15 packages of pencils which used to cost $14 for a dozen packages. The sale price is 15% off. What does she pay for the pencils? Jason buys pens at the sale price of 5 packages for the price of 4. They used to cost 29 cents a package. He buys 10 packages. What does he pay? (1987, 114)

Later, the teachers expand cooperative mathematics to include students building a board game, where they move and win by solving problems invented by other students. Such a class democratizes authority by having the students responsible for codeveloping the curriculum. Coming up with math exercises helps desocialize them from being passive learners isolated from each other by competition.

Democratic Study: Literature, History, and Society

In a democratic approach to a literary work, the teacher could ask students a transformative question about the narrative: "Are there different choices or different speeches a character could make at any point which would change the meaning of the story?" Students can be invited to question the authority of texts by imagining other possibilities for the human action portrayed, thus empowering their imagination of alternatives, rather than accepting the text as a fixed statement on human options.

To demonstrate a literature curriculum that invites students to question texts, I would like to consider Shakespeare's *Henry IV* and *Henry V*, with their marvelous characters—Prince Hal, Falstaff, Bolingbroke, Hotspur, and Glendower. In the opening scene of *Henry V*, Prince Hal, now king, has ordered a legal exercise about Salic law, a traditional code he wants his advisers to interpret to support his hereditary claim to the throne of France, as a pretext for invading that country. The advisers are scholastic and even comically legalistic. They go into lengthy explanations of the case. The king, impatient, finally demands a simple answer to his rights, and gets it—a legal justification for making war.

This nicely constructed scene offers a chance to study the text in relation to the themes of law, power, and making war. Such a discussion could be academic, topical, or generative, or all in sequence. One choice the teacher could make is to ask the students to act this opening scene, and then go on to relate their own experience and current political events to the scene. Another choice is to lift out one of the themes—power, perhaps—and ask students to explain what it means to them.

As a third way to launch a critical exploration of law and power through the Henry plays, the class could be presented with Salic law and Hal's family tree, to judge the new king's claim for themselves. They could examine the particulars of the case and debate Hal's rights. This would be a participatory, inductive way for students to engage an academic subject matter. It would require some initial research by the teacher to develop the materials. It would also encourage students to argue with texts, even masterpieces, rather than to accept them passively. The opening scene of *Henry V* could launch an exercise in which students research and judge events in the play. In this way, neither the authority of Shakespeare nor the authority of the teacher would be telling them unilaterally what things mean; students would be discovering meaning with the teacher.

Another critical-democratic approach is possible here with the Shakespeare play as the initiating text. For older students, it would be appropriate for the teacher to pose the issue: "Is law an unchanging body of rules?" The teacher would ask students to think of anything that used to be legal in the past but is illegal now, or vice versa. Students could discuss this problem in peer groups, get help from older people in their families or neighborhoods, and then report to the class as a whole. This is a difficult question to answer, so the teacher should prepare examples from history to demonstrate how group conflicts as well as changing conditions have altered the law. I think of some cases that would be relevant to the law changing as power and values in society changed: slavery and racial discrimination used to be legal; separate but equal facilities for the races were okayed by the United States Supreme Court in 1896, then declared unconstitutional in a landmark school ruling in 1954; trade unions were once illegal and repressed in the United States; the legal status of abortion has changed over the years; a woman's right to vote underwent a legal change in the twentieth century; the practice of child labor was unregulated before World War I, and mass education was once not compulsory; minimal health and safety codes for housing and for work are inventions of this century; the military draft was once the law of the land but that changed in the 1970s to an all-volunteer service; until the Freedom of Information Act was passed, citizens could not compel government to release files it was gathering about them; vehicle emissions were not legally regulated until recently.

The teacher could first find out whether students understand what the law is and what changes have been made in it and then could present material about changes outside their experience and knowledge. That material should include debates from various sides relevant to the legal changes, so that students can evaluate diverse positions and decide for themselves. In these discussions, the teacher can ask, "Who benefited from the change? Did the balance of power and rights in society change?" To encourage students to see themselves as participants in history and as potential agents for change, the teacher can also ask, "Did any of these changes affect you? How? What legal changes are necessary now? Why?"

Next, the critical-democratic teacher could assemble a media file of law cases which poses problems about unequal justice in society: "Should all people be treated equally under the law? Are minorities treated the same as whites? Are the poor treated the same as the rich?" Historical material could be examined describing how African slaves in the early American colonies were punished more severely than whites for the same crimes. Students could investigate whether the death penalty and harsher prison terms have been more frequently imposed on people of color. On the subjects of drug enforcement and class inequity, students could be presented with a 1989 case from North Carolina as documented by CBS in 1990: the wealthy heir to a local textile fortune received no jail sentence after his third conviction for cocaine possession, while a white worker at the family's plant was given a two-year sentence for possession and sale of two marijuana cigarettes. Students could be asked, "If you were the judge how would you have decided the two cases?"

To bring the democratic study of law and power to the context of war in the first scene of *Henry V,* the teacher could assemble files about recent wars that America has conducted in Vietnam, Grenada, Panama, and Iraq. In each case, Washington claimed the legal rights to make war. Students could examine and debate the legitimacy of these claims. Documents from the Contra War of the 1980s would also be relevant here; the World Court in 1986 declared United States support for the Nicaraguan rebels illegal and ordered reparations be paid by Washington to Managua. The Reagan administration ignored the judgment and pursued the war. Its claims could be compared to the World Court judgment as a case for students to decide.

The *Henry* plays also suggest generative themes that would be appropriate for older students willing to discuss them, themes relating to the students' individual, family, and group experiences with the law and with war: "How has the law crossed paths with your lives and communities? How have the police acted in your neighborhoods? Have you witnessed an arrest or visited a court or jail?" or "Have any family members been in the military or fought in Vietnam, Grenada, Panama, or Iraq?"

Law and aggression also invite attention to the democratic themes of class, age, and race inequity, because foot soldiers are young, often from poor working-class families, and disproportionately people of color, while those who declare war tend to be older, rich, powerful, and white. The teacher in high school, for example, can ask, "Why is the infantry disproportionately filled by minorities while air force pilots are disproportionately white? Would war be declared if it was up to young people to decide instead of older politicians and generals? Is there a generation gap in the way younger and older people think about war? When is war the right decision for a person or a society? If a person opposes a war being fought by his or her government, does he or she have the right to refuse to serve?" From these questions, students can write compositions, discuss them in peer groups, and then read them aloud for dialogue by the whole class.

After a student-centered opening, themes of war and the generation gap can be studied academically in the Shakespeare plays. Prince Hal has a difficult relationship with his father, the erstwhile Bolingbroke, Henry IV. The father's calculated moves had made him a shrewd politician, unlike wayward Hal, the delinquent heir-apparent. On his deathbed, the father, who usurped the crown in a coup that ended in the murder of the lawful King Richard II, righteously tongue-lashes his son for his ignoble behavior in taverns, which the worried Bolingroke sees as poor preparation for ruling the unstable kingdom Hal will inherit. The dying father educates his son in how to control the country: busy giddy minds with foreign quarrels to unite warring factions around a disputed throne.

Apparently, Prince Hal learns this lesson well. As King Henry V, he rejects his commoner cohorts and drunken good times. He plans a foreign invasion that takes English, Scottish, Welsh, and Irish commoners off to fight as one national army against the French. By triumphing at the great battle of Agincourt in 1415, the new king is strengthened by foreign intervention, a lesson understood by manipulative rulers before and since Hal's adventure. War helps him stabilize a shaky rule. In taking his father's advice, he transcends the generation gap by becoming like the former king. The critical teacher can ask students if Hal made the right choices or if he had other choices. Did Hal become a better person? Would they make the same choice as Hal? Could Hal have stabilized his nation without going to war? What would that take?

Reinventing Plot: Exercising Critical and Democratic Imagination

The text offers more opportunities for critical and democratic thinking. In *Henry V*, on the field at Agincourt the night before battle, the troubled young king expresses doubts about the pending human slaughter. But he is allowed to dismiss his guilt by insisting that war is

God's way of taking off those whose time to die had come. Shakespeare did not effectively challenge this convenient rationalization. He could have had other characters commenting on the king's weak claim to the French throne and how he is trying to be like his shrewd father who advised him to unify a divided population with a foreign enemy, to make non-English subject people's rally to his English crown. No such critical dialogue appears in the play; nor is there a strong counter to the king's insistence that God, not he, is responsible for the coming slaughter.

The text allows the king to explain away the dreadful moment created by his ambitions and power politics, but the democratic classroom does not have to agree with Shakespeare's pro-aristocratic tilt. Shakespeare's intentions were not to criticize monarchy. The tolerance and patronage of the aristocracy sustained his playwriting and his theater group. But if Shakespeare was predemocratic and royalist, those limits are not necessary in our context. Kings have been replaced by politicians who inherited the Machiavellian methods of previous rulers, but elected officials lack divine right and must answer to constitutional limits and to the democratic rights of the people. Teachers in our age do not have to worship monarchy, manipulative rulers, or the Great Books. They can critically question a predemocratic masterpiece.

Students can also be asked to reinvent scenes and speeches, to rewrite the text in a critical manner, as an experiment with alternatives. The teacher could ask, "What kind of character could answer the king's speech on the coming slaughter?" This is an interesting creative problem that encourages students to argue with masterpieces. It may also encourage them to question political leaders, not blindly accept their leadership, wars, or versions of events.

Besides rewriting parts of the play, the class could study one of the national cultures in Scotland, Wales, and Ireland, and learn about England's violent conquest of them. What image of the subject Britons do we get in *Henry IV* from the comic characters, like Fluellen? How is the historical Owen Glendower, a Welsh national hero, different from Shakespeare's Glendower? Why not compare a Welsh text on Glendower with this English one that makes Glendower something of a demon? This comparison would raise democratic questions about literature embodying ideology, rather than transmitting to students a perception of masterpieces being politically neutral.

Democratizing Authority: The Riot Act and the Last Word

The examples above suggest some ways to pose democratic and critical problems from academic subject matter. To further democratize curriculum, teachers can transform two behaviors that interfere with a democratic learning process: reading the riot act and having the last word.

The riot act relates chiefly to the teacher's behavior on the first day of class, when he or she lays down the law, the rules governing attendance, lateness, seating, exams, term papers, required texts, grading policy, and so on. Reading the riot act is a ritual that opens each new term and is repeated whenever a question of discipline or requirements appears. Although students expect a teacher to assert his or her authority, they also resent the unilateral power presented to them. They may feel adrift if the teacher does not impose structure; they may feel dominated if the teacher does.

This dilemma is complex because teachers who don't assert their authority invite chaos at the worst and testing behavior by students at the least, as students probe the soft rules to find what the limits are. In a class without traditional discipline, students can doubt the seriousness of the course, thinking that real education is not going on here because the teacher's authority is low-profile and nontraditional. Students have not had much chance to practice mutual dialogue, co-governance, self-control, and cooperative learning.

Students don't expect to negotiate such things as their grade, their homework, their rules for speaking in the classroom, the length of their papers. Teacher-centered schooling has given them few choices and little experience in democracy. Because of this lack of democratic practice, many students feel reassured *at the same time* that they feel resentful when the teacher reads the riot act. They expect the teacher to tell them what to do. They want to know right away the kind of authority they face and what is expected from them. By reciting the riot act, the teacher satisfies students' needs to have their situation clarified for them. This is an understandable desire on the students' part, given the kind of schooling they pass through. But the teacher's assertion of unilateral authority does more than inform students about their position; it also confirms that position as subordinate, which students react against. Reading the riot act triggers student behavior into its learned modes of silence, submission, or sabotage. This is a conflicted state of affairs.

To navigate the conflicts, to win some constructive participation in dialogue, it helps for the teacher to take a negotiating posture. This involves consulting with students as much as possible about the subject matter, work assignments, and classroom rules. Focusing at the start on rules set down unilaterally by the teacher can preempt the students' openness to talking. Many will be adjusting their defensive postures to a fixed regime. Their task, then, will not be mutual learning, dialogue, or co-governance but rather complying with or undermining the rules. Many will raise their protective silence instead of lowering their defenses and offering their authentic voices, which the dialogic teacher needs to hear to construct problem-posing situated in student reality.

When I avoid unilateral authority on day one, some students happily greet the openness of a negotiable classroom, while others are suspicious and awkwardly unsure how to behave. I have to offer a democratic process while also developing the students' confidence and skill in using that very process. This is not simple. To reassure students, I arrive with meaningful exercises and enough structure to give the class direction. I invite their questions about the subject matter and class requirements. In response, I refer to some reading and writing I plan to have them do. But I try to leave as much space possible for them to act on the course. The simple fact is that students are not expecting a democratic classroom and are not prepared to co-govern all at once. It would be naive to think that my sincerity or my good intentions are enough to transform their prior experience. I have to provide a democratic structure and invite them into it step by step.

Reassuring Structure: Understandable, Mutual, and Open

In offering some structure on the first day of class, I describe the course as a participatory workshop with discussion, reading, and writing, but not much lecturing from me. I tell students that I know how to lecture and have a lot to say on the course material but that I prefer dialogue. At this point, some students have asked me how long I have been at the college, suspecting that I am a new instructor who doesn't know how to teach. When I tell them I have been there for years, some may wonder if I am a veteran teacher who still doesn't know how to teach. I try to ride out their mixture of curiosity, doubt, and discomfort by saying that classes are more interesting and educational when students participate as much as possible. After my brief presentation, one group of students often says that it likes the idea of a discussion class because there is too little discussion and too much lecturing in their other classes. Another group of students does not react, keeping cautiously silent.

About the silent ones, I suspect they prefer a traditional class with lecturing. I think some prefer to be lectured at in a way that avoids adjusting to new social relations in the classroom. Lecture classes require less student participation. They are less challenging than problem-posing dialogue. It is easier for students to miss a lecture than a workshop discussion because a friend can take lecture notes for them to catch up on. Lecture classes are also easier to sleep through or to do homework in because the teacher is not looking at students as closely or expecting as much participation as in a discussion. Then there are those students who believe that education is serious only if the teacher does most of the talking, because the teacher is the one with the knowledge that counts. The pro-lecture group makes its presence felt in class by not participating in dialogue. This always concerns me. To appeal to silent students for participation, I try to make dialogue exciting and productive, so that it animates as many students as possible. This animated group does not have to be a majority; it can pull more students into the process if it is a dynamic minority.

To draw out a critical mass of participating students, I immediately practice problem-posing on day one, centered on questions like "What is good writing?" in freshman composition and "What is a good news report?" in journalism, and "What is a good speech?" in a class in public speaking. To value dialogue as part of the grading process, I propose that class participation count as part of the final grade.

On the first or second day, depending on the length of the class period, which subject I am teaching, and the quality of student participation, I distribute learning contracts for students to discuss and amend, as another way to negotiate the curriculum. My contracts specify three grade levels, A, B, and C. I say that if any of them start out planning to get a D or an F, I would prefer they drop the class right now, because it is a monumental waste of time to be here. (This is not something high school teachers can say because students cannot drop those classes, but even there the teacher can still send signals inviting students to set high goals.) For each grade, I usually propose different levels of participation, attendance, length of papers, number of papers, project work, books to read, and so on. I hand out the contracts, ask students to read them, discuss them, and then ask questions for whole-class negotiation. Then I ask them to take them home, think them over, and make one of three choices: sign the contract as proposed and amended in class at a specific grade level, or negotiate further changes with me individually, or throw the contract out and negotiate a new one of their own design. Some students like this arrangement; others do not accept the contract and refuse to sign anything. They want to be judged the old-fashioned way, solely on my own terms. Faced by this resistance to mutual authority, I accept their rejection and grade them traditionally.

In negotiations with students who agree with contract grading, I give in on some items and stand firm on others. In general, my students bargain for fewer words on each paper, for softer deadlines on homework, and for more allowed absences and latenesses. My position here is to maintain challenging minimums. I ask them to explain their changes on each item, and invite other students to agree and disagree with each proposal. Then I take votes to see how much support any counter-proposal has. I also explain my position on any item. After bargaining, we reach compromises. Students also have the right to negotiate individual contracts with me, which some do.

After this, in some classes, we have gone on to prepare a document called Rules for Speaking in Class. I ask students to each write down one or two rules they want me and them to follow in our discussions. They read them to each other in twos or threes and then I go around the room from group to group for reports, collating a first draft that eliminates duplications. We discuss each item, refine or rewrite it, and then vote it up or down, until we have a mutually agreed class protocol on speaking. Generally, students come up with such items as these: don't interrupt others when they speak; don't insult other people; keep your remarks close to the topic; don't go on and on when you're boring people; don't talk to neighbors when others are speaking; everyone is entitled to their opinion; and the teacher should not let students do or say anything they want but should say what he thinks and stop people from talking too much. From my side, I offer such items as these: don't wait for the teacher to respond first after another student has spoken but take the initiative yourself; ask questions right away when you don't understand something. Some classes vote to have discussion without raising their hands to speak while others want to raise hands and have me call on them. Every class so far has voted to sit in a circle rather than in rows facing the front.

Few students have experienced negotiating the curriculum, so they are unfamiliar with the process. Often I have to nudge them into deliberating on the class discussion rules and on the contractual minimums for A, B, and C grades. But after a while some classes take up negotiation with surprising enthusiasm. Some students get the message and become almost too eager to negotiate. They treat everything in the course as renegotiable. I have to set limits here and insist that there be a good reason to renegotiate something already agreed to. If I don't set this limit, the students themselves will not feel obliged to follow the contracts or other rules we set for the class. In this regard, it's my responsibility to open and to limit negotiation, but even here I encourage students to share this responsibility by disciplining themselves, by speaking up if something is wrong or damaging to the group process. A democratic process means that students cannot do what they want whenever they want. The structure is democratic, not permissive; it relates individual rights to group rights.

Occasionally during the term I want to change something, add a book, move up a date for an assignment, include a project not mentioned earlier, substitute one kind of thematic project for another. I propose the change to the class, explain my reasons, and consult with them for their agreement or disagreement. I bargain for their consent because I am also accountable to the group.

When students do not live up to the quantity and quality specified in their contracts, I let them know during the term and warn them that they are not qualifying for the grade they agreed to. When I do not live up to the contract, I am often reminded of my lapses by the students, which is a remarkable moment, because they are constructively disciplining the teacher, not negatively sabotaging the class.

I help students get used to the negotiating process by saying that in this course they do not have to stew in silence or act out their hostility when they are unhappy or in disagreement. I urge them to speak up when they are angry or confused or opposed to something. I assure them that I do not get insulted and do not hold grudges. I add that if they stay silent or act out their unhappiness, they will sabotage their learning and the class. They are free to complain or disagree, and so am I, but none of us is free to sabotage the learning process.

By presenting a negotiable curriculum from the start, I try to prevent the first day from being a traditional encounter with a teacher laying down the law. Instead of reading the riot act, I ask the students to think about the course and to decide what they want to do. This establishes them as decision makers who are responsible for framing purposes and intentions with me. I try to offer an experience of democratic authority, rather than one of a teacher unilaterally imposing rules.

Shared Decision Making: The "After-Class Group"

Another structure of democratic authority I have experimented with is an after-class group, which meets with me after each class to evaluate and plan the ongoing course. In one class, as part of the learning contracts negotiated in the beginning, I offered students a choice of projects, including participation in the after-class group. I thought to limit the group to six students, three male and three female, but in that class nine students wanted to join; I said okay, hoping that their interest would help make the experiment a success. When a day's session ended, the regular students would leave the room and we would stay on. The a/c students in that class did not have to go to jobs, to families, or to other classes, as did some others; so they had the time to choose this option as one of their projects. This is harder to do in evening courses because those students have little free time to meet outside class. Teachers in elementary or high schools can consider other times for such a group if meeting after class is not possible, perhaps during cooperative learning exercises while the whole class is in session and when all students are working in small groups. If students cannot meet during class or immediately after, then it will be necessary to find another time during the week.

I began each after-class session by first asking the students what they thought of the day's class. Did it go well? If not, why? What did they like and not like? Students would respond one at a time, then begin cross talk without raising hands or waiting for me to supervise the discussion. I would take notes, listen carefully, draw out their remarks, connect their individual responses, and comment on their perspectives. If some students always volunteered to speak first, I would try to begin with the less assertive ones the next time.

After a few tentative sessions, the group that met after a Utopia class became a small legend to the rest of the students, so much so that other students asked to sit in after class to see what we did. We had frank discussions about what was being learned and not learned in class. The students dropped their shyness in remarkable ways and confronted me directly with their pleasure and dislike about various parts of the class. They criticized me for taking too much time with each peer group when we broke up into discussion groups that worked on one aspect of a book or theme. I found each of the committee reports interesting enough to discuss in depth, but they told me I was taking too long and was ignoring other groups, who also had a right to report in the class discussion. I adjusted my timing and after a week or so was able to meet their expectations. On other occasions, I would preview for them what I had in mind to do with the next class, and ask them to comment on my lesson plan, which I adjusted from their input. They also complained that we were doing one too many class projects and winding up with too little class time to report and discuss their work, which was true, but too late to change, so I told them I would organize the projects differently next time I taught the course. The a/c group also discussed my ideas on how to divide up the book *Walden II* for thematic study, and recommended which themes they wanted to study. Many were hostile to *Walden II*, for its dull, pedantic narrative. They forced me to defend my choice in using the book. One or two thought we weren't reading enough and should have more assigned books. Others disagreed; after they had their own debate, I joined it. As part of this group's work, I asked the students to design a course evaluation form which the whole class would fill out at the end of the term, so that they would be assessing the course in their own ways. They developed this evaluation form through two sessions after class. Sometimes class would end with debates unresolved, and the after-class group functioned as a second class to reflect on the loose ends of the first session. In this way, it became a reflection on our reflection, a dialogue on dialogue. The after-class group evaluated itself at the end, and the students were all positive, recommending it as a regular part of all courses at the college. I should add that one or two students in the group were using it as a way to avoid doing a written project or presentation. They were not speaking much in the group or were leaving it early. I had to approach them individually to let them know that they were not living up to the minimum requirements for taking part in the group. The grade for the a/c group was subsumed under the grade contracted for individually in the contracts.

Democratic authority needs a variety of structures like the after-class group through which the teacher and students share responsibility. I found the a/c group extraordinary. I was compelled more than ever to explain my curricular choices to students, who asked challenging questions about their education. I could not win any argument by authority alone, and they did not win by simply refusing to participate or by sabotaging the class. The dialogue was mutual and frank, and actually influenced the direction of the course, a plain result of their interventions which justified their participation. With the after-class group, I was not alone in evaluating the class or in planning it. The students observed and codeveloped their learning with me.

Democratic Structure and the Learning Process

In my classes, I propose that any paper can be rewritten for a higher grade. I encourage students to rewrite as often as they like and count only the highest grade they get on any rewritten paper. By announcing this rewrite policy, I offer an open structure. I give grades, but grades are not final if students care to raise them. I want them to value revision in their development as good writers. Not everyone takes advantage of this rewrite policy, but a number of students do.

To encourage students to rewrite for a higher grade, I offer specific advice about revising their papers and tutorial time if needed. Because I want my responses to their work to be supportive, I respond to the ideas and skills they display in their writings first and to errors second. After commenting on the good aspects of their writing, I encourage editing for correctness and revising to develop their points. When calling attention to correct usage, I do not use a grammar code to correct errors. I ask students to hand in a rough draft along with the final copy of their paper, to encourage them to edit and revise, rather than turn in papers written off the top of their heads. On the final copy I read, I bring standard usage to the students' attention in a self-correction format. Where there are errors, I put small marks in the margins of the essay and ask the student to correct those lines. If they can't correct the errors on their own, they consult me. This is my attempt to desocialize students from expecting teachers to mark up their papers and be the sole source of correct answers. Students have to become editors of their own work, to break their dependence on authority, built from years of getting papers returned all marked up. Traditional schooling has taught them to think of themselves as error makers and of teachers as error finders. Also, I think it is more respectful to hand back a paper without defacing it. I don't want to humiliate students by trashing their work. Small, line-by-line marks send messages of self-correction and respect.

Many usage errors are simply the result of what I have been calling a performance strike, from their low attention to education in general and to writing especially. I tell students that they possess much greater knowledge of correct usage than they habitually display in their written work. They are not investing enough attention in their writing to perform at their best. By putting marks in the margins but not correcting the lines themselves, I throw them back on their own resources to use what they know before I teach them what they don't yet have. My students are able to correct many of their errors once they pay careful attention to the words and sentences. I make self-editing a routine expectation of the course, and if any paper is sloppy or poorly written, I do not give a grade but require a rewrite. Democratic classes should have high standards.

If certain errors appear often in student papers, I use those papers in class for writing lessons. I do not use grammar books or workbooks. When I see a pattern of errors or the same error appearing in a number of papers, I use the student texts for exercises in grammar, usage, and meaning. The literacy work is situated in real needs and texts, not in abstract, A-to-Z grammar lessons. The class becomes a group editing seminar where students focus on their own writing. I ask them to discuss in small groups what corrections need to be made in any student paper. This dialogic class develops literacy skills situated in the cognitive levels and linguistic products of the students. It also allows students to experience learning cooperatively. Often I ask them to give each other copies of their papers so that they can evaluate each other's work. In general, they prefer to write responses to other students' work but not to put grades on the papers. They feel it would be putting down their peers to give low grades. I agree to their evaluation without giving grades.

Using interactive language arts, the democratic classroom can be effective if it is based in cooperative relations. Sapon-Shevin and

Schniedewind (1991) said about the empowering effects of cooperative learning, "It has been found that all students, particularly minority students, learn more than in traditional classrooms, and the liking of school and the liking of others of different racial backgrounds increased" (167). Kagan (1986) reported on student achievement in cooperative classrooms compared to traditional ones:

Of the 46 studies reviewed, 63 percent showed superior outcomes for cooperative learning; 33 percent showed no significant differences; and only 4 percent showed higher achievement for the control groups. Most importantly, however, a dramatic difference emerged among the studies as a function of cooperative learning methods. Almost all studies (89 percent), which used group rewards based on individual achievement produced achievement gains. (244)

Kagan reiterated that gains in cooperative classrooms were more pronounced for minority and low-achieving groups: "In a relatively short time what appears to be a long-term minority student deficiency in basic language skills can be overcome by transforming the social organization of the classroom" (Kagan, 247).

By having students write a lot and collaborate, a cooperative class sets high goals for student achievement. Students take on the mutual task of reflecting on their learning processes. As they move back and forth between individual work and collaboration, I approach an individual student for tutoring whenever I notice that she or he does not understand a technical aspect of writing, such as comma splices and bidialectal transformations from Black Vernacular English to standard usage. I also bring in special readings or suggest special assignments to suit a student's interests or needs. In this way, I try to keep sight of both the group process and individual needs.

Writing has not been an empowering experience for most of my students, who come from the middle and low tracks of high school, often returning to college after years in the work force. Many work full time, raise families, take several classes, and commute, leaving little time for writing. In general, putting words on paper has been frustrating, demeaning, or irrelevant. From my own life as a writer, I know that good writing is not easy. My responsibility is to show optimism about their prospects and to negotiate a curriculum with high expectations, democratic structures, and critical themes in language meaningful to students.

I want to democratize learning, but I do not stop being an authority in the classroom. My authority changes. My teaching practices and my comments seek a democratic position in class instead of the unilateral and teacher-talk authority that students both expect and resent. From a democratic point of view, I try to unify process and content, to have the methods invite students to take responsibility for their own education while the subject matter orients their intelligence to critical thought on knowledge and society. Sapon-Schevin and Schniedewind (1991) have written that "more than commitment to process is necessary. It is also necessary to teach content that helps students develop a critical consciousness about the basis of inequality in school and society and the options for change" (174). They refer to teachers who use cooperative learning to teach the uncritical standard curriculum. In these classes, students study war, for example, in cooperative groups without ever being asked to consider whether wars are either just or avoidable. In other classes, students work cooperatively to learn mass advertising techniques without coming to terms with the "competitive, sexist, often exploitative, underpinnings of much advertising" (177). The invitation to democratic learning described in this book assumes that both the learning process and the subject matter reflect democratic values.

Who Gets the Last Word?

Besides avoiding the unilateral establishment of rules that comes from reading the riot act, I want to desocialize myself and the students from the ritual of the last word, which is a ceremonial summary of the class hour offered by the teacher. My goal is to have students speak more and do more of the intellectual work of summarizing rather than expecting me to do all of it.

Freire defined the summary as an important "inductive moment" (Shor and Freire 1987, 157–61), when loose threads and spontaneous utterances are gathered together into a meaningful framework. The summation can be a key cognitive activity. But in teacher-talk classrooms, the final word is traditionally a summation made by the teacher when students are anxious to leave the room. When I look around at the end of class, I often see students putting on their coats and gathering up their books as they anticipate my summarizing the session. When the teacher begins the last word, many students have learned to stop listening. They count the seconds until they can run out the door, from boredom or because their busy lives require rushing from class to class to jobs to family. The final word becomes in these circumstances a moment where the teacher formally certifies what was learned that day, just in case students missed it. Summarizing while students want to rush out is a pointless, awkward ritual.

To avoid talking to people who don't want to listen, I try to leave time at the end for students to offer the last word. I seek volunteers to reflect out loud on the class dialogue that day, and then I decide whether I should add anything. If no one volunteers, I call on one or two students. I ask what they think was important or what questions of theirs remain unanswered. I may also ask what interested or bored them during class. If they all reject this invitation, I decide to say a few things to warm the waters, and then invite other students to jump in. I accept their lack of familiarity in sharing this teacherly task of the summation, so I am willing to wait some weeks until students join in the process. The benefits from this small democratic practice are worth the wait. Sharing the last word desocializes us from expecting the end of the hour to be a ceremonial teacher's speech, the effort of unilateral authority to sum up, in the face of student power to sabotage the teacher's final remarks. Instead, this can become a moment of democratic communication.

Still, it would be naive to expect students to rise uniformly to this invitation to democracy. I have had classes where my attempts to replace the riot act and the final word with negotiated contracts and participatory exercises were rejected. I habitually try dialogic teaching several times before consistent rejection forces me to pull back to a traditional spot where students will take part. The degree of student resistance determines how dialogic any class can be; I judge the resistance and acceptance in each class and then decide on the profile of my authority. Students have the power to insist on traditional education or on no education at all. I only have the power to invite them into a critical classroom that practices some of the democracy they have heard so much about.

Socialization into Democratic Dialogue

Even if students like the democratic process offered in class, they may be shy from lack of experience. Many will take a long time to trust the teacher and the process. They need support in risking to show enthusiasm for the class, because they might get branded as the brownnose of the group, sucking up to the teacher for a grade.

The patient reconstruction of these habits involves establishing democratic speaking rights. The democratic teacher gives up the right to dominate the discourse, to go on speaking if few are listening and many are bored. This kind of teacher practices a new discourse with students, where they have a right to announce they are bored, to reject the theme and process of the class, and to suggest their own directions. In traditional schooling, democracy is much alluded to while students are unilaterally tested, tracked, lectured, ordered around, lined up, and told what to do. Students are talked at, talked about, and talked over when they speak. They are denied the essence of democracy, which I define as co-governance in private and public life; as a respectful relationship between people and authority in school, work, and society where the constituents assert the balance of power, not the bureaucracy; as the equal distribution of wealth and power in society, so that an elite does not control vast financial and political power, so that all groups have access to mass media and to educational resources; as grass-roots power in society at large so that municipal and community areas are governed from below; and as multicultural, nonsexist, and nonracist practices in society. Democracy means that ordinary human beings and subordinated groups have the power to act on their interests and to participate equally in developing the policies governing the life of the nation.

Students bring few democratic habits to the classroom because they have few opportunities to practice them in school. To reverse this situation, more than good intentions or friendly manners are needed. Teachers and students need a democratic practice inside a critical curriculum.

The futility of undemocratic authority is that the teacher silences students and talks to himself or herself, or the teacher repeats what students already know because they are playing dumb, or the teacher gets vacant mimicking of her or his words on examinations or papers written by students just getting by. Teachers and students are capable of far more than this. Meaningful education is waiting to happen. Democratic teaching can be a catalyst.

Critical Teaching and Classroom Research
An Interdisciplinary Field for Activist Learning

7

Dialogic Education Involves Research

The values discussed in previous chapters—participatory, affective, situated, problem-posing, multicultural, dialogic, desocializing, and democratic learning—can help students develop critical consciousness. This way of thinking prepares students to act as citizens who question knowledge and society. I turn now to the last three items on the agenda: dialogic learning as classroom and community research, critical education as an interdisciplinary curriculum, and empowering pedagogy as a field of knowledge and activism.

Essentially, the empowering education outlined so far offers students self-development in a cooperative and critical process. To think critically in this framework means to examine the deep meanings, personal implications, and social consequences of any knowledge, theme, technique, text, or material. Critical thought about any subject reveals its internal structure and its connections to self and society. This in-depth scrutiny is also research. To study something in-depth is to do research. In this sense, research implies detailed investigation, an extensive exploration of subject matter, thought, and language. Because the critical-democratic classroom involves in-depth scrutiny, it defines students as active researchers who make meaning, not as passive receivers of knowledge.

This critical classroom functions as a research center in a number of ways. First, the teacher examines student life and language to create a curriculum situated in their themes and thoughts. Second, students are invited to join the teacher in studying their community and conditions, as co-researchers of their own culture. Third, once a generative, topical, or academic theme is posed as a problem for critical dialogue, students and teacher become researchers again, investigating a specific subject matter. Fourth, both teacher and students research the learning process under way, to discover how teaching and learning are progress-

ing. Classroom and community research, the ninth value for empowering education, is the key to this approach.

Traditionally, the term *research* has not referred to teachers studying
their students' learning, or to students studying their own language,
lives, and thinking, or to students and teachers mutually scrutinizing
materials in class. *Research* has meant for most students the academic
ritual of preparing a research paper. Research has also been a special
activity of scholars, consultants, and graduate students in libraries, lab-
oratories, institutes, corporations, military centers, universities, and
field sites visited by specialists. This traditional universe of research is
what Boomer (1987) called the "elsewhereness" of scholarship—it happens everywhere else except every day in the classroom, where it is
needed.

Education researchers do show up in classrooms to observe and to
measure student and teacher performance there. But this nonpartici-
pant research is isolated from day-to-day teaching, published in journals, reports, and conference proceedings. Some scholars have done
very important work teachers can benefit from; some researchers are
careful to stay grounded in the realities of teaching; others make efforts
to reach teacher audiences. But for the most part, scholarly work does
not help the classroom. The reasons are obvious. For one thing, schoolteachers have little free time to study research publications, to write articles, to join in seminars with colleagues, or to attend conferences.
Classroom teaching is the low-status work of education. Teachers are
not paid enough or treated well enough to encourage their behavior as
collegial intellectuals and professional researchers. Moreover, the academy produces its high-status knowledge in a discourse foreign to
teachers. Researchers and scholars tend to talk to each other in a language accessible mainly to themselves.

An undemocratic hierarchy separates researchers from teachers and
students. This professional pecking order is also patriarchal and racial.
It places mostly white male scholars at the top and mostly female classroom teachers at the bottom. Some teachers do research and use research, but many are either silenced by or resentful of scholars, whose
position gives them a privileged distance from the challenges of mass
education. Yet despite their lesser pay, harder work, and fewer privileges, the teachers who educate each generation are as important as
researchers in universities or institutes. Teachers help develop the intellects of millions of people who then develop society. More than anyone,
they need to research the learning process in their classrooms. Unfortunately, the undemocratic division of labor and money in education

makes research a preoccupation of universities rather than of public schools and community colleges.

In reality, all serious classrooms already do a form of research because meaningful learning involves examining subjects in depth and from several perspectives. Further, effective teachers are those who examine their students' learning process, to discover what is being learned and not learned, so as to increase the learning already under way. But many schoolteachers and community college teachers lack the time and support to do in-class research, to organize students into research units, and to train them in research methods. This is a limiting factor, because the more the teacher researches student culture and learning, and the more the students research knowledge and their conditions, the more developmental the class can become. One dimension of education reform, then, has to include more free time for teachers, longer class periods to facilitate research projects, and in-service staff development so that more teachers can do classroom research and build it into the curriculum.

Democratizing Research: Teacher-Researchers, Student-Researchers

In the classroom, the dialogic teacher researches the students to learn their themes, cultural conditions, speech, and ways of learning. This knowledge is basic for problem-posing and for integrating formal bodies of knowledge. But students can also be asked to do research. In Freire-based programs, it is common for older students and community members to join educators in research, either prior to the start of a learning program or during it. The educators benefit from student participation in research because students are at hand to explain findings to the teachers who are less familiar with the community than are the students. This democratic co-research helps the curriculum avoid becoming teacher-centered or academically abstract.

To unify teaching, learning, and research, community members participated in research in the Adult Learning Project (ALP) in Edinburgh (Kirkwood and Kirkwood 1989). Community research enabled the teachers to codevelop curriculum with their constituency. The ALP also included specific training programs for community members in research methods. It may be easier to incorporate older students as co-researchers than it is to work with younger ones, but it helps to recall Schniedewind and Davidson's approaches to cooperative learning, where young students do out-of-class research into their favorite TV shows and the bulletin boards of their school. On this common ground, teacher and student co-researchers are learning with and from each other, and educators are democratically passing on their special research skills so that students share a function generally monopolized by scholars.

It helps if teachers can study the local communities before formal instruction begins and before a curriculum is designed. This will ground the teachers in student reality as the basis for a curriculum. Once class begins, the critical teacher can design the early weeks of the course as an exploratory time to become grounded in student language, cognitive skills, and affective levels. To do this well, the teacher needs a participatory approach with relatively short-term exercises, to get the students expressing themselves as soon as possible and as much as possible. A participatory opening invites students to write about their experiences and learning in their own words, producing the raw material that the teacher mines to construct the curriculum. What the teacher learns from student writing and speaking informs her selection and structuring of generative, topical, and academic themes. In an academic discipline, where specific texts need to be covered, the teacher can extract from those texts their key themes and questions, and ask students to reflect on them in their own words prior to encountering them in the text. Working from a student-centered discourse better prepares students to take on material in an academic form.

Research during class requires concentration and experimentation on the teacher's part. In one fifth- and sixth-grade "whole language" class, a teacher, Mary Kitagawa,

noticed that one of her students consistently misspelled the word "closet." Instead of merely correcting the child or taking points off for the error, she tried to discover why he was making the mistake. "He was writing 'clothit,'" she explains. "So I tried to listen to him to see if he was saying it that way. But he didn't have a lisp." When she realized that he learned the word clothes first, she suddenly saw the logical leap he was making. (Koepke 1991, 38)

By taking a researching attitude to her pupil's work, Kitagawa was able to discover the logic of an error—"clothes" to "clothit"—and to correct it in relation to the student's language experience. In her class, students "decide what to research, how to research it, and the length and form reports will eventually take." Besides exercising democratic choice in curriculum, students participate in mutual evaluation. They use self-surveys to assess their reading and writing in addition to receiving evaluations from the teacher. The habit of observing the learning process is thus generalized in class, not monopolized by the teacher.

Besides generalizing research habits in class and observing student activity carefully, a few things can help teachers who take a research approach to curriculum. One is keeping a classroom journal, written as soon after class as possible. This is one means for a teacher's self-education, to reflect on the learning process under way. A second aid is an experimental frame of mind, which invents teaching strategies from the actual activity observed in class, much like Kitagawa's effort to determine the source of her student's spelling error, rather than mechanically following a textbook or syllabus approach. The curriculum should be organically related to student learning.

The critical-democratic teacher invites and expects students to do research. They can be asked to examine key words and phrases used by them or by texts. A good example of this is Bigelow and Christensen's high school class, who were asked to analyze what it meant for Columbus to "discover" America. Students not only scrutinized language in relation to history, but they also compared several history texts to pull out differing conceptions of Columbus. In another class, Bigelow and Christensen asked students to research the collective text of the group—a narrative of group experiences that helps students see some of their common positions in society. In another setting, in a middle school in Detroit, one teacher has students brainstorm topics to research, questions to ask, and methods to follow, after which they undertake a two-month project requiring weekly written logs, a final oral presentation and product, and a self/peer/teacher evaluation (Ladestro 1991). In addition, students can also research their peers outside class, as in the topical investigations in my class of the arms race and the Contra War in Nicaragua, using questionnaires and opinion surveys. Lastly, it helps to do research/teaching with colleagues so that experiences in class can be shared.

Benefits of Classroom Research for Teachers

Goswami and Stillman (1987) summarized in their preface some of the transformative effects on teachers who do classroom research:
• They collaborate with their students to answer questions important to both, drawing on community resources in new and unexpected ways. The nature of classroom discourse changes when inquiry begins.
• Their teaching is transformed in important ways: they become theorists, articulating their intentions, testing their assumptions, and finding connections with practice.
• Their perceptions of themselves as writers and teachers are transformed. They step up their use of resources; they form networks; and they become more active professionally.

- They become rich resources who can provide the profession with information it simply doesn't have. . . . Teachers know their classrooms and students in ways that outsiders can't.
- They become critical, responsive readers and users of current research, less apt to accept uncritically others' theories, less vulnerable to fads, and more authoritative in their assessment of curricula, methods, and materials.

The transformative effect on teachers was also reported by Atwell (1987) in a classroom research experiment by fourteen language arts teachers in a Maine elementary school: "Six months into our inquiries, every one of us had dramatically altered his or her approach to the teaching of writing. . . . Teachers slow down when we engage in looking at and thinking and raising questions about our students' writing. . . . We stop focusing on presenting a lesson and evaluating its results and start observing our students in the process of learning, listening to what they tell us, and responding as they need us. . . . [The teacher] listens to what they have written, responds to their questions, asks questions about their drawing and writing, logs her observations, records data about skills she has noticed or introduced in individual writing conferences, writes, and shares her writing with her students" (89). In Atwell's school, traditional grammar lessons became longer writing sessions where teachers observed students and conversed with them about their composing. Publishing projects replaced skills drills and fill-in-the-blank exercises. Some students responded by carrying clipboards to the playground to continue writing at recess.

To research student learning, Emig (1987, 65) provided some preliminary questions based on her observation of the composing process of twelfth-graders:

- What are the attitudes toward literacy and the educational background of the family?
- When, and under what circumstances, did the child begin to write, and read?
- If the child remembers these experiences, what description does she give? What feeling tone?
- What does the learner think writing is for? What are its functions?
- What are the attitudes, constructs, and paradigms the student has about school, about English and the language arts, about writing?
- How can his process(es) of writing be characterized?

These guiding issues help direct the teacher's attention to the student experience as material to research. In addition, I repeat here some questions I offer students to give an active, critical opening to my writing classes: "What is good writing? How do you become a good writer?

What are the hardest and easiest things for you when you write? What questions do you have about good writing? When do you write? How much and for what?" I also ask them to examine their past classroom experiences by answering the following questions: "Who was the worst teacher you ever had? Why? Who was the best teacher? Why? What does it mean to be a good teacher? What does it mean to be a good student?" These questions stimulate critical thought about present and past learning; they also signal students that the learning experience is something to reflect on.

Heath (1983) researched the home and school language of young students in three communities in the Carolina Piedmont: higher-income white, working-class white, and working-class African-American. She found that the three socially unequal groups also had unequal successes in school related to the connection of their home language to the discourse of the classroom. Not surprisingly, the most privileged white group did the best in school.

The higher-status white families Heath studied had home speech habits favored in traditional classrooms. Through home-based storytelling and reading, more affluent parents introduced children to the form of printed texts and narratives (a beginning, a middle, and a conclusion). Children exposed to books and stories gained a developmental head start useful in school, where narratives and texts are central. In addition, by questioning children how items from books and experience related to each other and to new material, these parents helped their children develop an important speech habit and way of thought called decontextualization, which means using language to analyze, compare, and imagine other contexts similar to and different from the immediate one we are in. If a child reads a book about dogs and farms, the habit of decontextualizing means that she or he will relate the material in the book to other dogs and farms the child has experienced, read about, or imagined. This helps develop verbal fluency to express thought and observations, careful attention to detail, and habits of abstracting meaning from immediate experience.

The narrative, descriptive, and comparative uses of language are prized in school but are not developed equally in all children, Heath found. Children from upper-income homes in her sample were exposed to a discourse compatible with school culture. These youngsters were asked at home to notice details in books and in daily life, and to respond to questions like "What is this? What color is the house in the picture? Is this house like the one you saw yesterday in town?" Such exercises from parents helped those children develop verbal habits of generalization and description which served them well later on in school. In addition—a matter not discussed adequately by Heath— these children got from their parents the accent, syntax, vocabulary, clothing, manners, and skin color which marked them as members of a privileged group in an unequal school system with a long history of giving more advantages to the already privileged.

Heath also found that middle-class parents engaged their children in a lot of banter, a constant commentary on what was happening around them. She called this discourse "a lot of talk about nothing," to designate the running narratives which some parents maintain with their young children, to stimulate their attention to detail and their habits of verbally reporting on their perceptions. This discourse helps introduce them to school communication, which often requires students to produce instant commentary on printed texts, experiments, and statements.

But the language habits favored by school are not those she found in the white and minority working-class homes, which tended more towards concreteness in one regard and to creativity in the other. The religiously fundamentalist white working-class parents that she observed did not encourage their children to comment either generally or creatively on their experience but rather limited them with prescribed meanings and fixed morals. The speech community here was doctrinaire, not open, discouraging creative, critical, or subjective commentary from children. On the other hand, the African-American community encouraged in children a narrative discourse about reality that prized creativity in language more than detailed observation or rote repetition of doctrine. The creativity of these students was not rewarded by the narrow language uses expected in school, while the disciplined concreteness of the poorer whites limited their school performance in terms of the creative and abstract uses of words.

Educationally, to meet the needs of the two at-risk groups, Heath's classroom and community research pointed to more imaginative language uses in class and to a researching curriculum which employed "a lot of talk about nothing":

Inside a third-grade classroom described by the principal as "low-achievers," several pairs of children are working over tape recorders in dialogues with each other. One small group of children is in costumes performing . . . for a few kindergarteners who are visiting. Yet another group is preparing illustrations for a story told by one of their classmates and now being heard on tape as they talk about why the drawings illustrate the words they hear. . . . They spend as much of the day as possible talking—to each other and the teacher, and to fifth- and sixth-graders who come into the class one half-hour each day to read in small groups. (1987, 40)

Activities in that classroom are accompanied by a lot of talk about language and meaning, to accustom children to using their voices as aesthetic and research tools. The students themselves teach other students, use their own voices to discover meaning, and learn from each other as well as from the teacher.

To use the richness of discourse in daily life, teachers employing this method also invited community people to class, from grocery clerks to museum guides, to talk to the children about the way they use talk in their work. Further, the children, whom Heath called "language detectives," are asked to research their talk at home, the questions people ask each other, the answers they give, the material they read and talk about. Such a researching classroom acknowledges, uses, and respects the linguistic culture already existing in the students' lives. In this case cited by Heath, the researching classroom provoked latent language skills rather than silencing students with grammar drills and facts to memorize (Heath 1987, 40–41).

Research as a Teaching/Learning Process

Students have much to gain from classrooms where their teachers research them and where they do research. This applies not only to language arts but also to critical math classes like those described in the previous chapter, where research into the military budget, tax loopholes for the rich, subsidies to the nuclear power industry, or pay inequities for women and minorities revealed conditions largely ignored by the traditional curriculum and by the mass media.

Further, in a critical study of a theme like "Columbus discovered America," an academic subject can become a research project where students judge different versions of history instead of absorbing only an official story. By examining primary materials from a period, event, or public policy, students could become historical researchers. Giroux (1978) developed an intriguing method for this in social studies education, through which students became researchers and writers of comparative history. Judy (1980) also advocated a primary materials approach to studying humanities subjects, through research files of original documents provided by the teacher. The basic method for this approach is to invite students to reflect cooperatively on primary sources from which they draw conclusions and then compare them with those drawn by scholars. This exercises their complex powers of thought and avoids a passive transfer of information about any subject.

"Acquiring information can never develop the power of judgement," Dewey asserted. "Development of judgement is in spite of, not because of, methods of instruction that emphasize simple learning"

(1975, 55). Traditionally, the classroom is not a scene of complex learning. In traditional classrooms, teachers tell students what things mean and what to memorize. Students then feed this official syllabus back on tests and papers. What facts they do gather, they lose in a brief time. Trying to memorize facts, they don't get much chance to exercise research.

One way to develop critical judgment in students while also doing classroom research involves *thinking examinations*. When I give an exam, I tell students it is not a short-answer memory Olympics in facts and definitions. The exam asks them to think through the meaning of the material. To do this, they are free to use any notes, books, or papers they want. It's not cheating to consult sources. I present critical questions for students to choose from and often ask students to invent their own questions. Before an examination, I use a class session for students to write, debate, and choose questions they want on the upcoming test. Some of my tests involve cooperative work, for which a group of students gets a single grade for their group responses. Their group and individual responses are written at length, in essay form, not in short answers. The papers give me feedback for my research into their understandings of the subject matter, their existing writing skills, and their habits for cooperative work. In addition, I have tried a dialogic format for test taking. I begin by asking students what unanswered questions they have about the materials or issues or texts we have been studying. This discussion offers students a chance to clarify whatever confuses them before the test begins. Then I pose a critical question about our material and invite students to talk it over in small groups before writing on it individually. After they write, I collect their papers, and we discuss as a group how they each answered the question. When I hear their replies and read their papers, I get a lot of feedback on how they are understanding or not understanding the subject. This helps me pose new problems, introduce themes and materials, lead discussions of readings, organize peer groups for projects, respond to student compositions, arrange group work and change the curriculum for the next time I teach the course. In this way, the exam can serve as another opportunity for me and for my students to take a researching attitude to the work.

Earlier, I spoke about a freshman composition class which selected personal growth as its generative theme. This study of a generative theme can be understood here in terms of classroom research. When students wrote that personal growth is only a matter of individual talents or weaknesses, they did not include social factors that influence their success or failure. According to them, people had to make it on their own and had no one to blame but themselves if they failed. In their papers, they displayed primarily the values of self-reliance and blaming the victim. Observing this, I posed problems which asked them to re-think their ideas. To this end, I brought in readings about corporate and government economic policy and about discrimination in the work-place. I asked for critical dialogue on such issues as "Does success de-pend only on your personal qualities? Do corporate and government policies affect your chances? Are there obstacles and resources in so-ciety which can help or hinder your growth?" I posed sexual inequality as a topical theme through the following questions: "Are men and women equal in American society? Do men and women have equal chances for personal growth?" One essay I brought in concerned a woman scientist's account of her rocky road in a man's profession. After reading and discussing these materials, I asked students to rewrite their first papers in a new format, which began with individual factors like ambition and family support influencing personal growth and then went on to the obstacles and resources in society which can hinder or help the individual.

With regard to this freshman composition class, I did not plan in ad-vance to use a generative theme of personal growth or to introduce readings about corporations leaving New York or staying there only if the city yields long-term tax breaks. These problems came up in-process as I observed the students' responses. In problem-posing dia-logue, when students display their understandings of a theme in class they teach me the material to use when I design the curriculum. I am the first researcher in the classroom insofar as I observe student thought and learning, but I become part of a researching community when I re-present student material to them for mutual reflection.

Before a semester begins, I outline all my courses. I prepare lessons and readings. In August, I cope with my September anxiety by desig-ning a term's worth of projects, writings, and exercises. But I hope to discover generative themes in-progress from students. If I can discover provocative themes generated from student experience, I reinvent the syllabus. In short, a critical-democratic teacher comes to class with a structure and then reinvents that structure with the students according to their learning, language, conditions, and interests.

Thematic Research and Empowerment

To demonstrate some thematic possibilities in a research format, I will describe in detail some classroom approaches, from the elementary grades and college courses.

The elementary examples are from Schniedewind and Davidson

(1987). In one mural project developed as an interdisciplinary blend of art and social studies, the goals are "to give students an opportunity to cooperate in the creation of change in their community. To provide the community with a mural representing the contributions of people who helped their community" (178). The students make a community mural devoted to groups often left out of official history or else given only token recognition in the traditional syllabus: Native Americans, minorities, women, and working people. Making the mural is a long class project which can be started early in the year and continued over a span of months. This long-term project can be coordinated with smaller ones. If some students finish work on smaller projects, they can use their extra time on the mural rather than having to wait for the rest of the class. This gives students some constructive work always at hand.

The mural project itself begins with a problem-posing dialogue. Teachers elicit discussion around the following issues: "Does art have to be the product of one person alone or can it be produced cooperatively? Does art have to hang in private homes or museums or can it be displayed in public to inspire the community? Have students seen any community murals? What do they depict? What groups have often been left out of these pictures of history?" The students are then asked to begin researching neglected groups with the goal of producing a mural about them.

Working in the mid-Hudson region of New York, Schniedewind and Davidson provided examples of forgotten local history for students to research: about the food, clothing, and life of the indigenous Lenni Lenape people, who inhabited the area before Columbus; about the abolitionist and feminist Sojourner Truth, who had a home nearby where she hid escaping slaves in the Underground Railroad; about African-American women of a local college sorority who responded to hotel segregation in the 1880s by opening their house to minority travelers; and about Hispanic parents who organized in the 1980s a bilingual program for the school curriculum, to meet the needs of their children (179).

Students are given sources of historical information to consult about these forgotten groups, people, and events. Then they divide into research committees to investigate them. Each committee prepares a report while the teacher seeks out a wall for the mural, materials for painting, and local artists to help in the production. After the committees report their findings, the students debate which event from each group is the best choice for depiction in the community mural. With the help of artists and art teachers, they collectively produce a mural.

After the project, there is a "process" discussion in which the students reflect on the project itself. This processing of their own learning is a collective summary done after each cooperative learning exercise. It replaces the teacher's traditional monopoly of the last word. By sharing the summation, the teacher encourages critical reflection and researching attitudes in students.

This ambitious mural project is a research-based, interdisciplinary, and democratic way to teach history, visual arts, and language arts. Further, it can desocialize students from competitiveness and from passive learning, because it involves active collaboration. Such a project challenges the traditional history delivered to students by the official syllabus. It transforms the Eurocentric, male bias of traditional texts by focusing on women and people of color involved in local events. It introduces students to multicultural, nonsexist, and nonelite contexts. Naturally, teachers in other areas would have to situate this approach in their own local history, for example, in the urban Northeast, relating the experiences of immigrant Europeans and migrant African-American families.

In the cooperative classrooms designed by Schniedewind and Davidson, other democratic research projects include examining textbooks for racial stereotyping, analyzing a community problem (such as garbage disposal or the need for trees) to come up with a solution which the class can put into practice, studying nonviolent resistance (including the 1942 Danish rescue of Jews from the Nazis), and uncovering the hidden history of cooperative enterprises now operating successfully in the United States.

In another research project, Schniedewind and Davidson begin with a discussion of the students' breakfast and connect it to world hunger and the domination of Third World economies by multinational corporations. The problem posed is "Bananas for Breakfast: Healthy for Whom?" (1987, 379). This structured exercise encourages students to rethink their everyday activities and their consequences for life in another country, like Honduras. Students role-play two thirteen-year-old girls, a North American, Jill, and a Honduran, Elisa, plus their fathers. North American Jill eats bananas for breakfast, and her father owns stock in corporations reaping profits from the banana trade with Honduras. The Honduran girl and father discuss the hunger and poverty in their country in relation to the banana trade. After the role-playing, students consider how Jill's life affects Elisa's and how Jill's family could help the Hondurans—by raising money to send them, protesting corporate policy at a stockholder's meeting, and so on. Exercising math, they also study a chart that shows where the money goes when North Americans pay twenty cents a pound for bananas. (Hondurans get less than 10 percent.)

This focus on North–South inequality leads to a discussion of how the class could bring such information to the attention of others. The teachers invite student ideas. They also suggest some appropriate activities through using educational bulletin boards, sponsoring a hunger awareness day, selling locally produced Honduran products, and working with groups that are trying to change corporate policy. From the student-centered, generative theme of bananas for breakfast, the class can go on to research other food items popular with students, like chocolate bars, Coke, or hamburgers, to learn the politics of inequality in everyday terms. Projects like these situate critical research and action in everyday life and structure academic knowledge into the generative experiences of students. They are examples of what I call "extraordinarily reexperiencing the ordinary," which is a goal of empowering education.

The Researching Classroom: Questioning Inequality

For students in higher education, a good example of a researching classroom is a course taught by Solorzano (1989) at East Los Angeles Community College, listed as Directed Practice in Social Welfare. Solorzano offered it as a joint sociology and Chicano Studies course to students who were mostly Chicanos from the local area. Before he took on this teaching assignment, the course had been a traditional practicum, which placed students in schools and agencies. Solorzano set as his goal "to integrate a Freirean problem-posing orientation to the class," which could connect research and action (219).

He began by dialoguing with students on the social issues most important to them. This is a typical start for a critical-democratic class, where students are invited to speak about their concerns. In this initial dialogue, the teacher is doing in-process classroom research into student language, perceptions, and conditions. From these first dialogues in Solorzano's adult class, a student-centered theme emerged: concern about youth gangs in East Los Angeles.

Gang violence had been receiving much attention in the press and in the film industry in the late 1970s, when this class was first offered. (In the late 1980s and early 1990s, the film emphasis shifted to African-American gangs.) The *Los Angeles Times* ran a three-part series on Chicanos in the media just as the school term began. These articles became the first texts through which students began researching the theme of youth gangs. Solorzano asked, "What are some of the images of Chicanos in the mass media?"

The media dialogue centered on the negative stereotypes of Chicanos and on the Chicano-white culture clash as presented in Hollywood gang movies. Two weeks of discussion led Solorzano to re-present the following problems: "Why are Chicanos portrayed negatively in the mass media?" and "Whose interests are served by these negative portrayals of Chicanos?" These questions became the focus of an extended research and action project.

About the value of research, Solorzano wrote: "I believed that in order for students to critically understand the nature of any social problem, they had to possess the skills necessary to gather data and have a firm grasp of the theories used to interpret the data" (1989, 200). To accomplish this, the class divided into three research groups: (1) a library group to research images of Chicanos in the media now and in the past, using the *Readers' Guide to Periodical Literature, Sociological Abstracts,* the *Social Sciences Index,* the *Los Angeles Times Index,* and the *New York Times Index;* (2) a group to research public data on youth gangs in East Los Angeles, using the area census on Chicanos, information from the sheriff's office and from the police department, as well as sociological texts on deviant behavior and firsthand reports from gang members; (3) a group to research the film industry, including Hollywood studio executives, Chicano community members and groups working as consultants to moviemakers, and groups challenging the negative images of Chicanos in the media.

After several weeks, the research teams reported back to class. One discovered that the gang problem was being blown out of proportion. The percentage of Chicano youth joining gangs was not ten, as reported in the media but closer to three. Another group, examining images of groups in film and other media, found that "Chicanos were stereotyped disproportionately in subordinate and demeaning occupational roles such as bandits, thieves, and gangsters. Students also discovered negative Latino portrayals in films and in magazine and newspaper articles dating back to the turn of the century. . . . This popular media portrayal seemed to reinforce the social scientific image of Chicanos as stereotypic social beings whose problems could be traced to a deficient or disadvantaged culture" (221). They observed a blaming-the-victim ideology at work in the dominant media, which characterized Chicanos as having personal and group weaknesses.

After making their analyses, the students focused on how Hollywood was exploiting Chicano stereotypes to make a profit. They decided to take public action against the youth gang films to raise awareness of racist portrayals in film and to stop the further release of negative images of Latinos. They organized a boycott and an informational picket against some offending films. For help, the class approached outside organizations, which led to the founding of the ad hoc Gang Exploitation

Film Committee, to oversee the protests. After public protest and after mixed profit results from these films, Hollywood stopped producing Chicano gang films. According to Solorzano, no new Chicano youth gang movies appeared in the decade after this class. He comments on the impact of the project:

> It was apparent that the students developed commitment to and confidence in their own ideas, as well as research, organizational, and communication skills to test those ideas. They had become empowered for the "moment." In that moment they had exposed the larger community to an organized group of people who felt, acted, and succeeded in doing something they considered positive. . . . I can only hope that the students' critical curiosity, their new problem-solving skills, and the related sense of empowerment remain with them. . . . If they do remain, the Freirean approach has achieved its major goal of empowering students to reflect and act on real-life problems on a sustained basis. (223)

Solorzano, like Schniedewind and Davidson, offered the classroom as a research and action center. In regard to action, Solorzano reported that "to understand the problem posed and to empower students, one must take action on the problem and reflect critically on the action taken. Therefore, it is my responsibility as the coordinator to challenge students and to resist passivity, to take a more active role in their education generally, and to address the specific social problems they have identified. In some of my courses I have failed to do this, but, as most educators know, each class has a different personality and will react to issues differently" (223).

The potential of any class for action depends on various factors I will take up below. While research for social action is a goal, it is not always an appropriate or workable one given the limits of many classrooms. Solorzano also concluded that having a two-semester time frame helped his course evolve to the point of in-depth research and action, which would be harder to do in a shorter period.

In going from dialogue to research to action, Solorzano reported some feelings of disorientation in himself, as democratic authority was shared in class, shifting some control from teacher to students. As students took responsibility for the work, the teacher needed to direct the process less. To share authority with students is an unusual experience. Democratic problem-posing re-positions the teacher in the learning process, but the teacher does not become irrelevant or unnecessary. Her or his participation and expertise are still needed, but in a different way. When students accept the teacher's invitation to codevelop the curriculum, the dialogic process is democratizing authority. This transformation is a goal of empowering education—to have students share responsibility and authority for their learning. As this process evolves, the teacher's profile changes so that he or she supervises less while relating his or her knowledge more and more to student initiatives. In Solorzano's case, the new classroom relations stabilized as teacher and students grew accustomed to sharing control, but it takes some humor and resilience to cope with the transition, because both teacher and students are products of the old system and have little experience with the new relationships involved.

These examples of classroom research at the elementary and college levels are cross-disciplinary and action-oriented. I want now to consider the last two items on the agenda for empowerment, *interdisciplinary* and *activist* learning.

Crossing Academic Boundaries

Critical-democratic classes often cross the boundaries of academic disciplines. In the mural-making project described by Schniedewind and Davidson, students did reading, writing, speaking, cooperative learning, social studies, visual arts, and elementary math. In Frankenstein's adult mathematics classes, students practiced statistical analysis, developed skills in reading and writing, and used material from economics and sociology. In Solorzano's college course, the students did media analysis and social-historical research. These exemplify the interdisciplinary value of empowering education, the tenth item on the agenda.

When it comes to materials or to the learning process, a student-centered teacher integrates the subject matter and the methods appropriate at any moment. As critical dialogue evolves, the responses of the students signal what material and structure are needed. By using multiple formats––group work, whole-class dialogue, individual writing or exhibits, project presentations––teachers can avoid a one-dimensional structure to critical learning. Similarly, crossing disciplinary lines deploys multiple approaches and bodies of knowledge.

A critical-interdisciplinary approach can be applied to law and medicine. In general, legal and medical training are not self-critical about their professions or critical of conditions in society. To design them as critical, interdisciplinary curricula teachers could ask: "How have Western perspectives, patriarchy, and elite clientele affected the practice of law and medicine? Historically, what roles have women and minorities played in the practice, training, and research of these professions?"

Birth-control research and development have focused on the female, not the male. Was this inevitable? Cancer treatment emphasizes expensive, invasive, high-tech therapies. These doctor-centered approaches have cost billions of dollars, and failed to stop the spread of cancer. High-tech therapies have marginalized research and development into cancer prevention, dietary and environmental causes, and naturopathic treatment. In the case of law, critical studies could ask how disputes were settled before law became a massive institution in modern life. Wealthy groups in society have been the preferred clients of doctors and lawyers; poor and working groups have been underserved and underrepresented. Democratic medical and legal education would study this inequity and invite students to imagine how law and health care might be transformed to serve the needs of the majority. Lastly, some powerful interest groups in society (such as the food, chemical, and pharmaceutical industries) that have commercial stakes in costly health care practices and in traditional education for practitioners can be studied for their influence on professional training.

A critical-interdisciplinary teacher also draws on themes and texts from student culture as well as from academic disciplines. Printed materials from daily life—newspapers, magazines, junk mail brochures, signs, bulletin boards—are some of the texts people live with in the mainstream. The empowering class can turn to these materials as a starting point for critical study in language arts and in content areas. The list of ingredients on packaged food can be a foundation for science classes, to study the biology and chemistry of nutrition. Reports from local papers on air or water pollution can serve as starting points for a science curriculum. Magazine articles on the high rate of teenage pregnancy in the United States, or on the school dropout rate, or on the increasing wealth in the United States of the top 20 percent versus declining income for the poor, could open math/social studies classes.

In using TV news and daily papers to develop critical literacy, one interdisciplinary art educator, Perr (1988), has taken a special interest in challenging the mass media. Students redesign advertising so that the ads communicate a progressive message rather than sell a product; they rework magazine ads to make the words and images say something socially critical, in their own words. Similarly, students redesign the front page of a daily newspaper with their own texts, so that the news speaks in their voices, expressing their fears and hopes. In addition, students produce grass-roots television as a critique of the television now dominant. Art here is not abstract or alien to daily life but is rather a way to integrate media studies and social criticism, to rethink the imagery and messages pouring in from mass culture.

Interdisciplinary Literacy: Language Arts and Content Areas

Interdisciplinary education also means integrating reading, writing, critical dialogue, and cooperative learning across the curriculum. Linking content areas to collaborative language arts is an important step away from the disabling separation of language study and academic subjects.

To develop literacy and understanding about subject matter, teachers of content courses need a reading-and-writing-to-learn approach, in which students keep journals, do free writing, revise their essays in groups, write about and talk about their readings, as a means to grasp the material and express it in their own words (see Britton et al. 1975; Mayher, Lester, and Pradl 1983). Students need to talk freely in class about their learning, to work out meaning and to inform the teacher how they understand the subject matter. Frankenstein does this in her critical math classes, which include an unusual amount of writing, reading, discussion, and group work.

Making language arts integral to content areas is the basic idea behind "writing across the curriculum" (Fulwiler and Young 1982; Fulwiler 1987). This innovative development challenges the standard curriculum, which separates academic courses from language study. Typically, writing classes are thought of as service courses for other disciplines, serving their need to make students good readers and writers. This segregation of language arts from academic learning cheats both sides of the richness available when literacy and critical thought are exercised through a study of specific subject matter. In addition, learning and literacy would best be served if the notion of writing across the curriculum was expanded into critical-democratic learning across the curriculum. Every content area, from biology to economics to accounting to architecture, can pose its subject matter as critical problems related to social conditions and to student experience. Further, to lessen student resistance and to increase participation, all classes can be structured democratically. Students who codevelop the curriculum in content classes will gain a motivating ownership of the learning process.

Negotiating the curriculum and making it dialogic should not be restricted to communications classes. If those practices cross disciplines, the curriculum will become a holistic critical and democratic experience for students. They will receive from class to class a reinforcement of their learning. Given the rigid separation of academic disciplines from each other and from the language arts, this will not be an easy transformation. But until the curriculum becomes cross-disciplinary and critical-democratic, integrating language arts with content areas, education in school and colleges will remain an interference to learning.

Open Borders: Activist Learning

Crossing academic boundaries is curricular action that challenges the dominant structure of education. This leads to the eleventh and last value of this agenda: *activism*. Critical-democratic pedagogy is cultural action against the educational limits of the status quo. The basic process of dialogue—problem-posing—actively questions schooling, society, teacher-talk, and existing knowledge. It democratically invites students to make their education, to examine critically their experience and social conditions, and to consider acting in society from the knowledge they gain.

Dialogic problem-posing is a pedagogy Freire called "cultural action for freedom" (1985b, 43). At the classroom level, it influences individual thinking, behaving, and speaking, in a cooperative group process. It offers intellectual and emotional development to students through the cultural domain of education. In dialogue, students can develop critical re-perception of their powers, conditions, language, knowledge, and society, which they had before thought about uncritically. This reflective process opens possibilities for new thinking, feeling, and acting, once people examine received knowledge and the status quo, as well as their routine ways of living and learning. Such cultural action may lead to deeper change in self and society, but that depends on a number of factors: how many high-quality transformative classes and experiences are available to the individual; how many organized groups and coalitions to change school and society are accessible; how much support and free time private life offers to develop the conviction, knowledge, and social action to follow through on critical knowledge; and how open or restricted the political climate is when and where people undertake projects in social change.

Empowering education is oriented to self-transformation and social change, but this pedagogy is only one way to act against inequality and for democracy in school and society. Social movements for civil rights, for equal school funding, against militarism, or for women's equality could be called "mass action for freedom." In these movements, masses of people are organized for democratic change. Further, political campaigns to elect progressive politicians and school boards could be called "electoral or parliamentary action for freedom." Film and theater workers can undertake "artistic action for freedom" by making movies and plays critical of inequality and by telling stories which the official syllabus, major studios, and stages ignore, from labor history, women's culture, and minority communities. This alternative culture will offer critical teachers resources for adding diversity to school and college curricula. In the print world, alternative presses and dissident publications are engaged in "media action for freedom" as they produce materials useful for dissenting organizations, feminists, antiracists, environmentalists, consumer advocates, empowering educators, and opposition groups. Some small presses also support democratic diversity and freedom of speech when they produce critical books turned down by commercial publishers. Then there is "environmental action for freedom," which includes those groups targeting industrial pollution, deforestation, and nuclear power, as well as those advocating major investment in a recycling industry. When trade unions go on strike for better conditions, they take part in "labor action for freedom." Last, there is "consumer action for freedom," of the kind pursued in the United States by Ralph Nader's public interest research groups.

Critical education in classrooms is thus one activist way among many to question the status quo while promoting democratic values for self and society.

Activist Education: Transformation of Self inside History

Critical pedagogy is activist in its questioning of the status quo, in its participatory methods, and in its insistence that knowledge is not fixed but is constantly changing. More than just dynamic and filled with contending perspectives, critical knowledge offers a chance to rethink experience and society. As the examples from Schniedewind and Davidson (1987) and from Solorzano (1989) demonstrate, this activism is situated in the students' age and level of development, in the subject matter of the class, and in the political conditions of the area. Schniedewind and Davidson focused on the local history of forgotten peoples as well as on local problems for students to research and act on. Solorzano's class zeroed in on the nearby film industry to oppose its racial stereotypes in gang movies. Activism takes different shapes depending on the situation of each classroom.

At the least, the dialogic class acts against the traditional curriculum. It challenges passive schooling, where students learn that education is something done to them rather than something they do. It invites students to become active learners who question received wisdom, undemocratic relations, and unequal conditions, and who codevelop the curriculum. The critical teacher activates democratic potentials in students by posing knowledge and history as unfinished and transformable. Challenging undemocratic authority and student passivity in education is a significant action of the dialogic method.

As an example of acting against the ideology of the status quo, I can refer back to the freshman composition class which chose personal growth as its theme and where I brought in material about corporate economic policy and discrimination. In that class, the students blamed the individual alone if he or she failed to succeed. Through dialogue, reading, and writing the students were challenged to re-perceive the system in which they construct their fate. This learning process acted against the values of extreme self-reliance and of blaming the victim, and it raised the profile of arbitrary limits set by an unequal society.

In some circumstances, the critical teacher can also invite students to consider acting on social conditions, not just studying them. In upstate New York, Schniedewind and Davidson suggested that students question what their bananas for breakfast meant to Third World people and consider action to challenge the North–South inequality. In East Los Angeles, Solorzano invited students to research and act against racial stereotypes in Hollywood films. In New York City, Perr asked students to rethink media images and to invent their own political culture by making windows for peace, adorning buildings with antiwar messages and images. In the Bahamas, Elsasser and Irvine taught a woman's writing class that published a feminist manifesto in the local paper, challenging male domination. In New Mexico, they organized a community literacy program for Hispanic teenagers, which included a job service, a traveling family theater, and writing bilingual books for the impoverished schools of Bluefields, Nicaragua. Each of these projects connected knowledge to social action.

Activist Learning Is Oriented to Change-Agency

Change-agency in this pedagogy means learning and acting for the democratic transformation of self and society. It can take place at work, at home, in school, and in the community, wherever people take responsibility for rethinking and changing the conditions they are in. Teachers who help students develop as agents of change are what Aronowitz and Giroux (1985) called transformative intellectuals. Change-agency is action at the classroom level so that students rethink disabling ideologies and behaviors, such as self-reliance, classroom silence, getting by, playing dumb, political cynicism, anti-intellectualism, white supremacy, male dominance, excessive consumerism, dependence on authority, and so on.

Students can be introduced to the notion of change in the subject matter of a course. In no field is knowledge fixed; it is always evolving; schools of thought keep contending. The curriculum can present this diversity, so that students do not receive static or one-dimensional views of academic or technical knowledge. Contending thought in any field can be presented to students as a problem for their deliberation. Anthropology classes can examine the debate over the disappearance of the Neanderthals. Economics classes can debate the market system, to puzzle out whether profit-driven production is more just or efficient than an industrial system based on producing for social needs. Biology classes can debate whether gradual or catastrophic evolution most influenced the development of flora, fauna, and terrain. In science classes students can read debates on the impact of human exposure to toxic wastes and nuclear radiation. Which view makes the most sense to students?

Further, the knowledge of a discipline can be presented historically, comparing what is thought now with what was thought fifty or a hundred years ago. Students can be asked to analyze differences in the field over a period of time. How was Shakespeare read in 1920? How is his work being criticized now? In architecture, how does Frank Lloyd Wright's design of homes for people of modest means compare to what was built in Levittown after World War II and what is being built now? What do the changes indicate? Teachers can ask students to use their imaginations and write stories about how an academic field will look fifty years from now. What will people and society be needing and thinking in the future? Communicating the reality of change is one way to help students develop a dynamic intelligence that enables them to imagine change and perhaps participate in making change.

In terms of activating student thoughts about change, the teacher can raise the profile of change-agency under way now. Efforts to transform knowledge and society exist in every age but the status quo is hostile to ideas, values, and movements that challenge existing authority. Official culture has a stake in obscuring the opposition. The critical-democratic teacher can work against this by giving a high profile to alternatives and dissent in society. For my courses, I look for stories and materials of citizen activism and dissent, of groups involved in relevant campaigns and constructive projects, to give them some visibility in the lives of my students.

The activist teacher can also ask students to interview working people in a variety of jobs, to test their own career training in school against the realities of work (Shor 1988). Career curricula in school often romanticize occupations, but idealizing the work world does not serve students well. Occupational training supports the status quo when it uncritically funnels students into the undemocratic job market. A change-agency curriculum would reveal what working life is like day to day, on the job, in each field being studied. The critical career class can also research trade unions to discover if a job site is organized well, poorly, or not at all. Such a class can invite unionists to speak to students about labor organization and how to organize. Management can be invited to debate labor about the value of unionization. If local cooperatives exist, they too can become part of an activist curriculum that exposes students to diverse structures for work, profit, and ownership.

For an activist science curriculum, students can do research outside the classroom. An interdisciplinary science class studying sound and light might send students supervised by a teacher and equipped with cameras, tape recorders, and measuring devices, to different neighborhoods to see if wealthier areas have different sounds and different illumination from poorer ones. They could write up reports on their findings to integrate language arts into science education and could chart the differences they find to integrate math into this study. They could compare the housing, police presence, garbage, and printed messages on the streets. The comparative study of neighborhoods would be an activist introduction to social inequality, expressed here through living conditions.

Actively Studying Life to Change It

For a closer look at change-agency, community life, and critical learning, I can report in some detail the activist dimensions of the Adult Learning Project (ALP), a program for urban working-class students that was founded in 1979. In their analysis of the project in the Gorgie Dalry area of Edinburgh, Kirkwood and Kirkwood (1989) described the initial situation:

In Gorgie Dalry, ALP workers have found that the most prevalent theme is alienation and the increasing privatization of people's lives. . . . A major task implied by it is to encourage people to contact, communicate and collaborate with each other, and begin to see the possibility of taking risks and contributing to change in society. (137)

ALP educators researched the area with community members to prepare a curriculum in relation to the key themes of alienation and isolation. Faced with this community condition, ALP set an activist community agenda:

the attempt to involve as many people from the locality as possible; the identification and exploration of themes by participants; the carry-through from learning into action; the emphasis on taking responsibility and exercising authority; the stress on intentionality and shared purpose; the link with churchhouse groups; the outward-turned orientation, seeking to relate people from other cultures and areas, and those not yet involved; the emphasis on parenting and children; the provision of creches [family shelter for new residents]; and the regular social gatherings in the ALP shop, which are really celebrations of membership. (138)

Through ALP, three major problem-themes became learning programs for students: Living in Gorgie Dalry, Health and Well-being, and Parents and Authority. These three led to several action projects:

(1) Play in the Terraces—The theme of Living in Gorgie Dalry uncovered a problem of play space for children. ALP launched an extended student-led community project to deal with a conflict between automobiles and children playing in the housing area served by ALP (called "the Terraces"). The different needs of car owners, parents with children, and children themselves were negotiated at length by the community, which reached policy decisions on how to organize parking, driving, and play space in the area (101).

(2) The Skills Exchange—High unemployment in the area left many residents with unused skills and too much time on their hands. ALP students organized a mutual skills exchange called "Tit for Tat" which was open to all residents in the area. No money changed hands for services shared. The range of skills available free to members was great. Members registered their skills and a volunteer core group kept track of jobs done (106).

(3) The Parents Centre—The Centre emerged from and for parents who felt isolated, burdened with responsibilities, and lacking support. It included a family shelter for new members who had not yet settled into local housing. This welcoming place focused its talking groups on problems with kids, individual identity and one's role as a parent, living with teenagers, the influence of books and television on children, the transition from home to school, sibling rivalry and parental favoritism, feeding children, preventing accidents, and the function of play (110).

There were also action projects to set up a writer's workshop and a photo workshop to meet the interests of members. According to the Kirkwoods, the learning programs and action outcomes were directed to goals for empowering education:

facilitating people's emergence from their isolated position in the crowd, and their struggle to help create the good society, founded on dialogue and respect for each person as a subject, where people take responsibility for themselves and for others, where being is recognized as more important than having, where the need to have enough is seen as a necessary precondition for being to the full, and where the attempt by the few to accumulate great power and wealth is recognized as a denial of participation by the many. (138)

The ALP learning programs and action outcomes were situated in the depressed economic conditions of Scotland in the 1980s. Its constituency was being marginalized and depressed by economic policy in Britain, which resulted in high unemployment, an emphasis on privatization, and a withdrawal of social services. ALP activities put some flooring under the feet of its sinking constituency. It lessened the disempowering isolation of members so that they could stabilize in a social setting, organize to meet some immediate needs, and pursue their development even in hard times, in a mutual process with others in the same condition. Still, it was not a political movement that could work at larger social change. That would require a mass organization for transforming power in the political arena.

A different structure for activism and adult education has been under way at the legendary Highlander Center in Tennessee. A unique institution, Highlander was founded in 1932 by Myles Horton and Don West (Adams 1975). In the antiunion South of the 1930s, Highlander started as a labor education center allied with the Congress of Industrial Organizations (CIO) when that union was in its militant heyday. In 1952, when the Cold War and McCarthyism were chilling militant unions in the United States, Highlander remained oppositional and became a center for civil rights education in a Jim Crow southern state. Since 1969, it has served as an organizing resource for poor communities of the region on such issues as mining and flood disasters, health, occupational and environmental safety, and the control of land and resources. In the 1980s, it began making links with adult education programs like itself in other countries.

Highlander connects education to social change by helping local groups and activists clarify their goals and build alliances. At the Tennessee farm which is the Center, organizers, activists, community advocates, and critical educators take residential workshops with others working on the same problem. Highlander also does participatory research at the request of groups that need background to develop their program. If asked, Highlander staff will go to communities to lead workshops for the group's expressed needs. Lastly, to develop new leadership, Highlander has a youth and internship program at the farm (Highlander Education and Research Center 1987). These programs link groups and active individuals to each other while providing resources to promote their further development. Highlander's uniqueness extends over many areas, from its use of music, song, dance, and media, to knowing how to help groups develop their agenda, to challenging the racism, sexism, and conservatism of the area. Those coming to Highlander or asking Highlander's aid are not told what to do. Instead, they are offered a dialogic process to clarify strategies useful for groups contending in a variety of arenas for social change.

Empowering Education Is a Long Process of Redevelopment

With empowering education, in most settings, student activism will take some time to develop. However, students' interest in democratic education and social action will increase if the political climate in society changes to one favoring protest culture. A democratic climate favoring protest, with mass movements on the offensive, would orient more people to participate in making social change. But even in activist times, many students will resist critical-democratic education for a variety of reasons, including the lingering effects of passive schooling. On the other hand, even in conservative times, many will take part in critical classrooms and in action groups. The political openings in any age and in any situation need to be discovered. This is what it means to engage in situated pedagogy and politics.

The action of a dialogic teacher against teacher-centered education is change-agency by itself. But student-centered, critical classrooms are easier to organize than the participation of students in change-agency outside class. At my low-tuition, working-class, mostly white college in a conservative part of New York City, I do not expect students to be social activists by the end of a term. A few arrive as activists, and a few move in that direction through the term. But given the traditional college curriculum, the conservative community, and the reactionary climate after the 1960s, more than one or two semesters of critical-democratic education are needed to move numbers of students into activism. I do, however, expect to stir their critical thinking, to engage them in a democratic process of education, and to challenge some aspects of their traditional socialization. At the least, they will have faced questions and issues glossed over by mass media and mass education. And my critical-democratic problem-posing will have asked them to consider that human beings and history are in a state of constant change. If these students had an overall critical curriculum at the college, the numbers accepting change-agency would increase.

Critical teachers do not have to wait for everything to change before anything can be changed. What goes on in each classroom is significant. Critical learning is by itself a form of social action because of its transforming potential, its challenge to the dominant culture inside and outside us. Still, it is important to keep in mind the limits related to the age, the interests, the levels of development, and the commitment of the students. Students in formal schools and colleges will respond unevenly. Some will be more open-minded than others. Some will more willingly rethink official knowledge and dominant values.

The limits on teaching for self and social change also include administrative restraints. If a syllabus is mandated, with required texts, standardized tests, an official reading list, and an exit examination, then the open space to reinvent the subject shrinks, while the demands on the teacher's ingenuity magnify. This is a political problem requiring organized campaigns against the traditional apparatus of education. Campaigns for cooperative learning, critical teaching, multicultural education, and student-centered instruction are crucial for winning democratic rights for teachers and students. Winning parental and community support for these changes can push administrators to cooperate. At the college level, a campaign for writing across the curriculum and for critical-democratic teaching in all departments would also open up pedagogical space for transformative learning.

Teachers in some programs sponsored by progressive churches, unions, local organizations, political groups, or private agencies will have fewer limits on their activist goals. These nonformal arenas often accept that some action and transformation should take place. On the other hand, formal schools and colleges are institutions supervised by various authorities. If education was irrelevant to power, it would be regulated less. Part of the empowering experiment is researching what open space exists in any setting for critical teaching and activist projects. Another part is figuring out with like-minded colleagues and students how to use this space well.

Not for Oratory: Using the Political Opening

Cultural action in a classroom is not like political action in an organization or movement. A classroom in a school or college is rarely a self-selected group seeking social change. The mainstream classroom is a mélange of students with various motives in an institution structured against their empowerment. Most often, students do not come to class with a transformative agenda. Few are looking for empowering education. Some welcome a challenging democratic process while others resent it; some welcome an unsettling critical dialogue while others reject it. As Goodlad (1990) observed, "Students are largely passive and at least by the time they reach the upper elementary and secondary school grades, appear to assume that passivity is what best fits the nature of school. They even come to dislike disturbances of their passivity" (24). The way out of this situation has to be negotiated carefully and gradually.

Teachers who treat the classroom as a political meeting can expect stiffened resistance from students as well as more vigilant policing by administrators. In community-based, nonformal education, there may be more room for activism, but even there teachers can misunderstand the political limits of the sponsoring group. Activism needs to be situated inside the community's conditions and developed with the students, who dislike harangues. Sectarian teaching that promotes a correct line only mimics traditional teacher-talk. Dialogic, democratic teaching rejects sectarian posturing. Students cannot be commanded to take action and cannot be graded on their consciousness. They can only be presented with critical problems and invited to think and act on them.

Dialogic teaching is a challenge to authoritarian schooling, to student disempowerment, and to inequality in society. But single critical classrooms by themselves cannot transform school and the economy. Society gets transformed by social movements contending in a variety of political arenas, from electoral races to union organizing, from community action against discrimination to campaigns for peace, for reproductive rights, for environmental action, and for civil rights. Each movement is educational by itself and can also include formal educational programs inside the larger project. These are likely sites for empowering education, within movements themselves, in addition to empowering classes in schools or colleges. From the mass of students in formal education, some will take to activism and join movements for social change. Those movements take off in history when they reach a critical mass, develop seasoned leadership and coalitions, articulate widely held grievances and dreams, and find an idea whose time has come, especially when a crisis polarizes society and creates a political climate for change.

Education is not the center of power in society, but it can affect power because it is a vast cultural territory filled with contention. Conflicts in society spill over into education, and contentions in schooling spill over into the larger society. Freire was arrested in Brazil during the coup in April 1964, and his expanding literacy program was dismantled. The Brazilian elite and army, which banned his books and forced him into exile for sixteen years, did not consider his project harmless in a time of rising mass expectations and political ferment. In the 1988 elections, the success of Workers' Party candidates in Sao Paulo, Brazil, again brought schooling to the forefront. Soon after, Freire served for over two years as Secretary of Education for the new city government, where he launched major reforms in the schools.

In the United States during the 1960s education was a major front in the social movements for civil rights, for peace in Vietnam, and for women's equality. A militant phase of civil rights activism was launched by African-American undergraduates through their lunch counter sit-ins in the south in February 1960. Student protests also affected the government's ability to pursue the war in Vietnam. In the 1970s and

1980s, authorities in and out of school launched reforms to undermine the protest culture emerging in education. These reforms from the Nixon through the Reagan administrations—career education, back to basics, the literacy crisis, more standardized testing, and demands for traditional excellence—sought to limit the activism and cultural democracy opened up in the 1960s (Shor 1992).

The activist influence of education has been felt in other places from the 1960s onward. Student protests in Paris touched off an upheaval that nearly toppled the de Gaulle government in May and June of 1968. In South Africa, in June 1976, a student uprising in Soweto against white Afrikaans language in black African schools ignited a new militant phase against apartheid that led to the eventual release of Nelson Mandela in February 1990 and the legalization of his party, the African National Congress. In support of this successful campaign against apartheid, college students in the United States after 1985 forced hundreds of universities to divest stocks in corporations doing business in South Africa.

Further, before the immense rally against nuclear weapons in New York in June 1982, some 151 universities in the country held anti-nuclear teach-ins the previous November, to prepare the way for the million people who marched in New York. In 1987 and after, in the occupied West Bank, the Palestine uprising, Intifada, led the Israeli army to close down Palestinian schools and colleges in an effort to control the protests, but the local population organized its own underground education during this period as an adjunct to the rebellion. In Korea in the late 1980s, militant students kept the pressure on the government to democratize the country. In China in 1989, student protestors led the pro-democracy movement that spread to neighborhoods and brought the government to a halt for weeks. In the great changes in Eastern Europe in 1989, students also played a role, especially in Czechoslovakia and Romania.

Critical education and democratic activism in school are not marginal. They can support transformative projects in society at large, challenge the socialization of students into an unequal status quo, and democratize the education system. At some moments, education projects can propel activism in society, creating the potential for larger changes. Empowering education invites students to question school and society, to consider some alternatives and to imagine others, and to reject the inequality whose roots lie in the economic system. Society would be very different if education were critical and democratic.

Having discussed basic values for empowering education, I will focus the coming chapters on day-to-day problem-posing in class, on teacher transformation to dialogic methods, and on the discourse needed to help critical dialogue work in the classroom. In these discussions, I will offer a detailed model for problem-posing as well as one for classroom and community research. Finally, I will examine what I call the third idiom, which is the discourse of the democratic speech community created by teachers and students in a dialogic class. The third idiom evolves in dialogue from the noncommunicating idioms students and teacher bring with them. Against language that alienates, the critical-democratic process seeks language that transforms.

Becoming an Empowering Educator

Obstacles to and Resources for Critical Teaching

8

Turning Point: September Power or Pain

When sweet September rolls around again, teachers and students face their annual rush of hope and fear. September is rich in possibilities and cluttered with disabling routines. These early days can be a turning point if they reject the dismal practices of the old regime. September can be transforming if critical ideas and democratic discourse replace teacher-talk and the standard syllabus.

For an alternative to the traditional syllabus, the values discussed earlier provide some foundations. In this chapter, I will offer paradigms through which teachers can research the obstacles to and resources for critical learning. This research is basic to becoming an empowering educator. Specifically, I will contrast a *zero paradigm* in traditional education with a *critical paradigm* in empowering programs.

The zero paradigm is the deficit-model dominant in education. It defines students as deficits to be filled with skills, words, and facts, ignoring the culture they bring to class. About defining students as deficits, or zeros, Freire (1970) wrote that in the standard syllabus "knowledge is a gift bestowed by those who consider themselves knowledgeable upon those whom they consider to know nothing. Projecting an absolute ignorance onto others, a characteristic of the ideology of oppression, negates education and knowledge as processes of inquiry" (58).

In the zero paradigm, teachers function as delivery systems to transfer knowledge. Lectures followed by recitation questions, work-sheets, short-answer exams, and textbook assignments are the typical means for transfer-teaching. Such an approach is the dullest way to teach and to learn. With its passive role for students, the transfer-method also has the friendliest fit with top-down control, because it sends a disempowering message to students: knowledge and power are fixed from above, not negotiated or discovered from below.

Further, the zero paradigm creates artificial divisions between

200

teachers and students, between students and students, between students and knowledge, and between knowledge and action. When packages of subject matter or lists of facts are delivered to students, little more than memorizing is expected of them. Because knowledge comes at them in a one-way discourse, they have little need to interact with the teacher, with each other, or with the material. This passive process is so alienating that intellectual life becomes associated with boredom and imposition.

In contrast, the critical paradigm is egalitarian, interactive, and mutual. It says that *both teachers and students start out at less than zero and more than zero simultaneously* as the class begins. "Less than zero" means that some values and habits of both students and teachers interfere with critical learning. "More than zero" means that some of their thought and action support empowerment. Both bring resources and obstacles to class; both have language, knowledge, and intentions that can help or hinder critical study. In the critical paradigm, teachers and students are complex people in a position to make or derail transformative learning. The project, then, is what Kuhn (1962) called a paradigm shift, in this case a shift from the disabling zero model to the empowering critical one.

Paradigm Shift: From Cultural Deficit to Cultural Democracy

In the educational system, teachers and students are divided at the bottom of the ladder. They are alienated from each other by a hierarchy and a curriculum that establish the teacher's authority at the expense of the students. But empowerment requires their cooperation. They each know things the other must learn.

Culture is not the sole possession of one side in the democratic classroom. Every human being who speaks a language has culture and makes culture every day. Culture is what human beings do, make, and say. Students all come to class with culture and language from their community, from which they take values and to which they add their own culture-making action. Social experience gives people systems of thought, language, behavior, aspirations, and relationships. However, groups occupy unequal cultural positions in society; not all have equal power to determine the fate of society or of their own specific group. Power to set the terms on which individuals, groups, and society develop is unequally distributed by class, sex, race, age, region, and physical ability. Wealthier people and men have more power to develop themselves and to affect society's development than do female, poor, and working groups. Whites have more social, political, media, and economic power than do people of color. This hierarchy denies cultural democracy, which means equal power for all groups to develop themselves and the nation.

The zero paradigm supports cultural inequality. It delivers a dominant, Eurocentric syllabus that silences critical thinking about society and ignores the culturally diverse languages and experiences of students. It produces underachievement in the legions of students who resent and resist an alien culture imposed on them. Minority students especially face the dilemma of subordinating themselves to the language and values of white society. In regard to racial subordination, Cummins (1989) wrote that "in place of self-esteem and a strong sense of cultural identity, schools have systematically promoted ambivalence and insecurity in minority children by punishing them for speaking their first language and by devaluing their cultural roots" (6). In a similar vein, Goodlad (1990) observed that minority students in an unequal system "face an insulting put-down in the insensitive white expectation that they (and all other minorities) shed rich, evocative languages and cultural traditions to blend innocuously into the culture of the school and the community" (6). Goodlad's and Cummins's remarks also apply to white working-class students in an education system favoring upper-class language and culture.

The critical paradigm, on the other hand, respects the knowledge, experience, and language of students. It does not mythologize them as deficits. The first responsibility of critical teachers is to research what students know, speak, experience, and feel, as starting points from which an empowering curriculum is developed. Wallerstein (1983) discussed student-based research as a first step in a program of English as a second language she helped found:

We started the program by listening. Our team of five to seven persons conducted research for two months on the needs or "themes" of the community before launching into adult education classes. We talked to neighbors, met with church and community groups, observed people in parks, and visited social service agencies. Many of the themes we uncovered became the core of our ESL program. Our team consisted of two Chicanos and two Anglos from the community, and three Anglos who came from outside—all bilingual; two of us outsiders moved into the community before starting work. (Wallerstein 1983)

A teacher's education can begin before class through researching students, to discover their language and issues.

But affirming student culture does not mean that students know all they need to know or that teachers don't know anything special. In fact, what teachers know is crucial to the transformative process. Pedagogical skills and academic knowledge are required for critical teaching.

The question is how to use expert knowledge to facilitate rather than hinder student learning. The teacher is in a condition similar to that of the students when critical classes convene, possessing knowledge which can empower or disempower, depending on the learning process.

These dual potentials exist for various reasons. From the students' point of view, their thought, speech, and action are influenced by mass culture and mass education. Student culture is not an autonomous product. It is shaped by words and values absorbed from socializing agencies like school, church, mass media, and the streets. The status quo transmits an existing culture to them, which teaches them how to see themselves in the world. On the other hand, teachers develop in the same unequal society as students. Their professional culture of teaching is not their autonomous invention. The culture of schooling trains them in the dominant discourse and practices—teacher-talk, reading the riot act, the last word, short-answer tests, competitive grading and individualized work, commercial textbooks, standardized exams, tolerating the administrative monopoly on power, seeing students as deficits to be filled with grammar, and an official syllabus drawn from existing canons of knowledge. On both sides, the school culture of teachers and the mass culture of students are disempowering forces. Teachers and students alike need to desocialize from the dominant influences on their development.

Cultural empowerment, then, cannot mean the teacher unilaterally delivering the Great Books and the King's English to students. Neither does it mean uncritically praising or using the everyday speech and thoughts of students. Empowerment means teachers and students both reinventing the cultures they learned in an unequal status quo. In that mutual reinvention, they create a critical culture on the ruins of the zero paradigm. That new culture is a two-way discourse, a democratic achievement of dialogue that I call the third idiom. With a new language for learning and mutual communication, they can begin transforming their alienation from each other. When critical-democratic teachers lead a transformative class, they invent what Vygotsky (1962) called a zone of proximal development. This border culture is a learning area between students' speech and understandings and those of the teacher.

The critical paradigm of empowering education, then, calls for inventing a zone of transformation where the cultures of students and teachers meet. Teachers are responsible for taking the lead in discovering this zone. Once discovered, it is filled with a specific subject matter and learning process—a theme (generative, topical, or academic) and problem-posing (critical dialogue). Empowering education thus takes place in a symbolic frontier, a developmental borderland between the teacher's and student's existing cultures. As a place of mutual communication, this meeting ground of teachers and students is not owned exclusively by academic culture or by the culture of everyday life.

Borderlands of Transformative Culture

When academic culture reinvents itself by a democratic approach to learning, knowledge, and daily life, and when everyday culture becomes critical and absorbs academic study, teachers and students inhabit a border zone of potential transformation. They are challenging the divisive socialization inherited from the zero paradigm.

In this challenge, the teacher's expertise is important, whether in nursing, writing, chemistry, history, engineering, or economics. Most students do not possess academic knowledge, whether about paragraph development or chemical precipitates or blood components or labor movements or Balzac's novels or quantum physics. Most do not possess the political skills needed to organize cultural democracy in the classroom and in society. Most have not exercised the critical literacy that might help them analyze the texts and media in their lives and produce their own alternatives. Because of these gaps in student knowledge, the teacher has the task of posing problems, providing exercises, and offering readings that develop skills and knowledge not yet held by them. But in the critical paradigm, students do not leap out of their cultural territory into the teacher's academic terrain. Instead, teachers pose problems in a learning process situated in student thinking. In this process, the teacher does not transfer knowledge but rather poses it as a critical problem relevant to student perceptions.

To inform a borderland where all positions are questioned, teachers research student culture. These might be appropriate questions for researching students at various levels:

• What do students talk about, read about, and write about? When do they read and write, for what purposes? What books do they buy or have at home?

• What do they watch on TV, read about in newspapers, and listen to on radio? Do they think the media give them an accurate picture of events? What news are they *not* getting? Can they define the politics of their newspapers? What political words are already in their vocabulary?

• What aspects of their language appear often as good choices for classroom study—repeated words, phrases, sayings, references, favorite songs, typical expressions?

• What images and texts do they have on the walls of their homes?

- How do they discuss their aspirations? What do they want from life?
- For older students—Have they taken part in any political action? Do they belong to any unions or organizations? Do they vote?
- What do they say are the most important problems in their lives? What do they say are the most important problems in society?
- What music is popular? What do they do for recreation?
- What do students eat? What clothes do they wear? What kind of housing do they live in? What kind of medical care do they get?
- For younger students—Do they show signs of neglect or child abuse? Do their parents ignore their schoolwork or pressure them to do well? Are they read to at home? What stories do they invent or tell? What situations, themes, phrases, or characters fill up their play? What are their favorite games and toys?
- For teenage and older students, are there signs of drug or alcohol abuse? How do they get and spend money? What kinds of jobs do they hold, if any? What are their income levels? Are they sexually active? Is teenage pregnancy a problem? Do they receive effective sex education?
- Were the parents and students born in the United States? If foreign-born, how do they speak, write, and read English? How do they see their own ethnic identity? What do students say about other ethnic groups and races? What is the racial and ethnic makeup of their area? Do they see race relations as a problem?
- What are the typical relationships between men and women in their homes and communities? How do they see masculinity and femininity? Do they think men and women are equal, or should be? Do women feel free to express themselves? Do male students interrupt the women who speak in class? Are young or adult women students under family pressure to not go to college? Do they experience sexual harassment in the neighborhood, school, or college?
- What about other social relationships, like those between tenants and landlords, citizens and police, workers and bosses? How do they talk about them? Which present problems?
- How do they feel about schooling? Do they think they are getting a good education? What are the local schools and colleges like? What level of education do people in their families and neighborhoods have? Are there any community-based education programs?
- What are community conditions—density, housing, religion, health care, mass transit, crime, playgrounds, sanitation, commercial and government services, race relations?

Responses to these questions ground teachers in community culture. Out of them come generative themes, the words reflecting powerful subjective conditions around which learning programs can be developed. This research can help in using topical themes about social issues not situated in student conversation or academic themes drawn from scholastic bodies of knowledge. The teacher who knows about student language and conditions can relate topical and academic material to the words, needs, and experiences of students. The student context offers reference points from which to integrate content areas like tax law or biology or history, which are best studied as critical problems related to student perceptions.

To learn about my students' contexts, I observed them in class and in the community over a period of several years. In class, I studied their reading, writing, speaking, ways of working in small groups, and behavior in whole-class dialogues. I read their papers carefully and discussed them with individual students to make sure I understood their meaning. I consulted with other teachers about our student population and their academic performance. I took notes after class to help me think through the learning process we were undergoing. I hung out in the cafeteria, the library, the lounge, and the gym to listen to students, to watch the way they related to each other outside class, to talk with them, and to play basketball with them. At my desk, I spent hours of office time conversing with them. I lived in their community for a few years, shopped there, got to know auto mechanics, supermarkets, bakeries, and diners, to observe their life and language outside schooling. On campus, I learned about the institution by reading college documents and by speaking with administrators and veteran faculty. Further, I considered the political climate in the community, city, and nation as factors in learning. What I can accomplish in a critical classroom depends on the community and social conditions outside. For example, the state of the economy influences my students' attitudes towards learning. In hard times, they act less patient with experimental and liberal arts classes, anxious to finish degrees in career majors to help them earn a living. Prolonged budget cuts in the public sector damaged the quality of education at my public college, increasing tuition and class size, reducing the number of classes available, thus making college life harder for students. Lastly, the racial climate surrounding the college is bad. As a consequence, minority students in class tend to be withdrawn. These are issues I keep in mind when researching the student context.

One Context: The ALP Research-Learning Process

One model for research and curriculum design comes out of the Adult Learning Project (ALP). As reported by Kirkwood and Kirkwood

(1989), ALP developed a ten-stage process which began with educators investigating the community they were to teach in. As in Wallerstein's experience in founding an ESL program while living in the neighborhood of the students, community research is a typical first act of empowering educators. The educator is not extending an alien academic culture into the community but is rather constructing a critical culture with the participants.

The mutual observation of community life is sometimes called participatory research, to distinguish it from academic research done in archives or done without community participation and review. Participatory research means investigating students' culture from the bottom up, as they see themselves, with the community as joint researchers, authors, reviewers, and users of the research. This makes the teacher a researcher who is allied with students but who can also pose questions the students are not yet asking themselves.

To show this process concretely, I can summarize the Kirkwoods' report of the ten stages that led from participatory research to curriculum design to community action:

1. *Secondary Source Investigation.* Before a learning program is offered, ALP educators visit libraries, local and central government, and universities, for background information. The research group meets regularly to discuss findings about work, schools, census data, health, employment and unemployment. This gives the group a preliminary grounding in the area.

2. *Primary Source Investigation.* ALP educators walk through the area to observe the people and terrain, how residents relate, shop, relax, speak, and so on. The researchers also contact local clergy, politicians, community organizations, managers of workplaces, and trade unionists, asking: "How do people see the area, its boundaries, its physical and social characteristics, its history? What are their feelings about the area and their hopes for its future? What is their personal experience and knowledge of its problems?" (8). This firsthand research is compared with the factual information gathered from secondary sources. The group is now doubly grounded in its territory.

3. *Finding Coinvestigators.* While research is under way, ALP professionals seek out community coinvestigators. They knock on doors, hold public meetings, and turn to existing adult classes for community residents who might serve as researchers. The research is carried out jointly by professionals and local citizens, who compare perspectives. The community coinvestigators learn interview methods from the ALP staff. They also speak about their experiences in the area, serving as subjects and educators of the ALP staff.

4. *Coinvestigation.* Community coinvestigators meet with ALP educators to evaluate the research program. One ALP educator serves as group facilitator and the other as an observer and recorder of the discussions. The research group works in pairs to tape interviews with relatives, neighbors, and shopkeepers, and to observe moments in community life. Members of the research group report to each other and try to identify significant situations and recurring themes in the community.

5. *Making Codifications.* The research group decides which are the most significant issues emerging from its community study, and then builds a codification of that generative theme—a pictorial representation of a typical and problematic situation in community life. The codifications are familiar enough to be easily recognized and responded to but open-ended enough to suggest a personal problem with social dimensions, worthy of extended discussion.

6. *Decoding.* Other residents join ALP educators and coinvestigators to discuss the codifications. Several decoding groups meet at different times of the day to get a cross-section of responses from area residents. One ALP educator leads the decoding dialogue while another observes and records the discussion, which proceeds in four steps:
• *describing* what you see in the picture,
• *identifying* with the people pictured to interpret their thoughts, feelings, and action,
• *relating* the situation to the discussants' lives,
• *probing* why the situation exists as it does, to grasp the wider social and historical factors in it.

The teacherly ritual of having the last word is democratically reconstructed here in four parts:
• at the end of each session, the ALP recorder summarizes the decoding dialogue, quoting key phrases from individuals, and offering any contradictions or outstanding issues the group has not noticed;
• next, the group responds to this summary and analysis, confirming or challenging it and adding reflections;
• third, the ALP discussion coordinator then seeks agreement from the group about the most important themes emerging from the decoding;
• fourth, a written summary is sent to each member, with the coordinator's remarks on the session. These notes serve as the basis for deciding which generative themes are best represented by the codification discussed. Those generative themes become the base for building a curriculum around such issues as parenting, powerlessness, unemployment, and health.

7. *Building the Curriculum.* After ALP educators and community coinvestigators have jointly decoded the pictures, they codevelop an interdisciplinary learning program from it. The goal is to engage different levels of the theme: personal, local, national, global, "the inner world of feeling and the outer world of facts, the influence of the past, the impact of the present and the potential for the future" (13). Outside experts in specific disciplines like history and psychology are consulted as resources for group dialogue.

8. *Learning Programs.* After the decoding group and the academic experts decide how to structure a curriculum from a generative theme, community residents are invited to enroll for group dialogue sessions usually lasting eight to ten weeks, which begin with codifications. ALP educators trigger discussion at these sessions with a question for decoding the pictured theme. After reflection by participants, not before, an expert makes a presentation, followed by more dialogue to reflect on the academic presentation.

9. *Action Outcomes.* Action grows from the dialogue groups. Action plans go through prior investigation of their feasibility as well as continuing evaluation as they evolve. The areas for action include community action with people or organizations around a specific problem; creating a new organization in the area; and individual action to change one's personal life.

10. *New Investigation.* After a dialogic decoding of a generative theme and after an action project has been researched and undertaken, ALP educators and community members begin a new investigation into another problem in the area, thus initiating a new cycle.

The ALP model, which evolved over a decade through trial and error, is not followed rigidly. ALP workers found that each stage can be longer or shorter, depending on the theme and the group. They discovered, too, that action can occur along with reflection in a learning group and need not necessarily come only at the end. In the course of the process, community co-researchers took on more responsibility. This democratic sharing of the research and teaching functions is a key feature of empowerment, which can often go furthest in nonformal adult programs.

ALP's academic consultants sometimes had a hard time integrating themselves into the dialogic process. Because of their learned habits of teacher-talk, they were used to dominating discussion instead of working in dialogic and interdisciplinary ways. Still, the academic expert remained an integral feature of this community program, demonstrating the role of academic knowledge in a dialogic curriculum.

Mutual Development Begins from Less Than/More Than Zero

The ALP used community research to situate critical study in student culture. It democratically included students as co-researchers and co-developers of the programs while democratically absorbing expert knowledge as well. This approach brought academic experts into a student-centered process where human development goes both ways. Empowering education is not something teachers do to students for their own good. In a dialogic process, the groups influence each other. ALP educators learned their craft with the students. If the students had not codeveloped the research and curriculum, the educators would have lacked a fertile grounding in community experience. If the educators had not organized dialogic learning in the community, participants would have lacked a transformative program.

All constituents created the ALP's learning culture. But while teachers and students both bring resources to the classroom, each also carries in obstacles to critical learning and action. In the ALP program, some conflict occurred concerning the traditional lecturing favored by academic experts serving as consultants. Other conflicts stemmed from the desire of some students for short-term skills courses instead of long-term projects for self and social change. Still other divisions occurred inside dialogue groups, where the desire for self-expression competed with the requirements of group discussion. Some people talked more than others and talked about very private needs or issues, which at times distracted from group dialogue. In addition, there were community conflicts between the needs of children and those of drivers— play space for the kids versus parking space for the cars.

Group differences and individual conflicts are inevitable but not necessarily destructive. Critical dialogue does not seek unanimity or conformity; it draws out authentic differences among participants and seeks to discuss them in cooperative, nonantagonistic ways. Managing conflicts constructively in class requires agile leadership on the teacher's part. Conflict is even more likely in formal schools and colleges where students are required to take courses they don't want, by contrast with the voluntary association of adults in programs like ALP. More compulsory than community education, schools and colleges provoke some legendary student alienation. Formal institutions usually place more restrictions on teachers as well. For these reasons, research into the resources and liabilities brought to class by teachers and students is crucial, to anticipate conflicts and to be well-grounded when they appear.

A Paradigm of Four Domains

The critical paradigm asserts that learning is helped by the resources and hindered by the obstacles students and teachers carry into the classroom. Using the assets and overcoming the liabilities of both helps the critical class become a culture for democratic empowerment.

In researching the resources and obstacles to empowerment, the critical teacher focuses on four coexisting conditions: students less than zero, students more than zero, teachers less than zero, and teachers more than zero. What actual resources and obstacles, assets and liabilities, do students and teachers bring to class?

To demonstrate the four coexisting domains of the critical paradigm, I will outline some assets and liabilities of teachers and students at the College of Staten Island, where I began teaching writing, literature, and mass media in 1971. The campus was founded in 1957 as a community college of the City University of New York and was merged with upper-division Richmond College in 1976, after which it began offering two-year, four-year, and some graduate degrees, as well as a noncredit English Language Institute. It is a low-tuition, low-budget, commuter campus in a largely white, conservative, and semisuburban part of the city. In applying the critical paradigm here, I will first offer a narrative description and then a series of notes on the situations of students and faculty.

The students at this nonresidential college are mostly white (78 percent), reflecting the dominant white population on Staten Island, in a city where the overall public school enrollment is primarily students of color (70 percent). The college's minority group is mainly African-American and Hispanic, with some Asian, Haitian, and Arab groups. The English as a Second Language program is substantial, but minority and nonnative students are marginal; communication among the racial groups is chilly and limited.

The white student group, which I will focus on in the coming pages because of its dominant position, is mostly Italian, with Irish being the second largest ethnic cohort. The white students are often the first in their families to attend college. Many have gone to parochial schools. They and their public school peers come to class with traditional expectations. In class, they wait for the teacher to do education to them. They expect college to be like high school: teacher-talk, textbooks, short-answer tests, and memorization. When I ask about their college classes, they report that their traditional expectations are largely confirmed.

From the 1970s on, these nonelite students entered college at a bad time. The City University, free since 1847, imposed tuition after an orchestrated fiscal crisis in New York in 1976. Open Admissions, fought for and won by student protests in 1969, was stifled after 1976 by tuition increases, by severe budget cuts, and by newly imposed entry exams in writing, reading, and mathematics. Many younger untenured faculty members were fired, while older faculty hunkered down for years of shrinking budgets. Classes became more crowded. The college became shabby, a discouraging environmental message to students about the low esteem in which intellectual life was held on this campus. In perpetual budget crises, the college's programs expanded evening and weekend sessions, to fill up enrollments with returning adults, cash-paying part-time customers receiving few services and amenities for their tuition dollars. This gave birth to a large part-time adult group competing for college resources with the younger day-session students. The college began serving three different constituencies who barely saw each other—the day student, the evening student, and the weekend student. These developments, resulting from conservative budget cuts in the public sector, fragmented life on campus, demoralized faculty, and diminished the intellectual quality of student experience.

The younger students fresh out of high school and the older students returning to college are similar in that many work for wages while taking classes. Undergraduates at some elite colleges may be enjoying the best four years of their lives, but my working students live hectic, exhausting lives. College, jobs, and family combine to give them busy weeks. Older students especially have full-time jobs and full-time families.

Day-session students typically hold low-wage jobs as helpers, cashiers, deliverers, counter clerks, porters and janitors, medical aides, gas-pump jockeys, gardeners, office assistants, file clerks, data entry personnel, mailroom and security staff, customer service workers, and burger pushers in fast-food chains. The jobs held by adult evening students and by the parents of younger day-students are likely to be in the police, fire, parks, school, and sanitation departments, in city health, social, and fiscal agencies as well as in the gas, telephone, and electric companies, as low- to mid-level functionaries on Wall Street, in direct-mail enterprises, in big department stores as well as in small businesses, and as nurses, nurses' aides, medical technicians, repairmen, self-employed tradesmen, computer operators, craftsmen, salespersons, and real estate agents. The white adults often own modest homes in the areas surrounding the college, though many students commute across the Verrazzano Bridge from Brooklyn. Some adult students are struggling to make ends meet. College holds out to students the hope of higher wages and promotions down the road, a dream that flutters across their tired eyes in evening class.

The dominant white student group cherishes a middle-class identity which to them is more respectable than being either working-class or poor. Not poor and not affluent, they can pay their bills with some left over for extras. They are upwardly mobile, sometimes studious, sometimes awed by and sometimes cynical about professors, and immersed in a mass culture of TV, cars, fashion, sports, celebrities, music, family life, and consumerism. Families tend to be large, extended, and close. But parents and children have difficult relationships. Youth culture is oriented to drinking, drugs, rock music, sex, partying, fast money, trendy clothes, and reckless behavior. The drugs, drinking, teenage pregnancy, and sexual diseases of adolescence are not yet out of control here, but parents are worried about their children's safety and their future.

The students have a fondness for alcohol and tobacco, their drugs of choice. The older students especially work hard for their money, put in an honest day's labor without complaining, pay high taxes, get little help from government, and come to class as often as they can, dressed neatly and modestly. They display admirable expertise in their jobs, which they take pride in doing well, even though they would like to be paid more. They often express resentment at welfare freeloaders, students on financial aid, and ungrateful foreign countries that allegedly get large amounts of their tax money for free. They are devoted to family life, but some grouse about their costly, unambitious children. In general, students of all ages are fascinated by the rich, whose power and luxuries bedazzle them. The admiration for the rich is often accompanied by a distaste for the poor, whom they see as lazy minorities with no jobs and a penchant for crime. Many students live fearfully at night behind locks and guard dogs, worried about crime and violence. Yet as hunger and homelessness spread in the city, more students have expressed genuine feeling for the desperately poor and think something should be done to help them. Their church background is predominantly Catholic; a few are Jewish, while others are born-again Christians. Their diets include fast food, sweets, coffee, and soft drinks. But among young and old, an environmental consciousness is slowly spreading, a growing concern about health and about toxins in the air, water, and land, which included a successful Island-wide recycling program launched in 1990.

On the whole, with family responsibilities, earning a living, commuting, and taking courses, they work too hard. They have too little time to develop their intelligence, their artistic talents, and their imagination. Their harassed lives and limited time for study or rest contribute to their conservative support for the status quo, because they have little opportunity to read materials critical of society or to imagine alternative ways to organize life. Their position in society above the poor and the minorities also contributes to the white students' support for the existing system, which apparently gives them more than those below them. At the same time, their political cynicism and alienation are awesome. They complain bitterly about politicians, government, and the way things are run. At election time they are unenthusiastic voters, but those who do vote reelect the same conservative politicians year after year, while continuing to say that something is very wrong with the country and that America is going down the tubes.

Teaching this complex, contradictory, and bright group of students is a faculty of intelligent, mostly traditional educators. The full-time faculty is dwindling from a long period of budget cuts and early retirements, while the part-time staff is large. In 1991, about 50 percent of classes were being taught by part-timers, whose low-paid work sustains the college budget. The full-time faculty tend to live farther from the college than do the students, in more prosperous urban and suburban areas. The full-timers can be generally divided into two groups: an old guard hired from high school staffs and from colleges in the 1950s and 1960s, and a younger, more liberal group hired in the late 1960s and early 1970s. The latter group came out of higher education at a time of campus activism.

In 1969, after Open Admissions was won by student protests, the City University was opened to more working, poor, and minority students. Enrollment nearly doubled by 1975, requiring a sudden hiring of young faculty. Many of the newly hired young teachers were later fired in the budget crisis of 1976, the year in which hundreds were to have been awarded tenure and thus a permanent place in City University. The fiscal crisis of 1976 gave the university an apparently nonpolitical opportunity to retrench, when about a thousand members of the junior faculty were fired on the eve of their tenure. Not only was this more liberal group prevented from consolidating its position in the university, but the costs of Open Admissions were reduced by replacing full-timers with adjuncts and by imposing tuition on students for the first time.

The events of 1976 were thus a political watershed, an offensive against cultural democracy in the guise of a fiscal crisis. Claiming fiscal woes, the multicampus university expelled a thousand younger teachers who were more supportive of Open Admissions than the senior faculty, while also reducing the student group by nearly a hundred thousand. This assault on cultural democracy tilted the politics of City

University and my college to the right, returning the initiative to traditionalist administrators and faculty who had dominated in the pre–Open Admissions days before 1969.

Under the influence of Open Admissions and the newer faculty, my English department and some others enjoyed an experimental period from 1970 to 1976, when the campus administration was liberal and the university, state, and city authorities had not yet stifled the evolving cultural democracy. At some moments, when mass movements dominate the political climate or when social crises go out of control, authorities allow more freedom to experiment or are simply unable to restrict alternative programs or even promote alternatives, hoping to contain the upheaval. Such was the case when the protest culture of the 1960s erupted in City University in 1969. Some authorities gave way to change and even promoted it; some had no choice but to tolerate change; and still other authorities and forces began organizing a counterattack against the changes. After the battle of 1976, the counterattack won, imposing tuition, restoring some traditional requirements, and setting new entry exams in writing, reading, and math. These apparently simple exams produced enormous amounts of failure, frustration, and bureaucracy, thus damaging students' morale and progress toward their degrees.

Overall, from the mid-1970s through the early 1990s, when the college, the city, and the nation were in the grip of a conservative restoration, I observed that students changed *less* than the faculty and the institution. This surprised me when I reviewed the critical paradigm I will detail below, because teachers often complained in these years about student conservatism, weak literacy, low achievement, and poor motivation. My assessment across two decades of teaching at my college is that the institutions of society—such as government, mass media, corporations, and education—moved farther to the right than did the students themselves. The political climate was pushed to the right, but not by the students or by the American people. City University and my campus at Staten Island are politically different from what they were in 1971. Responding to conservative policy shifts and regressive budget cuts, they became more bureaucratic, less egalitarian, and less experimental, thanks to tuition raises, new requirements, and more testing. Fiscal austerity and authoritarian control were imposed from the top down. Students did not vote for tuition, entry testing, and tougher access to four-year programs. They did not want larger classes and fewer courses to choose from. These policies are decidedly not in their interest and were not chosen by them.

In this period, the powers that be in public and private spheres withdrew support from education more dramatically than my students withdrew from learning. As the students' educational needs came under attack in the conservative period from Nixon through Bush, their self-absorbed behavior was a response to the hostile, declining conditions they found in school and society. Their educational and economic aspirations suffered as an outcome of an official backlash against the egalitarian changes of the 1960s, when authorities were on the defensive, making concessions like Open Admissions to mass movements. If students began giving less in the classroom, it is because education and society began giving less to them, to restrict the egalitarian trends and protests emerging in education and elsewhere in American life. In the conservative decades after 1970, students became concerned with personal needs in an age when the private and public sectors cut jobs, lowered wages, took back benefits and social services, raised prices, and increased tuition and taxes.

Students did not invent the local and national turn to the right after 1970, as official agendas for education went from careerism to back to basics, to intensive testing, to remediation, to higher tuition, to demands for excellence. The turn to austerity did not originate with students, but rather began with policies designed by the elite in business, media, government, and education. This reactionary turn of events, a sharp change in the political climate, affected student behavior in the classroom.

With this narrative of the local, larger, and long-term situations, I can now outline a critical paradigm of the obstacles and resources brought to the classroom at my college by teachers and students.

Using the Critical Paradigm: Classroom and Community Research

In this section, I will outline some assets and liabilities of students and teachers at my college as I have observed them across two decades. I will focus in greatest detail on the white students. They are the dominant group among the nearly twelve thousand students at the college. Some of their conditions and behaviors will be familiar and applicable to students elsewhere.

My comments on teachers will summarize my working conditions and that of colleagues in relation to the larger profession of education. While the students bring a combination of community and mass culture to the classroom, the faculty is marked by an academic culture. Their socialization into academic life took place in the universities where they learned traditional models for knowledge and teaching, based in teacher-talk and the transfer of existing canons. Although a number of teachers at the college have changed their practices, students report that most still follow traditional discourse and methods, that is, a passive, one-way transfer of information.

Students Less Than Zero: Student Obstacles to Empowering Education and Critical Thought

1. *Resistance.* In class, students are alienated by teacher-talk and remote subject matter, leaving many uninspired by intellectual work; many respond with passivity, resentment, and grim determination to get through; they resist in various ways—sabotage, silence, submission, playing dumb, getting by, dropping in and out of courses, not doing homework, coming late, being absent, getting friends or family members to write their papers; their subjectivity (relationships, work, sex, food, recreation, everyday language) is visible and invisible at the same time, a parallel life separate from the official language and themes of schooling; their expectations from school are generally low and traditional; their actual cognitive skills (reading, writing, thinking, speaking) are half-buried because schooling has depressed their performance levels; they are clever and know how to yes the boss or teacher to get what they want or to keep authority at bay or to avoid a challenging discussion in class; because they lack a critical curriculum and student organizations to protect their interests, much of their potential for activism and much of their intelligence is held beneath the surface.

2. *Uneven Levels of Development.* The uneven cognitive skills and affective development in students make it hard to take anything for granted when teaching the same course from term to term; day students are younger and poorly employed, evening students are older working adults with better-paying jobs; some read, write, analyze, and debate surprisingly well, while others are withdrawn or less developed in one or another literacy; some are unsettled adolescents, distracted by sex and growing up, with a lot of physical energy, fidgety in their seats, easily bored by or offended by the teacher; some are happy with a participatory class that stimulates their attention, expects a lot from them and gives a lot to them, even though others reject high expectations for writing, reading, speaking, or thinking; another group passively waits for the teacher to tell them what to do and what things mean, and respond without enthusiasm; some are eager to learn as fast as they can, while others are too harassed by jobs, other classes, or family lives to stay in class or to do much academic work out of class; some are conversant with academic conventions like correct usage, the expository essay, the Great Books, and so on; a number write florid or stiffly formal prose, mimicking the language of texts and teachers; others struggle with writing; a few keep up with national and international events, while

many follow crises sensationalized by TV and absorb official explanations from mass media (for example, their fear of terrorism as a threat to American life); they know about media darlings (celebrities, disasters, sports, and scandals); many have in-depth knowledge of specific jobs as nurses, mechanics, skilled labor in the building trades, which they relate to as experts, while other students have never held a steady job; they know when a question, reading, or issue is critical of traditional behavior, received knowledge, or the status quo—a moment when some defend the way things are, some resist by silent nonparticipation, and some risk opening up to the critical dialogue.

3. *Vocationalism.* Careerism in high school and college has depressed much student intellectualism; vocationalism has distanced many from academic life by aiming them at narrow careers; careerism is appealing to many students because the subject matter is closer to daily discourse and to earning a living; they want and need more income; the high cost of books, tuition, and daily living makes them anxious to finish college as soon as possible and get a good or better job; the saturation of everyday life with consumer messages overstimulates their desire to buy things, and they want to earn more money fast to become successful consumers living the good life; this distracts their attention from the liberal arts, where classroom discourse is more foreign to daily talk and which many resent as a detour to finishing degrees and starting careers; as hard times spread and unemployment stayed high, they became increasingly worried about how a course fit into their economic plans; economic austerity has made them anxious about the dollar value of a course for their future careers; students are not socialized into seeing themselves as change-agents, thinkers, artists, citizens, activists, critics, reformers, policymakers, environmentalists, organizers, global residents, peacemakers, or public interest defenders; these social roles are invisible to them or else appear as luxuries for people of modest backgrounds; school and society send them lesser vocational images; they learn they are the "working hands" of society; in the hope of getting ahead in life, and because occupational courses are more understandable than are the humanities, they enroll in career programs at the college, which take up a lot of time and also discourage critical thinking about work itself—work is an instrument to make money, and school is an instrument to make more money at work; critical thought (questioning the status quo) appears irrelevant to making money and is even risky (talking up or talking back can get you in trouble in school and on the job).

4. *Prior Schooling.* Numbers of students arrive with strong literacy and academic interests; in high school and below, these students bene-

fited from creative and critical teachers; students speak fondly of those teachers who were devoted to their development, used class time well, and made them feel smart; but most students arrive in class with uncritical intellects and average literacy; for them, prior schooling taught low performance; they have been trained to memorize rules, facts, and definitions for short-answer exams, leading them to conclude that education is a ritual of responses to questions for which the teacher already has the answers; they carry forward fragmented advice about how to write well and fragmented information about society, history, and the economy; uninspired by intellectual life, they turn to nonscholastic leisure time for fulfillment (friends, sports, music, sex, hobbies, shopping).

5. *Acceleration/Amplification in Mass Culture/Mass Media.* Everyday life has accelerated and amplified student perceptions—fast cars, fast food, fast music and loud videos, fast money, fast talk, fast action films, fast commuting between job and home and college, fast and frequent shopping, yelling over the street noise and over the expressway near the college, packing into loud discos and bars, ears plugged into a walkman, racing from class to class in a crowded schedule through crowded buildings; in a throwaway market economy, in a commuter college, an electronic society, and an automobile culture, student perception is speeded up and amplified unnaturally; it needs to be *decelerated* and *de-amplified* to human scale; they are used to fast talk and fast action, to high levels of stimulation, and to dealing with a *product* (in education— papers, grades, credits, or transcript entries certifying motion towards a degree), so they are uncomfortable with the deliberate pace of a critical *process*, which emphasizes reading, writing, and extensive dialogue; to overcome this acceleration, they need subject matter related to their personal contexts, classroom discourse accessible to their thought, as well as participatory formats, a negotiated curriculum, challenging issues, complex emotional textures, and projects that yield cooperative and personal products from the process (publications, exhibitions, and presentations); a decelerating/de-amplifying pedagogy is needed to effect a gradual transition from speeded-up mass culture to deliberate critical culture.

6. *Exposure to Regressive Ideologies.* Students come of age exposed to regressive values: racism, sexism, machismo, self-reliant competitiveness (making it on your own, taking care of number one, making a killing), magical hopes (lady luck, lotteries), national chauvinism (America, love it or leave it), authority dependence (tell us what to do), fascination with the rich and powerful (money talks), environmental waste (throwaway products), excessive consumerism (shop till you drop), glamorous

militarism (the Gulf War as an antidote to the Vietnam syndrome), and homophobia (queer bashing); the conviction that you must win or lose on your own (self-reliance) helps students deny the value of cooperative learning and action; they turn to friends and family for help but have few organized groups to defend their interests; buying power, not political power or intellectual power is success; chief among divisive values, racism evolves from their experiences in segregated schools and neighborhoods; minorities can't peacefully live or walk in many white areas; minorities appear in mass media as stereotyped poor people or as criminals; some white students think minorities have already won equality and nothing more needs to be done; other whites think that the courts and the job market favor minorities; some white students oppose racism but are weak in asserting their position in class; another divisive ideology, sexism, is absorbed in everyday life; females are presented in media mostly as sex symbols or helpers, the weaker dependent sex, while males are seen as tough guys, executives, career successes, and leaders who drive fast cars and get the gorgeous women; males also have more freedom in family life, because daughters are more restricted in their behavior than are sons and because wives are expected to work at home as well as in the job market; further, men and women students see that the genders have unequal earning power in society; typically, most of their professors are male, unlike their experience in the lower grades, where almost all of their teachers were female; even though they absorb regressive values from the status quo, many students know they have problems and that society isn't working right, but they don't have good explanations for social ills; getting more money appears to be a way to solve some personal problems; the world of the rich is their strongest image of the good life, not an alternative society.

7. *Short Time in Class and on Campus in an Unattractive Setting.* There is too little time, quiet, and repose on campus for intellectual, cultural, or political life; the campus is crowded, rundown, and unattractive—cinder-block walls, tile floors, fluorescent lights, Formica surfaces, fiberglass chairs; the environment does not invite students to spend more time on campus; the busy class schedule also limits their free time, leaving them few chances to visit professors' offices or to nurture extracurricular interests; after-class cultural and political events are hard to schedule; class hours are often too short to permit serious discussion; the college is either noisy at peak hours or else deserted at odd hours; the library is crowded, the cafeteria unappealing, with bad food, high prices, and poor environmental practices; classrooms and buildings are shabby, making it hard for students to think that education counts in a place like this; after twenty years of poor conditions, the college is mov-

ing to a new campus with nicer surroundings but with an even longer commute; poor public transit to the new campus means students coming late to class, dropping out, or buying cars to commute, producing more air pollution, traffic jams, parking problems, and bills for insurance and repair, which will require students to work more and study less, to pay for the car; education is entangled with the culture of everyday life, so the college environment and location will impact intellectual work.

   8. *Language/Discourse.* Textbooks are expensive, dull, and not in student idioms, mainly varieties of nonstandard dialects; students report being bored, baffled, and angered by them, especially when they pay a lot for a required text and use it little or understand little in it; teacherly discourse in the classroom is also in an academic idiom, which drives many students into silence; the linguistic form and abstract content of regular classes push them out of the discourse; in their own community discourses, minorities have the most variant forms of language, from African-American English to Afro-Caribbean English to Haitian Creole to Hispanic and Asian languages; their dialects, their oral community literacies, are not studied in class; the language conflicts they experience are not discussed as problems of power in school and society, that is, Whose form of language is dominant? so students develop the habit of blaming themselves for their "bad" English; minorities are reluctant to speak in front of white students, because of their nonstandard dialects and because of the racial separateness on campus and in the community; many women have learned to keep quiet, deferring to men in class, while others speak up and challenge the men; many male students have learned they can interrupt women when they are speaking; in general, students do not have experience with democratic dialogue, and confuse it with conversation and arguments in private life, so they often speak all at once when an issue provokes them, or they overpersonalize and digress, or they speak only to me when commenting on the dialogue, rather than to other students they should be addressing.

   9. *Literacy.* Students do a lot of communicating and decision making each day; they use language constantly, sometimes with ingenuity and style, sometimes for fun, for business, or for learning, and sometimes to make tough choices and to navigate difficult relationships; but for the most part, everyday discourse offers few chances to reflect and discourse critically about society; literacy in daily life is mostly conversational exchanges tied to immediate experience, as students tell each other many stories and communicate with family or with co-workers on the job; their reading matter is uncritical or commercial, such as period-

icals filled with advertisements and mainstream politics, popular novels emphasizing romantic, horror, or sports themes, how-to books, technical manuals, advertising circulars, mail-order catalogs, official forms, letters to families and friends, applications for jobs, financial aid, or college admission, Bibles and religious pamphlets, and campaign fliers; students fill out applications, write letters, prepare bills, invoices, order sheets, and estimates, and write reports for work or school; many have trouble writing because they do not write or read enough and because their writing and reading have not helped them make critical meaning from their knowledge, experience, and society; the mass media in their lives fill their attention with loud ads and bursts of disconnected information; the media encourage shallow attention to world events, keeping students out of touch with a critical view of reality; they do not read or hear critical commentary on public life because the mass media lack political diversity; they watch for and read about scandals involving sex, politics, stars, crime, and big money; their exposure to social problems through the media prevents them from understanding root causes and workable solutions; they see social ills with no way to understand them in terms of the system they live under; this information leaves them feeling confused and immobilized in regard to being citizens in society; it is frustrating to be saturated with fragmented facts on problems without understanding their causes or being able to act on them; what the media show and tell helps make many of them impatient with public life and pessimistic about finding solutions.

10. *Family Life.* Student home life often interferes with intellectual work; many live in large families with little room or quiet for study; students who are parents or single mothers are especially short of time for academic work; they have trouble getting child care; because women students at the college (but never men) sometimes bring small children to class, the classroom has to serve as makeshift child-care quarters, which range from calm to distracting to disruptive; younger students living at home have family conflicts; forced to live without a sex life in their parents' home, they can't have partners stay over; this leads to frustration; posing this frustration as a social problem and not as a personal failing is a generative theme here, to reflect on the housing shortage, underemployment, and lower wages for young workers as the social issues keeping them dependent and restricted; asking whether the status quo supports family life is a way to challenge the pro-family posture of conservative politicians; with long work weeks, long commuting, low wages, high cost of living, shortage of decent housing, underfunded schools, inadequate playgrounds, and unsafe streets in

many areas, the system is undermining the family life many students cherish.

11. *Health and Nutrition.* Fast foods and junk foods have become a national way of life, especially for people on the run, like my busy students, who take classes, hold jobs, and often raise families; accelerated and amplified lives also produce extra stress; in addition, they live in an especially toxic environment from nearby oil refineries and a massive garbage dump, which add to their health problems, while the health care available to them is traditional rather than preventive or naturopathic; the area around the college is notorious for air pollution, for oil spills, for toxic waste sites, and for the largest landfill in the world; students have begun to notice the high rates of respiratory disease and cancer in the community; still, their diets remain high in fat, salt, sugar, alcohol, preservatives, additives, and caffeine; students often come directly from work to the evening sessions without having had dinner, so they eat candy bars and potato chips, and drink soda and coffee, to help them keep awake in class; many smoke in hallways despite local anti-smoking laws, which are not enforced at the college; drugs appear to affect a small number of students in comparison to tobacco, alcohol, stress, and bad food; some students have become interested in holistic health, and choose themes of good eating, exercise, and environmentalism for their research projects, stirring up interest in some of their classmates, but others are unwilling to change their habits, especially about food, which they associate with cultural heritage, family life, and success (eating lots of meat); personal energy lost to bad food and class time lost from illness limit what can be accomplished; absences are frequent for ill health and accidents, especially among the younger students, who often underdress in bad weather, as well as live and drive with adolescent recklessness; to form a learning community the class needs a critical mass of students in regular attendance, willing to take part in a dialogic process; some students resent being graded on participation and attendance, because they are too busy to come to class or because they do not want much from education; others approve of counting attendance and participation in the grade; to help cope, students sometimes link up, so that if one is absent, the other fills her or him in.

Students More Than Zero: Student Resources for Empowering Education and Critical Thought

1. *Extra Abilities Hidden by Their Performance Strike.* Students have extra cognitive and affective resources which they don't use or display in alienating classrooms but which can be brought out by student-centered pedagogy; they know more and possess more skills than they show in passive, teacher-centered classrooms; they can read, write, listen, and debate with more care than they habitually demonstrate; they feel more deeply about experiences and ideas than they let on, withdrawn as they are into boredom or defensive silence; teacher-talk, standardized testing, commercial textbooks, shabby environments, and dull academic courses have produced resistance and low expectations, depressing their levels of performance; they are on a *performance strike,* having learned to withhold full performance in passive schooling; they are brighter, more articulate, and have more emotional depth than the standard syllabus allows them to show.

2. *Speech.* The bulk of students are withdrawn, but some talk a lot; assertive students can be a mixed blessing, sometimes dominating discussion and silencing other students, sometimes serving as lightning rods that provoke and encourage other students into dialogue; organizing small discussion groups where students take turns reporting for whole-class dialogue is one way to have more students involved; in terms of correct usage, white and native minority students come to class with a lot of standard grammar in their speech and writing; their speaking voices are available as good self-editing tools for developing reading and writing skills, limiting the need for workbooks and lectures on correctness; in class, they can learn how to read their essays out loud, in groups, in pairs, or individually, to become better able to notice and correct their own small errors; in peer discussion groups, they can learn how to give each other advice on revising work for a new draft; peer revision groups and reading their essays aloud for self-editing create participatory formats in class which help decelerate perception for intellectual work, because the class is deliberate, active, absorbing, and meaningful enough to hold student attention; students are encouraged to speak more in classes with a variety of learning formats, from whole-class dialogue to individual work to cooperative groups; they can speak passionately about themes important to them when they feel the teacher does not talk down to them or use jargon; they withdraw from teachers whose talk is condescending, obscure, or contemptuous; they prefer teachers who are fair, prepared, understandable, dynamic, and consistent; student speech is rich and colorful when they let teachers hear their authentic voices; they display lively imaginations, interesting thoughts, deep feelings, and humor; city life also makes them verbal in their daily relationships, if not in class; they are used to talking a lot in private life; their talkative habits can become academic tools in class if they accept the process of dialogue.

3. *Life and Work Experience.* Students bring many work experiences

to class, a mother lode of generative themes, stories, language, and issues for dialogue, into which academic knowledge and topical subjects can be integrated; they have experiences in school, in family life, in street life, and in relationships that are worthy of inquiry, like teenage pregnancy, abortion, drugs and alcohol, suicide, broken families, racism, sexual harassment, exploitation on the job, pressure to earn a living, conflicts in education; they don't expect the classroom to take this material seriously; they have not examined such issues in depth, so the critical class that absorbs themes from everyday life can open up scholastic talents students have not yet mined.

4. *Desire for Self-Esteem.* Students want to be liked and respected by other students and by the teacher; they seek self-esteem but have not developed much of it in the classroom; they also seek self-esteem in the jobs they take, where they are underpaid and underappreciated; they want to be listened to and consulted; few authorities ask them what they think and what they want, so the dialogic class can be a refreshing chance to feel that their lives, thoughts, and words matter; to encourage their self-esteem, I listen carefully to what they say and take notes in class from their comments; I ask them to repeat their statements and to reread their papers aloud, so that they have more practice speaking in public and so that other students can focus on the words of a peer as serious material for discussion; I also start a class hour with some reference to what students said before in the last one, to reinforce the importance of their words; I use their themes as problems for dialogue, to indicate the value of their perceptions and lives; I invite them to suggest themes and to bring in reading matter, so that they help construct the curriculum; lastly, the learning contracts I offer them are another means to communicate respect and co-ownership of the classroom.

5. *Curiosity.* Students are human beings and humans are a learning species curious about new things; they like the feeling of intellectual growth; they have unmet needs and unanswered questions about their experience, education, and the world; students are willing to listen to others who approach them with respect; but they need more mentoring by people who practice democratic authority, who do not boss them around, so that they develop in relationships that are negotiable, rather than dependent or dominating; they have some of these mutual relationships in private life, with caring and negotiable parents and relatives, with older siblings, with some sympathetic teachers or priests; they need more of this mutuality associated with intellectual work and public life; students also prefer to be busy instead of bored, because it helps the time move faster in class or on the job; their affinity for being active can help ease them into participatory and cooperative formats,

which they have not had much of in their classroom lives; they want to use time well in class instead of wasting it; they like to feel smart and to see accomplishments each week; they also have dreams of a better life, which can help critical classrooms to explore self-improvement through social and cooperative values instead of through the privatized idea of self-reliance.

6. *Democratic Attitudes.* Students have a healthy dislike for bosses, big shots, politicians, and arrogant pundits; they are sensitive to indignity and don't like to be pushed around by arbitrary authorities, haughty supervisors, and bureaucratic chiefs; they resent following rules they did not make; their democratic values include beliefs in justice, equality, tolerance for differences, fair play, and free speech; these values compete with antidemocratic ones developed by community and mass cultures, like male superiority, white supremacy, homophobia, narrow-minded ethnocentrism, competitive self-reliance, environmental disregard, excessive consumerism, and glory in military force; also contradicting their democratic values is the glamorous media image of the rich and powerful, which develops in students a fascination with the elite (big money); they see that the people who can get things done in society are the rich; they don't see individuals and groups winning improvements through concerted democratic action, so their orientation to activism is virtually nonexistent; students express cynicism about moneyed power in society but want to live like the rich; they believe in democracy despite few democratic experiences in school, at work, at home, in the street, and in their traditional classrooms; many like the dialogic class as an experience of democracy even though others resist the challenge to participate in an unfamiliar process.

7. *Racism.* The college is in a very white borough noted for racial intolerance; students come from largely segregated neighborhoods and schools; white families frequently chose to live in semisuburban Staten Island as part of the "white flight" from the city; though white students who come from integrated neighborhoods are mostly silent about their experiences, a few speak ill of their minority neighbors and others say they are happy living in a mixed area; attempts to integrate housing and a local high school have met with violence; the campus had a racial incident in the late 1980s, but few confrontations in general, perhaps because minorities are relatively few in number and maintain a low profile; in class, some white students express hostility at people of color while others talk of racial harmony and express disgust for racial attacks; some white students relate well to minorities in class, while others are distant; minority students are generally withdrawn in my classes, which are often 80 to 90 percent white; the positions of white students

on racism at my college appear to have four forms—(1) militant racism, (2) passive racism, (3) passive nonracism, and (4) antiracism; the militant racist group, assertive but not a majority, stereotypes minorities as criminal, hostile, lazy, unambitious, uneducated, pampered by government help, and as people who have too many children, take drugs, and live off welfare; the second white group in class, the passive racist one, tends to be larger, shares some of the sentiments of the militant group, but is less assertive vocally; this passive group is more discreet, more concerned about sounding racist in public, and displays less anger at and fear of minorities; still, the passively racist students oppose what they see as the favored treatment of minorities by government; they and the militant group agree that special financial aid, open admissions, and other affirmative action programs are reverse racism which give unfair advantages to minorities who are less deserving and less skilled than white applicants; the passive racists will sometimes admit that society is stacked against minorities, but it blames them for not trying harder, for complaining, for thinking that "white people owe them a life because of the slave-driving times," as one of my white male students wrote; militant and passive racists as well as nonracists in class often accuse the media of inflaming racial violence by playing up racial attacks; they think that race relations would be better if racial incidents were less reported; besides the typical issues raised by the racist group —that affirmative action is reverse racism, promoting unqualified minorities (and women) ahead of qualified whites (and men), that welfare is a giveaway program which discourages minorities from working, and that minorities are getting too many advantages now—white students sometimes say that they are not responsible for minority conditions because they did not enslave Africans hundreds of years ago and do not oppress any African-Americans now, and that the prisons and courts are soft on people of color, encouraging them to flout the law; these positions are expressed with less intensity when a class includes a number of minority people in it, more when a class is all white; the white students who hold these opinions come primarily from white ethnic communities that experienced prejudice against their own Italian and Irish ancestors, who feel insecure about their own social position one notch above the poor and minorities, and who are now feeling overtaxed and underserved by government in a society running out of good jobs and buying power for the middle class, which doesn't appear to be getting any help with its problems, so, they ask, why should minorities complain and expect aid and why can't they make it on their own like we did and do; besides the militant and passive racists in class, there is a third group of passive *non*racists, which can be as large as the passive racists; these white students disagree with the other two groups but they maintain a low profile in class; they don't think minorities are inferior human beings; white supremacy is not a value they support, but they are not as militant about their respect for minorities as the racist group is militant about its prejudice; this third group avoids stereotyping people of color because it says that people are the same everywhere, some good, some bad, and you have to judge all people equally as individuals; the fourth group, the antiracists among the white students, sometimes angrily confront the racist positions they hear in class, which is a time of fireworks in the dialogue; the antiracists are clear about the history of racism in the nation, as I hear from them in their papers, in their spoken remarks, and in private conversations; beyond tolerating or respecting minorities, they believe that a white-controlled society and racist whites are the problem behind the long-term discrimination in American life; they acknowledge that people of color face obstacles which whites never encounter; often, though, the antiracists and non-racists tend to be low-key, partly because they do not see themselves as the victims of racism in society or of the racist feelings of other white students, partly because they do not want to argue with other students in class and make enemies who might threaten them; those who are the immediate victims, minority students, generally do not speak up in classrooms where they are few in number, in a community where race relations are tense; where minority students are more numerous in a course, some do assert their position against racist remarks and stereo-types verbalized in class; this means that racist expressions by students in class are generally not balanced by antiracist voices raised by other students; because minority and passive white students do not equally assert their antiracist position against the bigotry expressed by some white students, class dialogue is often unbalanced; my role as leader of the dialogue is to pose problems and provide materials that balance the discussion; I intervene with questions, comments, exercises, and read-ings, to raise the profile of the pervasive discrimination faced by people of color and not by whites, and to encourage unprejudiced students to speak up and question their peers, so that I don't remain the leading antiracist voice in class; I also try to encourage minorities in class to speak, but this is difficult for them in a room packed with whites; I try not to lecture students on good and evil; I cannot moralize or sermonize them as if I am a superior teacher who considers them awful or dumb; any superior attitude on my part will only make the racist students de-fensively cling to their beliefs; I do what I can to treat racist remarks with patience to keep the dialogue open; I continue asking questions and making comments in a manner that helps students feel free to express their authentic values; I try to treat all students as intelligent people who want to do the right thing; students are generally reluctant to discuss racism while listing it often as a big problem in society needing discussion; once a discussion gets off the ground, the debate is usually heated, taxing my leadership to keep it organized and fruitful; one pedagogy I found helpful in regard to racism uses a problem-posing format beginning with a dialogue around the question "What is 'racism'?" so that students define their understandings of this word, after which I present more questions such as "What causes racism? What can reduce racism?" and readings about real discrimination in society, which I pose to students as concrete situations for them to solve.

8. *Sexism.* The students' relations to sexism in my classes have generally divided into three positions: (1) a militant sexist group composed mostly of males but with some traditional female support, both white and minority; (2) a passive group of men and women, some of whom favor sexual equality, some who oppose it, and some who don't care about the issue; and (3) a militant pro-feminist group of younger and older women students, sometimes joined by a few nonsexist men; these three positions produce more student-to-student debate on sexism than there is on racism, because some women students regularly and articulately defend women's equality and criticize male dominance, while other women and men may voice agreement, to challenge sexist positions in the room; as the dialogue leader, I have a smaller gap to fill with the theme of sexism than is the case with racism; part of this difference between dialogues on race and on gender comes from the fact that the immediate victims of sexism are also numerous members of the class; the injured parties, when it comes to sexual inequality, are women in class who are often a numerical majority outnumbering the males, unlike students of color, who are few in number, or nonracist whites, who are not the immediate victims of racism; adult women have been returning to college as a major social trend since the 1970s; by 1990, women undergraduates outnumbered men; many have been influenced by the feminism spreading since the late 1960s, even though they are not politically sophisticated or organized, don't march for women's rights, and don't want to be known as women's libbers; their feminism is unorganized, but when challenged by sexist comments in a group process in the classroom, feminist-inclined women frequently find their voices and each other; their challenges to sexist remarks often begin a student-to-student cross talk that can draw nonsexist males into the dialogue; besides the presence of immediate victims of sexism in large numbers in class, another factor making gender dialogues more balanced than ones about racism is that men and women live together in

everyday life in ways that whites and minorities do not; the sexes have not been physically segregated from each other in the way the races have been separated in American society; this means that men and women have a long history of conflict combined with negotiation, collaboration, and communication, even though patriarchy has favored male dominance in their interactions; the fact that the sexes live and often work together, talk regularly, raise families, and have to find ways to keep their home lives, job sites, and relationships functional, opens up space for women to assert themselves around men, in their negotiation of male supremacy; the situation is different when it comes to racism because white students lack an ongoing discourse in everyday life through which they process their own differing positions on racism; most white students do not bring to class a community discourse that negotiates the problem of racism among them in the way that women have had to negotiate their position with men in everyday life; further, minorities have had centuries of violent subordination, in terms of slavery, race riots, police brutality, vigilante attacks, assassinations, and fire-bombings; male dominance of women has also been violent, in terms of rape, battering, incest, harassment, and intimidation, but this physical assault on women did not reach the scale it took in race relations; because of the scale of violence and physical segregation in regard to racism, the races do not have everyday contact in the way family, work, and neighborhood lives bring men and women into association and negotiation; the race issue is also partly complicated by class, because people of color are stereotypically perceived as a poor and competitive underclass threatening the middle-class position of whites, some of whom need white supremacy to feel secure against minorities perceived as beneficiaries of social services paid for by taxes on the middle class and as needy people wanting access to the jobs and neighborhoods controlled by whites; the class factor complicates gender relations less because women are not perceived by men as alien poor people but rather as an "undercaste" within the same class as their male associates; those women who advocate equality do threaten the men but not as intensely as competition from people of color; racism may also provoke more anxiety and hostility than does the theme of sexism because male-female conflict is perceived by many students to be part of the battle of the sexes, which is sometimes a comic experience in the folkways of everyday life, connected to romantic courtship rituals, strange episodes of falling in love, and the playfulness of sex; because romance, dating, sex, and erotic fantasy are part of the battle of the sexes there is occasional hilarious laughter in class when we debate sexism, laughter which is rarely present when we debate racism; thus, because of historical and experiential differences between racism and sexism in society and in the lives of students, there are limits to considering the two issues together; in dialogue, some typical assertions made by the sexist group in class are that women want to be like men, that women aren't able to do men's work (trucking, firefighting, police, sanitation, and construction are cited most often), that women who get jobs in male fields are taking money away from men who have to be breadwinners to their families, that women work for spending money and extras instead of for family support, that women will oppress men if they get into power (that is, they will act just like the men they replace), that women don't know how to be tough leaders and problem-solvers (that is, they will *not* act like the men they replace), that children and marriage will suffer if women have the same rights to careers as men, that women have a special knack for child raising (the maternal instinct) and that it's in men's nature to be promiscuous while women shouldn't play around; when these themes appear in dialogue, the voices of the injured parties often challenge them, balancing male assertiveness with an antisexist reply, opening a debate; where appropriate, I intervene with questions, background information, readings, and examples; I also stop men from silencing women, because men often interrupt and talk over the women in class.

9. *Business Attitudes.* Students have mixed feelings about capitalism even though they rarely use the word because it is rarely used in school, mass media, or daily life; *capitalism* is a negative term generally avoided by capitalist media, by traditional curricula, and by political leaders; instead, students are taught to call capitalism by political euphemisms like free enterprise or private enterprise or the market economy or the free market or the American way of life; students are also taught to think of the United States and the West not as the capitalist world but as the free world; these euphemistic concepts encourage them to celebrate the system and to avoid criticizing its problems and undemocratic practices at home and abroad; hearing mostly uncritical rhetoric, and without access to alternative media and books, students learn that the market system, business, democracy, freedom, and the American way of life are synonyms; still, life is not easy for students from nonelite homes; they are the ones without political power or wealth; white working men have had a hard time maintaining their incomes in recent decades, as the best-paying industrial work has declined; working women have a hard time balancing family duties and wage labor; minorities are in a declining economic position; everyday problems are mounting, which limits the students' celebration of the system; even though students often hear that private enterprise is the best system in the world and that no country is as free as America, many still feel that big business runs the

country for its own profit, not for the public good or individual welfare; many feel that corporate leaders are overpaid and that politicians are in the pockets of big business; they also worry about industrial pollution ruining their neighborhoods and their health; these divided feelings about big corporations also apply to the American Dream; many students doubt the openness of American society to their success and to the future success of their children; they worry that there is not enough to go around, that they will have a hard time making a decent life for their families; on the other hand, students also want to do well in the business world; they want career success and buying power in the marketplace; but they are doubtful and will often consider critical questions; materials on the economic decline of working families (the sinking middle class) and on tax loopholes for corporations and for the rich are interesting and accessible to students, a state of unequal affairs that a critical class can examine.

10. *Humor and Emotional Tone.* Because students expect class to be emotionally flat, because they expect the reading, writing, and discussion to be uninspiring, they often react with surprise, delight, or shyness when class dialogue is emotional, not just analytic, and when texts convey intensity through printed words, from humor to sadness to outrage to hope; some take a while to laugh or express strong emotion in class because it is new to them, that intellectual life in a classroom should have emotional qualities besides the boredom, resentment, and self-doubt many have already experienced; they can be appealed to in a class with positive emotional and moral tone, but years of listening to teacher-talk make it hard for many to notice or to trust an affective transformation of classroom discourse, so I have to be patient and keep the verbal environment textured with humor, surprise, and curiosity, as well as with open discussion and structured reflection; I laugh in class when something is funny, and I react to the emotional or moral seriousness of an issue in our dialogue, to model the appropriateness of feelings in our work; those feelings can decelerate their attention and draw students into dialogue because the classroom intensity helps critical learning compete with the loud, accelerated pace of daily life and mass media.

Teachers Less Than Zero: Teacher Obstacles to Empowering Education and Critical Thought

1. *Traditional Training.* The lower and higher educations of most teachers at the college were traditional, modeling teacher-talk, teacher-centered syllabi, unilateral authority, short-answer questions and standardized tests, commercial textbooks, correct usage as the only idiom, male and Eurocentric readings; our academic preparation lacked models

of dialogic process, democratic authority, problem-posing, student-centered methods, and multicultural approaches; it took me a number of years to learn how to listen to students, to avoid teacher-talk, to develop participatory approaches, and to integrate academic knowledge into student experience; teachers need patience to develop experiments over a span of time, so that our habits can make a transition from traditional practices to critical and democratic pedagogy.

2. *Publish or Perish.* Scholarship or committee work carry more weight than teaching for tenure and promotion at my college, pressuring teachers to publish or sit on committees; to publish, do committees, and also be a good teacher is very demanding; college faculty who want to further our careers find that teaching is the weak link we can most easily ignore; doing classroom research is one way to merge teaching with publication, but such research is not yet high-status knowledge rewarded by colleges and universities; in lower grades, teaching does not compete with publishing, but teaching is still lower-status work, harder to do than administrative work and less rewarded.

3. *Departmental Limits.* The departmental structure discourages our faculty from experimental teaching; students get little exposure to interdisciplinary or student-centered learning; most courses are organized around one department's skills and subject matter, which are transferred to students by lectures; writing and reading instruction are considered English department concerns, whose function is to service the communication needs of other departments; writing instruction is considered the least desirable work; writing across the curriculum has not spread through the college.

4. *Teacher Burnout.* Severe budget cuts mean that little new blood has entered our college over the past decades; the faculty at my college and in my department are aging; it is hard to maintain experimental enthusiasm in a declining educational system; in an endless budget crisis I have to work harder to keep my morale high, to remember not to blame students for the system's decline and for institutional decay, to present a hopeful attitude to help students overcome the depressant atmosphere, so that they commit more intellectual energy to the class.

5. *Teaching to the Tests.* Limits from required syllabi, reading lists, textbooks, and workbooks are not operative in my department; our highly tenured faculty is not policed in its classroom practice; there are no standard syllabi and required tests of the sort faced by many schoolteachers, but our remedial courses are tied to exit writing/reading exams, burdening them with teaching to the tests; many remedial and composition courses are taught by poorly trained and underpaid part-timers, without status in the profession or the department; bad experi-

ences in writing courses affect student development and make them less willing to write, read, and speak in other classes.

6. *Fear of Freedom.* Some faculty fear losing control of the class if there are nontraditional rules, self-discipline, cooperative learning, negotiated syllabi, and student-centered methods, instead of traditional machinery such as term papers and final exams; they assert unilateral authority in class, which limits student experience with democratic learning; so, in my classes, to ease students into rarely practiced democratic habits, I have to offer some reassuring structure while introducing a participatory process.

7. *Large Classes, Rushed Schedules.* Our large writing classes leave little time for personal attention or tutoring of students; the working conditions at the college are rushed and crowded, with not much quiet or comfort; I stay after class to speak with students, but most of them run to other classes, to jobs, or to families; few students have time to come to faculty offices and talk, thus limiting the working relationships teachers and students can build.

Teachers More Than Zero: Teacher Resources for Empowering Education and Critical Thought

1. *Articulateness.* Our English teachers are especially good talkers; they and some faculty from other departments develop the verbal fluency that can help them lead dialogue and re-present student remarks as themes for discussion; the articulate voice of a teacher can be an effective tool for explaining materials and issues if the teacher employs a dialogic, student-centered process that first encourages a lot of student expression.

2. *Thinking Skills.* Many of our faculty studied philosophy and theory in college and continue analytic thinking through course design, classroom research, or academic publication; this philosophical background is helpful for questioning subject matter and student comments in class; teachers have spent a lot of time doing intellectual work, which gives them the ability to listen carefully, to organize fragments into meaningful wholes, to synthesize generalizations from extensive examples, to contrast different items, and to abstract issues from an ongoing dialogue.

3. *Love of Learning.* Many teachers in the college care deeply about knowledge and hope to pass it on; many try to model the love of learning to students; the knowledge that teaching is a public service, that education is a career for human development, is a positive value in society that supports a teacher's morale and surrounds her or his work with some dignity and prestige.

4. *Authority.* Because our faculty are experts in knowledge, they are

expected to take charge in class; they begin with the authority that comes from their professional training, their expertise in a field, their place in the school hierarchy, and their position in society as cultural workers who help others develop; the prestige of educated people who are also helping professionals can win some student cooperation, but it can provoke even more resistance if used in an authoritarian way; this authority works best when it is democratic, which means among other things that the authority of the students to coauthor their education is built into the curriculum.

5. *Conviviality.* Many teachers I work with want their classes filled with student participation; silent classes are frustrating, dull, and embarrassing; unresponsive students make teachers feel like failures; teachers feel rewarded by lively student participation; when classes respond, teachers get a boost in morale, which helps protect veterans from burnout and younger teachers from the despair that leads them to leave the profession; the teachers here also enjoy collegial relationships with their peers, so that they feel less isolated in their classrooms.

6. *Training in Research.* In graduate school, many teachers learned about research, which can help us examine the learning process in the classroom; teaching the same courses for several years gives us an ongoing laboratory to refine methods, accumulate observations, bring in outside consultants and collaborators, and test new approaches.

7. *Deviance Credits.* Teachers who attempt to transform their classroom, department, or institution are working against entrenched traditionalism; colleagues, administrators, parents, and students are most likely to have traditional expectations and values; because of this status quo, critical teachers have to discover what open space exists in the school, program, or college for an empowering project; one way I tried to ease resistance to critical projects was to take on some institutional tasks in my early years at the college and in the department, like writing parts of the college catalogue or meeting with student counselors or being a faculty mentor for internship programs or setting up a departmental colloquium; other institutional work could be selecting books for the library, supervising the yearbook, newspaper, or senior play, serving on the parking committee, accompanying students on field trips, setting up art exhibitions, poetry readings, or scientific lectures; this institutional activity builds up something that could be called deviance credits, a teacher's account of official approval for doing recognized tasks, which establishes his or her institutional citizenship and roots, so that he or she earns some political capital that opens space for deviating from the official curriculum into critical teaching and activist projects; longevity at a school or college can be helped by having one

foot firmly planted in the institution so that the other foot can deviate from the norm; participating in some approved activity can make it harder for an administration to isolate and fire teachers for their dissident activities.

8. *Institutional Clout.* Business, career, and technical departments at my college have overshadowed liberal arts in recent times, but our humanities programs have resources to draw on for raising issues more easily ignored in the hard disciplines; working out of English or social science departments has benefits because their traditions of social concern and interdisciplinary approaches make it easier to begin experiments there; some creative pedagogy has been emerging from English studies, especially in the last decades; in the age of the literacy crisis what English and humanities departments think and do has special significance.

Doing the above critical paradigm has clarified the territory where I attempt empowering curriculum and projects. This research has an egalitarian philosophy built into it. The critical paradigm promotes mutuality as a central egalitarian idea: Teachers and students alike possess knowledge, language, and attitudes which contribute to the success or failure of empowerment; both develop through the process. In addition, the critical paradigm acknowledges that education is cultural politics deeply connected to conditions in the community and society. This paradigm situates the classroom in the world surrounding it, which influences what teachers and students can accomplish.

Inside a critical paradigm, teachers have Promethean roles as change-agents and leaders of empowering education. They initiate a democratic learning process and promote critical perspectives on knowledge and society. Such teachers do not stand above or apart from students. They observe and illuminate the environment for learning, to reveal which conditions help or hinder transformative education, a hope brought to life by many hands and voices.

"The Third Idiom"
Inventing a Transformative Discourse for Education

A Model for Problem-Posing

Problem-posing is an art as well as a science. If there were only one way to do it, dialogic teaching would be easy and dull at the same time—easy because teachers could memorize the one best way and dull because the one best way would suppress creativity in education.

The dialogic process is self-evolving, not standardized. Developed in process, dialogue assumes the unique profile of the teachers, students, subject matter, and setting it belongs to. It requires democratic teacher authority, student codevelopment, meaningful subject matter, critical thinking, and creative adaptation to local conditions. These various inputs give each dialogic class its individual character as a complex emotional and intellectual experience.

Because problem-posing dialogue is creative, not standardized, it is helpful to report experiences of it, to see how it has worked in the classroom, with the caution that a report is not a prescription for the only way to do it. The following model I offer is one example and experience of problem-posing. I do not rigidly follow the model, but adapt it to the learning process under way in each class. The phases outlined below help me focus on dialogic practices.

1. *Posing a Problem.* Dialogue begins with posing a problem, whether generative, topical, or academic. Some sample problems I have used include "What is 'news'?" (in a journalism course) or "What is 'the American dream'?" (in a literature course) or "Why do people use cars so much?" (in a Literature and Environment class) or "What factors in society can limit or help personal growth?" (in a freshman writing course) or "What is good writing?" (in another writing class) or "What do you know about Columbus?" (in an interdisciplinary humanities class) or "What makes a story good?" (in fiction writing). In other fields, teachers could ask: "What are addition and subtraction?" or "How do you use math in your everyday life?" or "Where do your breakfast ba-

nanas come from?" (in social studies) or "What is illness?" (in health sciences) or "What is profit?" or "What is a monopoly?" (in economics).

A problem can be posed verbally, in writing on the board or through handouts, through a printed text or excerpt, through visual media like sign language, film, video, drawings, photos, and illustrations, or through performance art like dance, song, dramatic skits, or poetry readings. This first step in posing a problem focuses critical attention on a substantial issue or situation, not on a short-answer question.

I have also asked students themselves to come up with the problems that launch dialogue. I ask "What questions do you have about good writing?" or "What questions do you have about the mass media?" or "What issues in society and everyday life are important to you?" Teachers researching everyday life may pose problems about the sexual harassment of women on the job, or the difficulty of finding good jobs or affordable housing, or the high teenage pregnancy rate and the inadequate access young people have to sex education and birth control.

2. *Reflecting on the Problem.* After a problem is posed, students reflect on their understandings of it. For classes able to write, students can be asked to compose rough drafts on the problem. If the students are very young or preliterate, the problem can be posed for discussion or for an artistic response like drawing or acting in short dramas. More advanced classes that write may find it useful to vary writing with discussion, drama, or drawing. To prompt student response using a pictorial illustration from daily life, perhaps a picture of a woman leaving a day-care center and running for the bus, the teacher can ask, "What do you see? What's happening here?"

In academic or technical courses, the dialogic teacher can also present the subject matter as a problem to be written about or discussed rather than as a lecture to be memorized. In a statistics course, for example, the students could be asked "What is statistics? Have you seen or used any statistics? What statistics are most important for your needs and life? What questions do you have about statistics?"

After posing a problem, I typically ask students to think it over for a little while, make some notes, and then write for ten to twenty minutes. I often ask students to discuss the problem in pairs before writing, to use their strong oral skills for clarifying their thoughts. Students routinely ask if these papers will be collected, because they will write with more care if they know I plan to read or grade their work. I regularly collect them to encourage serious attention to writing and to use them as material for my classroom research into their thinking. But I announce that their rough drafts will not be graded, to relax their performance anxiety about writing spontaneously in class. I routinely write with the students in class, but to focus on their thought and participation I read my work only occasionally and at the students' request.

In responding to the problem posed, students express their sense of it in their own idiom, rather than passively absorbing the teacher's words from a preemptive lecture. They offer the first commentaries that begin the dialogue, instead of teacher-talk unilaterally establishing the idiom of discussion. By posing a problem and inviting student responses, the teacher immediately deploys a curriculum built from student thought and language. This is a way to begin class by democratizing authority. Students are authoring the first discourse and meanings for class inquiry.

3. *Literacy Development/Skills Exercise.* My classes compose rough essays on the problem, either after I pose it or after they have discussed it in pairs. With their compositions ready, I ask them to do some literacy development exercises.

As I understand it, dialogic pedagogy is concerned with developing skills, so a focus on literacy is important. I explain in class a variety of literacy exercises that develop reading and writing skills by asking students to read out loud, to self-edit, to edit in pairs, and to read their essays to each other in groups, for discussion and revision (Shor 1987a). I talk to students about the purpose and method of these exercises, expecting that some will take to them readily, some will resist, and some will need a few weeks to get used to them. This early focus on good writing sends a message that this class is a place of serious work.

Besides focusing on skills, the literacy development phase also develops cooperative relations. Students work collaboratively in a community-building activity. In editing teams, they help each other focus on correcting minor errors. In discussion groups, they compare their ideas and suggest revisions to clarify meaning. These are some ways to desocialize students from authority dependence, that is, from waiting for the teacher to tell you what to do, what things mean, and what is right and wrong. Besides shifting some of the responsibility for evaluating from teacher to students, peer editing and revising teams are valuable because they decelerate perception and communication, slowing down the anti-intellectual, accelerated attention spans developed in mass culture. Self-editing and peer editing can develop deliberate habits of scrutiny and communication, because chunks of class time are devoted to careful observation of written work.

Literacy development takes place here in a meaningful context situated in student thought and language. This dialogic exercise is not abstract skills development taken from a textbook or workbook. It is not a lecture on correct usage. It is an active exercise based in student expression. In sum, literacy work includes students reading essays aloud to use their speaking voices as grammatical tools to refine their writing skills; cooperative peer relations in discussion groups where students help each other revise their essays; peer education without teacher micromanagement of the process; and deceleration through a deliberate task requiring careful communication among students in relation to self-created texts.

When students read their essays to each other in groups, they compare their ideas and then select a paper, or a synthesis of their papers, to read aloud. I also ask each group to come up with a thinking question for class discussion based on the papers they have discussed. (A class can bypass writing and editing rough drafts and go directly to discussion groups, if students can't yet write or if class time is too short to allow writing that day.)

4. *Group Reports/Class Dialogue.* At this point in my classes, each student has written a response to the problem, has done preliminary editing on her or his rough draft, and has taken part in a peer group that discussed the ideas in the papers and chose material to read aloud with a question for discussion. They have listened to each other's essays, specified agreements and disagreements, devised a discussion question for the class, and selected one essay, a synthesis of positions, or a summary of conflicting opinions to report for whole-class dialogue. If the class is small enough and time allows, all students can be invited to read. In large classes, time is better used when each group selects one reader. At the least, every student has had an opportunity to read her or his paper in a small group, so the process involves everyone actively, not only the most assertive or the most skilled in writing. This process of peer-group discussion draws all students into some cognitive activity. Even though student participation in the peer groups is uneven, the fact of universal participation is important and reassuring because I am always concerned about the silent students when we reconvene for whole-class dialogue. The small-group readings and discussions are places where shy, passive, or alienated students can more easily talk than in the larger setting of the whole class. By talking, they are involved at least minimally in the process.

Also, by selecting a reader, a text, and a question for discussion by the whole class, the students do some codevelopment of the curriculum. They choose which paper, synthesis, or summary to read and which question to pose. Their choices codevelop the class because they select some of the foundational material for dialogue.

When the group reporting begins, I start by asking each spokesperson to give a brief overview of the group's deliberations, so as to encourage the habit of generalizing. Then, as students read their texts one by one, I take notes at my seat, copying down their questions, summarizing and conceptualizing their statements, noting key words and phrases, recurring themes, conflicting opinions, political perspectives, affective relations to the work, and literacy levels. This is part of my in-process classroom research. From this raw material, I fashion in my mind questions and comments for re-presenting their material back to them as critical issues for discussion.

This reflexive dialogue evolves from the students' responses to the first problem. I conceptualize student talk and writing in class under the pressure of an ongoing dialogue, but I also reread the student papers and my class notes at home to study the learning process and to prepare the next session.

In class, I not only take notes as students read their selected essays, but I also speak during student readings for several purposes:
• to give emotional and intellectual validation when a paper or remark is creative or insightful
• to support speaking students who are shy or nervous
• to ask questions that encourage withdrawn students to extend their written or spoken ideas
• to ask if students see connections or disagreements among reports, so as to focus their attention and to invite student-to-student dialogue
• to test if I and others heard the essays correctly
• to model an engaged listener of other people's speech and writing (in order to develop students as an audience for their work)
• to ask students to read and speak slowly, to reread their work and repeat their comments, so that their accelerated voices do not rush the words by the class without them having a chance to think about them. By taking notes as students speak, I have a built-in reason for asking them to slow down and to repeat, because I cannot write as fast as they can speak. This method of small-group discussion, whole-class dialogue, deliberate readings of essays, and synthesis of issues helps decelerate their speeded-up language and thought
• to model the use of the voice as a learning tool by taking the risk of thinking out loud before you have the material fully grasped.

5. *Synthesize and Re-present Student Responses: Second-Level Problem-Posing.* My notes from their readings contain raw data which I re-present to students. I read aloud my notes on their remarks and ask them what questions and issues they see as the main ones for us to focus on next. I dialogue with them to offer my perceptions of the key issues. In this way, they join me in synthesizing a new problem for the next level of dialogue. Their questions and papers are first reflections on the

initial problem. From them, we synthesize and generalize issues that go deeper into the problem and their thoughts. (I often ask students to take papers home and refine them for the following week. This is another way to deepen their reflection on the problem and also to encourage revision as a literacy skill.)

The second level is a reflection on the first level. We think about and discuss what they thought about and discussed in regard to the original problem. Students practice critical thinking about their thinking. In the aggregate, eight or ten group reports based on thirty student papers will produce a fertile ground of issues to examine, even if no one paper is deeply critical.

Sometimes students disagree with each other and me on the main questions emerging from the first-round essays. I turn the disagreements back to the class for dialogue. For example, in a mass media course some students write that "news" means reports of important events that affect people while others write that it means dumb stories about famous people and scandals. I re-present this difference back to the class for their reflection and writing. In a Utopia class, students often define Utopia as a perfect world we can never have, which is one way they express their pessimism about changing society for the better. I pose the problem in various ways: "Do only perfect changes count? How much improvement in society is really possible? What stands in the way of making improvements?" In this class, students have also disagreed about which themes are the most important ones to use to study the novel *Walden II;* I pose back to them choices for them to deliberate on, like education, family life, or work. In a literature class, some students write that the American dream is a fake while others insist it's alive and well. I present this disagreement to the class so that students wrestle with the issue. In a composition class, some students say that good writing is correct grammar and spelling while others say that it means expressing yourself in an interesting way so that readers don't get bored. Again I re-present this disagreement to them for their deliberation. A final example of second-level problem-posing is a disagreement students had about racial prejudice. After initial responses to the questions "What is racism?" and "Is racism a problem in American society?" some students said that racist violence and evidence of discrimination should not be publicized in the media because it only stirs up more trouble, while others say it's better to bring it out in the open than to leave it hidden. Once again, I re-present this issue for dialogue, so that the students exercise authority in making choices for the syllabus.

At times I disagree with the students about which synthesis, question, or issue best summarizes our first-round dialogue and best launches us on our second cycle. I mention my choice and argue for it as the next problem to work on. If my synthesis or question is not convincing, the students select one of theirs, and I wait for a chance to pose my issue in the dialogue.

After a new synthesized problem is invented by me or by them, I ask students to write again on the re-presented issue.

6. *Literacy Development/Skills Exercise: Second Cycle.* Again, students write, this time on a key problem synthesized from their first responses. Once more, they do literacy development exercises, then read their papers and discuss their ideas in small groups, and finally select an essay, synthesis, or report of disagreements from each group to read to the class as a whole, with a discussion question.

The class assumes a rhythm of formats here, moving into and out of a variety of structures, from whole-class dialogue to small-group discussion to individual writing to paired editing teams to group reports to home revision. The changing formats of problem-posing help stimulate student attention and make a critical class feel busy, to compete with the accelerated habits developed in mass culture.

7. *Group Reporting/Whole-Class Dialogue: Second Cycle.* This is now the second-level whole-class dialogue. As each committee delegate reads her or his report and question, I once again take notes, record their questions, and begin mentally synthesizing their texts into critical problems to re-present for dialogue. I again draw students out by encouraging them to go deeper into their ideas and to relate their thoughts to other students' ideas by questioning each other. I ask about concurrences, disagreements, and anomalies in the series of reports, to encourage their attention and critical habits of mind. Lastly, I provide intellectual and emotional feedback to individual readers to help them feel at home as public speakers. The discussion groups provide us with questions to pull the inquiry forward. I restate the group's questions and ask students to vote on which one they want to begin the next dialogue.

As the dialogue evolves from cycle to cycle, I think about appropriate materials to integrate into this discussion. What media and readings about personal lives, about social issues, and from academic bodies of knowledge will fit this ongoing dialogue? What would the students themselves choose to read for the learning that is under way?

8. *Integrating Materials.* To deepen thematic inquiry and critical literacy at this point, I integrate printed matter; I have also used films, videotapes, audiotapes, charts, and illustrations. To continue codevel-

opment of the curriculum, I also ask students to bring in materials, such as short stories, news articles, or magazine reports which they think are relevant to our dialogue.

When I integrate reading matter, I speak briefly about why I chose it. In basic writing classes, I often read the title or first paragraph out loud, and then, to prime attention to it, do "prereading" exercises that ask students to generate questions the text might answer. Sometimes I dictate the first few paragraphs for students to copy down, and then ask them to compare their grammar and spelling with that in the text, as an active, self-educating way to study correct usage. I go around the room and consult individually with students as they do this exercise, to learn what specific corrections they are making and to identify the level of their writing skills. When they finish comparing and correcting, I invite questions on the exercise. My observation of their self-correction and their asking specific questions about usage help me target instruction at the actual needs of the group, rather than teaching grammar from A to Z.

In other classes, I ask students immediately to read the whole text and then write a summary of its main points and their opinions, including one thinking question they want to pose for class discussion. Next, to develop cooperative deliberation on the material, I ask them to read their summaries and opinions to each other in groups, to compare how each understood the text, and then to choose one of their summations and questions to pose to the whole class for discussion. Each group reads, consults on their interpretations, and then makes a report, including its main question, to the whole class. I take notes and ask the class about similarities and differences in the responses we are hearing, and then read back their questions so that students can vote on which one they want to begin with. If there is no clear choice, we have a brief discussion on the most popular issues and vote again, at which point I go ahead with the question that wins the most votes. Once they have chosen their main question about the reading, I lead a whole-class dialogue on that issue, integrate comments of my own, and go from question to question until it's time for me to ask questions of my own not yet raised by students. This first reading is often followed by other readings on the problem under discussion.

In this way, the dialogue remains student-centered even though I integrate outside reading materials, because students develop the questions through which the reading matter will be engaged, without a preemptive lecture telling them what the text means, without a teacher-centered question-and-answer period on the material. I also ask students to evaluate the readings to let me know which they thought were best and which least helpful for our thematic inquiry.

By selecting readings, I make a higher-profile intervention into the process than before. When I provide reading matter, I bring a new discourse into our ongoing dialogue. Outside materials can disrupt the dialogic process if they violate the thematic and idiomatic contours of the discussion, that is, if they are too remote from the subject matter and the language of discussion evolving in class. My selection of reading matter has to respect the participatory process under way.

Texts of any kind brought in by the teacher remain dialogic and democratic experiences as long as students have the right to select their own texts and to criticize those offered by the teacher; as long as they have the right to first develop the summaries, opinions, and questions through which to discuss them without a teacherly lecture preempting their perceptions; and as long as any text is examined in a multicultural way and is related to the students' context. Their voices constitute the primary discourse, taking precedence over any printed text brought in. To maintain the democratic politics of critical education, texts enter a student-centered process rather than students entering a text-centered discourse.

By selecting reading matter at this point, I am doing what all teachers do when they select materials—making a value-laden choice. I seek reading matter that raises critical questions about society, knowledge, daily life, and the broad consequences of the subject under discussion. Integrating texts elevates my philosophical profile in the process. When I introduce readings or read aloud my own essay responses to problems posed in class or offer my own critical commentary in dialogue, I am making a thematic intervention. I say *thematic* because I am responding to the theme under discussion. My thematic interventions act on the meaning of the dialogue, its subject matter or content, so as to promote critical scrutiny.

In class I make two other kinds of interventions: for usage (literacy development) and for dialogic process (maintaining a critical-democratic discourse). I make *usage* interventions when I suggest literacy exercises to help students become strong users of language—through composing, editing, revising, reading, analyzing, and listening, individually and in groups. Standard usage is not learned here in isolation from a thematic study; critical thinking is not a set of abstract logic skills or problem-solving techniques; they are activities in a meaningful inquiry. Thinking or writing skills are not assigned as disembodied language arts. They are developed in a critical and democratic process as part of a meaningful context.

Third and finally, *process* interventions are moments when I organize, refine, and direct problem-posing. I exercise my judgment and democratic authority to lead the process. I have to gauge whether the dialogue is advancing, stuck, or digressing; whether it has critical depth or has become an exchange of casual opinions; whether it is democratically open to women, minorities, and shy students or is being monopolized by men, whites, and aggressive people; whether it is challenging intellectual passivity, regressive myths and ideologies, traditional thinking, and habits of resistance (playing dumb, getting by); and whether students are humoring me with clever performances cued to my words and values or are authentically examining critical issues. My responsibilities are to maintain the critical rigor, skills development, creative openness, emotional tone, and democratic quality of the process.

These three interventions—thematic, usage, and process—are different roles for the teacher. They require different forms of expertise: academic and multicultural subject matter and conceptual habits of mind for thematic interventions, student-centered literacy techniques for usage interventions, and democratic problem-posing for process interventions.

9. *Interim Class Evaluation.* With a few cycles of dialogue under way and some reading material integrated, I find an opportune moment to ask students to evaluate the class. I ask them to write anonymously what they like least and most about the class, how I am doing as a teacher, and what changes they think are needed. I collect these responses and summarize them at the next class hour. In class, I consult with students about the changes they suggest, before discussing and voting on the proposed adjustments they want, some of which I argue for or against. At the end of the term, I do this evaluation again as a final student assessment of the class, of me, and of their learning.

10. *Dialogic Lecture by the Teacher.* After evaluation, several levels of critical dialogue, and integrated readings or other media, I can choose here to make a more extended thematic intervention that I call a dialogic lecture. I call it *dialogic* to distinguish it from the *didactic* lecture common to teacher-talk in traditional classrooms.

The didactic lecture is the heart of teacher-talk. It begins a class hour with the teacher's voice. This didactic presentation by a teacher frontloads subject matter. Students are presented with extended comments which establish a teacher-centered discourse as the dominant idiom of the classroom. By preempting their speech and their thought on the subject matter, this unilateral discourse alienates most students. Therefore many simply don't listen when the teacher begins a lecture (or any other narrative), while others actively disrupt the class, making it impossible in some schools for teachers to lecture, forcing them to turn to worksheets and workbooks instead, to keep students quietly busy at their seats.

Problem-posing turns lectures and unilateral authority on their head. It reverses traditional classroom discourse. While didactic lectures frontload teacher-talk and backload student response, problem-posing backloads lectures and frontloads student expression. The dialogic teacher avoids preempting student participation with a lecture on a body of knowledge. Dialogue does not establish the teacher's academic language as the dominant idiom in the classroom. To practice democratic authority, the critical teacher poses a problem in language accessible to students, in a participatory format where student responses become the foundational discourse into which the teacher then fits her or his knowledge.

By posing problems to begin dialogue from students' words and perceptions, the critical teacher is free to comment in the discussion and at a certain point to make an extended presentation of her or his views. This extended and structured presentation by the teacher is what I call a dialogic lecture. Even though the teacher is speaking extensively in her or his own academic voice, it is a legitimate intervention in a democratic process, as long as the teacher begins with a student-centered dialogue whose content is integrated into her or his remarks. The dialogic lecture accepts the democratic discipline of the process. In a dialogic lecture, the teacher structures her or his expertise according to what students have said earlier rather than having students structure their remarks to follow a discourse unilaterally imposed by the teacher's lecturing voice.

The dialogic lecture is a valuable and delicate moment in problem-posing. The teacher, backloading her or his comments, has earned the right to speak by honoring the student-centered, dialogic process. Serious educators have a right and a responsibility to share their academic knowledge and perspectives. They must not impose their values or interpretations on students, but when their turn comes in a participatory process they can set an example of the love of knowledge, of a well-informed mind, and of a critically thinking intellectual and citizen. Mutual dialogue is not a know-nothing learning process. It is not permissive, nondirected, unstructured. It is interested in skills development and in systematic knowledge. The teacher must know a lot and must actively use that knowledge in a dialogic way. The dialogic lecture allows the teacher's knowledge an important place in the study as long as the students' idiom, perceptions, and right to disagree have been established first.

After some phases of problem-posing, where the teacher's voice is primarily interrogative and activating (by asking questions and re-presenting students' words), the teacher's *expository* presentation (a dialogic lecture) is democratic because it follows from and leads back into the mutual process under way. This dialogic intervention is a lecture because the teacher is speaking at length in her or his own voice about her or his point of view and expertise. The teacher draws on bodies of knowledge for the presentation, but dialogic lectures succeed not only because the teacher knows a lot but because she or he speaks in a way that stimulates students to respond critically to the lecture itself, not sit silently overwhelmed, baffled, or angry at the teacher's scholastic performance.

With this guide for the dialogic lecture, I will offer an example from a Literature and Environment course I taught for evening adult students. I began the course by asking the students to write about the main problems of their environment, so that they generated the opening themes of the class. On the first day, I posed the problem like this, "What are the most important environmental problems you live with?" Students wrote for about twenty minutes, did literacy skills exercises with their rough compositions, read them in small discussion groups, and presented their summaries to the whole class for discussion. What emerged from this material were two major generative themes, cars and kids cursing. The first was fairly predictable in a semisuburban area like Staten Island and at a commuter college like ours, but the second was unique. The dialogic process opened the syllabus to them, so it was wonderful for me to see students generate a theme I had not studied with any class before—kids cursing as an environmental problem. Eventually, from our extended dialogues on both themes, the students wrote two booklets. Their self-created texts became a backdrop of ideas against which we discussed official texts that I assigned from literature about the environment.

In terms of the unique theme, students explained why kids curse in a few ways: vulgarity in the mass media, poor upbringing at home, the bad influence of older kids, and adults' use of vulgar language. As we discussed their analyses, I saw that the causes most apparent to students were those most visible in their lives—loud mass media, troubled families, divorced parents, neglected children, undisciplined older siblings, and angry or immature parents who cursed a lot. As I listened and took notes, I heard them blaming the victims more than the social conditions that can produce these behaviors. The problems from their point of view was largely personal, one of family failures which led to kids cursing, a sound that polluted their environment.

A second problem was their attack on the media. Their criticism of the mass media needed scrutiny. They blamed the media for kids cursing. But when I asked, "Is there more cursing on TV, in films, in the newspapers, and on the radio than there is in everyday life?" they reflected, debated, and decided that there is far more cursing in daily life than in what they see, hear, or read in the media. So why blame the media? Because many students at my college feel that sensationalizing media add a dishonest, invasive quality to life, they often condemn the media when considering social troubles. Here they did not make a connection between the media's fondness for violence as a contributory cause for cursing, an issue I will say more on shortly.

While noting to myself some gaps in their criticism of the media and in their virtually exclusive attention to personal explanations for children's behavior, I observed that they ignored the way family life and individual attitudes are affected by the economic system. I wanted to question their laying blame on individuals for kids cursing and their ignoring the economic conditions of families. Thus, I asked, "Is our society providing families with the conditions needed to raise children well?" To make this broad question more specific, I asked, "What do families and children need to maintain a good home life?" Students thought it over for a few moments, then jotted down some thoughts and read them aloud for discussion. They specified such family needs as adequate food, decent clothing, comfortable housing, good schooling, regular health care, safe playgrounds and streets. "Are these needs being provided by society?" I asked. Students acknowledged that they were not. I decided the time was ripe for a dialogic lecture, to raise some still unasked questions about the economic system behind the social climate that contributes to family distress and kids cursing.

I began talking about the urban life around us. New York is home to many corporate headquarters as well as to media and tourist industries. But at ground level, where most people live, the city during and after the Reagan era of the 1980s was a decaying metropolis with some gentrified neighborhoods and worsening slums. Affordable housing for working families became harder to find. While unemployment and the cost of living remained high, full-time workers had a five-day, forty-hour workweek, a heavy schedule that the business world has not reduced since World War II. The long workweek, the high prices for groceries and goods, and the absence of affordable housing near work require parents to commute to their jobs, to be at work long hours, with both parents working to make ends meet. Single-parent households have an even harder time, and welfare families and the homeless have the hardest time of all. Working, commuting, the high cost of living, and the loss of jobs, I argued in class, have contributed to unstable family life and to inadequate attention to children, which in turn contribute to the anger in kids that encourages cursing. I posed a number of questions for extended class dialogue: "Could we have a shorter work week that gives parents more free time and also creates more jobs? Could we have work closer to home? Could we have housing policies favoring the working family and not the gentry or the tourist or the corporate front office? Could we have more invested in education and family needs and less in airports, convention centers, luxury hotels, and high-rise office buildings? What would economic and urban policy look like if we wanted to take care of children's needs?" After discussion of these issues one at a time, we took up some of them again in the Utopian novels we read, *Walden II* and *Ecotopia*.

Besides presenting economic policies as negative influences on families and children, I wanted to adopt the notion of "symbolic violence" (Bourdieu and Passeron 1977) to characterize the aggressive experience of children, from their exposure to violence and loud music in the mass media, to fast cars roaring through the streets, to their miseducation in understaffed public schools. Kids reflect the culture and values around them. They give back the kind of treatment they get. Cursing is one aggressive response to the aggressive and violent atmosphere in schools, communities, and the media. Even when there is no physical violence done to kids in school, many witness aggression and are treated with contempt or casual disregard, as nonelite students in underfunded, traditional school systems (Kozol 1991). They also see and hear a lot of aggression in the media, if not outright cursing; so it is in this way that the violence on TV, in film, and in music can make the speech of children more aggressive. The streets they inhabit are not tended by the city, not kept clean or safe. Kids receive disrespectful messages about the unimportance of the people living there—another invitation to resentment and cursing.

There are of course real physical abuse and sexual violence in the lives of many children, but there is also symbolic violence in school from overcrowded classes, standardized testing, discriminatory tracking, shabby classrooms, and authoritarian teachers and administrators, and in the macho atmosphere of the streets. The aggression kids reflect is a degenerate quality of everyday life in many cities. Kids not only copy the violence around them; they act out their anger at the way adult society treats them. In a city like New York, with several hundred thousand children living in poverty, the education and health of children are grossly neglected. Many affluent and middle-income kids also crave more attention and better mentoring than they get. They too are pushed to behavior that is resentful and angry.

Such ideas were the critical points of my dialogic lecture. They also anticipated the social and economic policy raised in the Utopian novels I assigned. In this way, my remarks grew out of the dialogue and fed back into it.

From the dialogic lecture, the next step is student discussion of the teacher's presentation. The dialogic lecture should be followed immediately by an invitation to students to challenge what the teacher said, so that the teacher can discover if his or her discourse was silencing or stimulating, accepted or resisted.

11. *Student Responses to the Dialogic Lecture.* Dialogic lectures are risky because they can silence students if the teacher talks too long, too pedantically, too rhetorically, or too remotely from the themes already under way. They are successful when they provoke student responses. In speaking and in writing, students should be urged to debate the teacher's lecture, as a means of assimilating the material, as well as informing the teacher if his or her presentation moved students to critical thought. Immediately after a lecture, students can be asked to write a summary and their opinions about what was said, including one question each wants to ask for discussion. After writing, I ask students to read their remarks in pairs or small groups to help them develop their own positions, before convening as a whole class for dialogue on the lecture.

In some classes, my dialogic lecture missed the right content, length, and style for provoking student responses, but in the environment class the students responded thoughtfully. They especially wanted to discuss the notion of symbolic violence. They also pondered the decline in public education as one social influence on children. They agreed that families would do better if parents had a shorter workday, less commuting, and more money to make ends meet, but they were pessimistic about making these changes in society. In a dialogic lecture in a journalism class, I tried to connect the White House decision to go to war with Iraq in 1991 with reports of a hostage deal between the Reagan–Bush campaign of 1980 and the Iranian regime. But this time the students were unconvinced. They listened to my presentation, using evidence available from mass media sources, and then rejected it in the ensuing dialogue.

In the context of a participatory dialogue, backloaded lectures do not silence students merely because they are at a level of critical analysis unfamiliar to everyday life. By backloading lectures instead of beginning with them, I gain student participation in critical learning and a working relationship which allows me to offer academic commentary that people are more likely to listen to, even if they reject it. Still, while the dialogic lecture is an option, it is not a required part of problem-posing. Other classes I teach develop a dialogue which makes a lecture inappropriate. In any case, the dialogic lecture is not a harangue or diatribe where the teacher rides her or his polemical hobbyhorse. The language of the lecture must be respectful of student opinion and of the dialogue out of which it emerged, or else the students will be driven into silence or into fake agreement with the teacher just to get a good grade.

12. *Solutions/Alternatives/Projects.* Where appropriate, given the age of the students, the subject under study, and the local political climate, the teacher can ask, "How do we act from the issues suggested in this inquiry? What action makes sense from the knowledge here?" Most students I teach come from conservative communities and are not inclined to activism to change the status quo, which many of them defend. My classes offer a reflective process and some challenging ideas not available in their everyday lives, in the traditional curriculum, or in the media. Some students develop interests in action projects or activism in society, and some have these interests validated by the class. By itself, problem-posing is already active because it challenges passive learning, undemocratic authority, existing knowledge, and social conditions. In the environment class, for example, students went to their neighborhoods and did research. They took up the final three weeks of the class with their presentations on what was wrong and what needed to be done. For my part, I brought in information on two local campaigns, both relevant to the study of the environment: a political project against toxic waste sites in our area and a campaign to prevent the use of a nearby harbor as the home port of a nuclear battle fleet. In regard to action, the teacher can organize projects or refer to ongoing projects in which knowledge is used for social change, but such activism cannot be a requirement, only a suggestion and a choice.

In general, this model for problem-posing dialogue follows a plan of pose a problem, write on it, invite peer-group editing and discussion, follow with whole-class dialogue, question students' responses and encourage students to question each other, pose a second-level problem, write on it, do peer editing and discussion, do an interim evaluation and adjustment of the process, integrate reading matter and bodies of knowledge for student critique, offer a dialogic lecture, hear student feedback, discuss solutions/actions, reflect on action, pose a new problem, do a final evaluation. I could diagram it like this:

Pose a problem → *Write on it* → *Literacy development* → *Peer group discussion/selection → Class dialogue → Pose a new problem → Write on it → Literacy development → Peer group discussion → Class dialogue → Integrate reading material → Writing/dialogue on the readings → Interim evaluation/adjustment of the process → Dialogic lecture → Student response to lecture → Discuss solutions/actions → If possible, take action and reflect on it → Pose new problem → End-term evaluation*

It is of course easier to diagram dialogue than it is to make it work in class. This model should not be followed as a prescription or taken as guarantee of success. It is one experience of dialogue structured into phases. The last thing a dialogic model should become is a rigid formula for how to do it. Teaching requires the creative reinvention of even good suggestions so that methods reflect the local situation. The best teachers discover what each classroom needs for the students and for the learning under way there.

Language, Learning, and Life: Dialogue and Local Conditions

As one example of adapting problem-posing and dialogic lectures to local conditions, I will return to Elsasser and Irvine's bicultural, Creole-English class taught at the College of the Virgin Islands. As I have said, the Afro-Caribbean students there had trouble passing the required writing examination in standard usage.

The students were freshmen who graduated high school only to fail the college's entry exam in writing. This failure surprised and deflated them. Noticing the situation, Elsasser and Irvine posed it as the first problem of the writing course: "Why do we lack the skills needed to pass the writing exam?" The students wrote on this question, giving the expected response that they did not know good grammar and the unexpected one that their *spoken* Creole was in conflict with Standard English on a *writing* exam. A community idiom had run up against the official language, adopted from the former colonial masters of the island.

When Elsasser and Irvine opened the dialogue to this issue of Creole versus standard usage, the class erupted. Students expressed anger at the language conflicts in their lives. They were not allowed to write and to succeed in the language they grew up speaking, which was their strongest idiom. They were being tested on their linguistic weakness, the alien white English left behind by the British. They spoke passionately about this condition once the classroom was open to their authentic feelings and ideas. They no longer had to maintain silence about this cultural inequality.

After consulting the students, the teachers decided to invite a native linguist and author, Vincent Cooper, to lecture on Creole. His dialogic lecture was a formal presentation by a scholar, but it was not didactic teacher-talk. It fit into an ongoing critical dialogue. His expertise entered as a dialogic lecture after a generative theme had been discussed in class. Because the theme was situated in student experience, the purpose of the lecture was mutual and apparent, giving academic knowledge a democratic and crucial role in the process.

Cooper was called in at a self-aware moment in the students' development, where his expertise was a resource to them and where his comments were situated in the dialogue already in progress. That he was from the students' own community legitimized the value of Creole as a distinct language. In a nonpedantic voice, he revealed the politics that had relegated their idiom to inferior status. The students received him well and wanted to find out more about their own language and their problems with Standard English.

The dialogic lecture will enhance the problem-posing process if the teacher's discourse starts from inside student life and is on the side of their empowerment, in language they can understand, while integrating academic knowledge they do not possess. In this class, the effect was to raise the status of Creole in student perception. Hearing Cooper's dialogic lecture in a problem-posing context, the students were motivated to invent a written form for their spoken Creole; as they did so, they absorbed the required Standard English. In this case, the teachers' choice of a generative theme (the clash of community speech with the official idiom) launched an empowering bilingual study of Creole, the language of everyday life, and of Standard English, the language of power (Elsasser and Irvine 1987).

Problem-posing dialogue signals to students that they know a lot, need to know more, and can experience intellectual work as relevant to their lives. They can successfully study themselves, their world, and bodies of knowledge, and come out of the experience equipped to learn more. The critical dialogue described here addresses students as complex, capable human beings, who are still developing, not as ignorant, deficient, or cultureless people.

Inventing a "Third Idiom" for Dialogue: A Voice for Empowerment

In dialogue, the teacher's voice, whether posing problems, responding to student remarks, or delivering dialogic lectures, heavily influences the success of critical learning. In large part, how we learn and make ourselves in the world depends on how we speak and how we are spoken to. Our speech indicates our position in school and society, as does the speech others use in addressing us. Classroom discourse can confirm or challenge existing uses of language. The classroom is the academic center of the day and the voices of the teacher and students are at the center of the classroom. Education is a social activity carried out through communication. It is a developmental relationship between human beings built by the exchange of language. When we transform the discourse of the classroom, we open up new potentials for student development.

In traditional classrooms, students learn that education is something done to them by the teacher's voice, not something they do in their own idiom. The discourse reflects unilateral authority. The students' role is to answer questions posed in teacher-talk, not to question answers in their own ways of speaking and seeing. They absorb the rules of an undemocratic discourse: The best student is the best answer-giver who says what the teacher wants to hear. The failure of this teacher-centered discourse lies in how little information and critical thinking students take away. The bulk of students do not benefit from the transfer of facts and skills. Traditional teaching especially underdevelops students who do not come to school with a privileged dialect or culture. To challenge this inequality, problem-posing frontloads student expression as one foundation to invent an idiom students need to make sense of their education and their conditions in society.

When critical dialogue works, teachers and students reinvent their relationship and their modes of communicating. They create a dialogic discourse in a mutual inquiry. I call this invented discourse the *third* idiom because it is different from the two conflicting ones brought to class by students and teachers: nonacademic everyday speech and academic teacher-talk.

The dialogic third idiom is simultaneously concrete and conceptual, academic and conversational, critical and accessible. As dialogue begins, the students' language of everyday life is familiar and concrete but not critical or scholarly; the teacher's language is academic but not colloquial or concretely related to student experience. The dialogic process overcomes their noncommunication. It transforms both idioms into a new discourse, the third idiom, which relates academic language to concrete experience and colloquial discourse to critical thought. Everyday language assumes a critical quality while teacherly language assumes concreteness.

This invented third idiom philosophizes experience while experientializing philosophy. As a discourse evolved in a democratic process, it rejects the unilateral transfer of culture from the teacher to the students. A mutual transformation of academic and community cultures is necessary because teacher-talk and everyday talk are both products of an unequal society. The knowledge and language that exist in daily life and in the academy cannot by themselves produce social and intellectual empowerment. The culture of schooling and the culture of everyday life in nonelite communities need something from each other to transcend their own limits. The current academic canons of language and subject matter need to be transformed in a multicultural way with and for students, to reflect their language and conditions.

Existing canons cannot be delivered to students as universal standards of excellence because they are the products of undemocratic knowledge making in an unequal academy and society. Elite groups have had the power in history to define the standard knowledge and language. Some educators define cultural democracy as transmitting existing canons to all students; this existing knowledge is often falsely called a common culture of the best that is known; this assumes that democracy means giving out *widely* what has already been canonized *narrowly* as the best. In reality, existing academic canons represent the taste, usage, and knowledge of an elite, developed over centuries in the virtual absence of women, minorities, and ordinary people. This exclusive canon and discourse need multicultural, nonsexist reinventions to become democratic and representative.

As separate products of unequal power relations in society, the teacher's academic culture and the students' community culture meet in dialogue to challenge their separation and inequality. In a mutual process of making knowledge, the two idioms are transformed into democratic communications between teacher and students. When dialogue philosophizes experience and experientializes philosophy, students become critical and the teacher situates her or his expertise in student culture. These are the transformations of discourse suggested by the third idiom. Because the transformations are mutual, affecting both teacher and students, the process is egalitarian, not a one-way transmission of values.

Without a process to invent a third idiom, teacher-talk and student silence will continue to dominate and undermine education. Both parties need each other to overcome the limits of their separate discourses, but it is up to the teacher to lead the change. The teacher prepares, initiates, and leads the process, inviting students to codevelop it.

The third idiom is invented anew in each classroom, situated in the students' language and developmental levels, in the specific subject matter, and in the political climate of the school, college, or community. It is not a standard discourse with one form. Because it is an in-process invention, it calls upon the teacher to be unusually attentive to student expression. Teachers clinging to one-way monologues, didactic lectures, abstract concepts, remote themes, and existing canons of subject matter can avoid the challenge of inventing a third idiom in each class, but they pay a price for nesting in traditional discourse: the loss of a communicating relationship with students through which critical learning can take place.

Students not allowed to invent a third idiom inhabit classrooms where teachers give answers to questions nobody asked, about issues few can relate to, in language fewer can understand. When teachers pose problems inside student language and experience, it will be possible for students to speak as members of an open learning community, not as monosyllabic prisoners in an alien discourse.

Overall, the third idiom is a linguistic, aesthetic, and political achievement of dialogue. It transcends the divided discourses spoken before. It redefines education. In the third idiom, traditional knowledge becomes what it has always been, an historical product reflecting inequality and needing critical perspectives and multicultural reconstruction.

Comedy and the Third Idiom

The invented third idiom can help the empowerment of students if it is humorous as well as critical. The humor I have in mind is not the teacher's witty repartee or sarcastic asides. Some teachers are known for making jokes and telling funny stories. For some, this behavior helps relieve their anxiety, cope with fatigue, or motivate students for a study of difficult or dull material. Others engage in witty remarks or sarcastic one-liners to act out their hostility to students and their jobs. Sarcasm can help keep students in their place; it is the humor of repressed anger, a verbal way to display hostility. As symbolic aggression, it throws a cynical pall over the classroom, letting students know that the teacher is not happy to be there with them. This same depressing message to students can be sent by the witty teacher who punctuates student utterances with comic rejoinders.

The humor I have in mind for the third idiom is not competitive wit, negative satire, aggressive sarcasm, narrative digressions, or stand-up comedy. Instead, when leading dialogue, I listen for opportunities for humor related to the material under discussion. This humor is not at the expense of anyone's remarks. It is amusing in the context of the dialogue. It is not pre-scripted but is part of the texture of the developing discourse. Sometimes the comedy is simply my expression of joy at an insightful remark by a student or my enthusiasm when I understand a problem we are working on. I try to express my joy of learning something new.

Besides joy in moments of illumination, I also seek humor when offering a dialogic lecture. I speak humorously during my remarks, sometimes poking fun at myself—the comedy of noticing my own foibles, like my excessive concern for the right words, or my academic tendency to use bookish phrases, or my habit of referring to unfamiliar texts and remote events, followed by my appeal to the students to see if I am making any sense. As I try to find the right register and vocabulary for my voice in the dialogue, I spontaneously use the comedy of overstatement, understatement, novel comparisons, unexpected convergence of apparently unrelated items, exposed contradictions, motifs (repeated themes in the ongoing dialogue), and discovering something to be the opposite of what it seemed. I see this humorous discourse as part of the dialogic experience, not for mere amusement. Such a discourse prevents critical study from becoming a one-dimensional rational analysis. I want to invent with students a third idiom rich in emotions, including laughter, outrage, indignation, compassion, awe, and delight. I am not there to amuse students, but neither is critical dialogue always sober. I see the critical classroom as holistic in thought and emotion, so I intuitively use humor.

There are many moments of humor and laughter in my classes, though I can't recall much that would sound funny in the retelling. I do remember the excitement when I brought to class some pathetic hamburgers from the college cafeteria for critical inquiry (Shor 1987a). I also remember the joy of some classes that made television shows examining their sexual and educational lives. There was humor as well in those classes that studied the politics of the classroom chairs we sat on. Just imagine, we were sitting on oppressive ideology and didn't even know it. Further, I recall laughter in a Utopia course as we dramatized the intimacies of parent-child and teacher-student conflicts. Another class, fiction writing, laughed when we examined the tangled gender issues in short stories about women facing changes. The humor was situated in the context rather than in a professorial performance. Humor is part of everyday life. It should belong also to the third idiom.

Intuitively looking for humor, I draw on classroom events over the course of the term. Events are a living archive to refer to for prior statements and actions that create humor. I remind students about what we said together and did before. In one interdisciplinary humanities course I mentioned above, Utopias, I intuitively began the term by posing a problem about the garbage strewn on the floor of the classroom. I had not planned to do this but followed a hunch when I entered the room and noticed the floor littered with coffee cups, candy wrappers, sandwich bags, notebook papers, soda cans, and so on. I rescued myself from some depression at having to teach under these conditions by rebelling against the garbage and using it as the first problem. I asked the class, "Why is there so much garbage on the floor?" An initial cycle of writing and discussion on this problem led to a second-level question, "What should we do about the garbage?" This theme evolved into a short-term garbage project, which included action to clean the room and to post notices about keeping it clean. Students made some clever signs and brought in paper towels to take care of wet spills and sticky spots; and I got the jobs of moving a garbage can from the hallway into the room and of recycling soda cans at the end of class. This activity also raised the issue of budget cuts concretely, because I put the conditions of the college into the context of the economic austerity being forced on the public sector, including education, which meant less money to pay for cleaning classrooms. Lastly, this project provided a means to build a cooperative learning community as well as a cleaner room and some humorous memories from an academic encounter with litter.

A learning community emerges from mutual communication, meaningful work, and empowering methods. This community can be built if I situate critical study inside student language and experience, listening carefully to students and drawing out their ideas, encouraging them to listen carefully and respond to each other, and then remembering what was said. This careful attention to the actions and words of students shifts the focus from teacher-talk to the students' learning process. By careful observation of our communication and interaction, I demonstrate to students that the curriculum is being built from them, for them, and with them. When I recall students' statements made during previous classes, they laugh, surprised that I remember them. The seriousness with which I take their remarks is a new experience of self-respect for them, and it elicits some laughter emerging from novel feelings.

Humor can also help students accept the problem-posing approach. The invitation to critical dialogue and empowerment can provoke resistance for a number of reasons, including fear of public speaking and of relating in unfamiliar, democratic ways. In the critical-democratic classroom, personal themes, social issues, and academic subjects are studied in ways that emphasize student participation, questioning received knowledge, and challenging the status quo and our socialization into it. Through problem-posing dialogue, the reality we often uncover is not the one learned in school or through the mass media. The language we use and the relationships we evolve are also new. Uncovering the upside-down nature of knowledge and reinventing relationships can provoke anxiety. What if our prior understanding of the world is not the way the world really is? What if we grew up thinking that Columbus discovered America, when he actually came upon a land already populated with Native Americans whom he enslaved and pillaged? What if minorities have just claims against society or if women have been cheated of equal rights to their development or if working students have been tracked downward through school into lesser programs and jobs? What if American military might has not been used for justice overseas? Critical pedagogy invites students to re-perceive, to examine what they know and how they learned it, to question existing conditions, all of which can arouse anxiety and resistance.

Seeing something fresh includes the joy of discovery as well as the fear of the unknown, the risk of breaking old habits and rules, and the fear of questioning the way things are. Laughter may emerge from students feeling growth or the importance of their ideas, but this process creates anxiety about hidden knowledge given voice. Humor helps ease some of the uneasiness provoked by a transformative process and its new third idiom.

In the Third Idiom: Critical Dialogue Is a Counter-Structure

While the third idiom is an alternative form of communications for learning, the dialogic model as a whole is a counter-structure to traditional education. It is important for students to see the alternative structure and authority of the problem-posing classroom. The structure of critical dialogue may not be automatically apparent to students, who can mistake the negotiable classroom as having no rules. This is one reason why participatory formats, problem-posing techniques, and skills-development exercises are valuable, to communicate the presence of a counter-structure rather than the absence of rules.

The structured process outlined in this book rejects permissive or shapeless education. Students are not free to do whatever they want in the dialogic classroom, just as the teacher is not free to do whatever he or she wants. There are limits and responsibilities on both sides.

In the transition from teacher-talk to dialogue, students and teachers will feel lost if they move from too much structure into too little. The third idiom is not a formless conversation. Dialogic discourse is not a vacuum. Transition to the third idiom means codeveloping counter-structures to replace the old practices. Educational life inside transitional structures is experimental, demanding, changeable, stimulating, and gradually desocializing. Years of traditional socialization cannot be overcome at once. Habits of democratic dialogue can be learned only through extended experience in counter-structures.

Students in a dialogic structure do not mimic the teacher's tastes, words, or knowledge. They are invited to criticize the cultures they examine, including their own. They are also free to reject critical studies and to defend the status quo. When knowledge is examined rather than prescribed, when the learning process is negotiated rather than unilaterally imposed, when the discourse is codeveloped rather than set solely by teacher-talk, students and teachers find themselves in an alternative structure for learning and authority.

The dialogic teacher comes to class with a lesson plan, questions, materials, and reading relevant to the subject matter and the students' culture, but he or she is open to change, to exploring outside the plan, based on what emerges from student speech and writing. There is a risk here, because some explorations will be dead-ends, and some students may abuse the openness with eccentric digressions. Still, to maintain a participatory and democratic classroom, the teacher has to be open to student initiatives. Without this openness, students will not feel free to exercise their voices. They will think they must agree with the teacher and mimic the teacher's words, which will discourage them from participating.

An open process helps desocialize students from their long-practiced passivity, making the structure grow from their thoughts and interests. But they will need time to feel comfortable thinking out loud, using their voices to work out ideas in public, a risky and unfamiliar undertaking for most students. Some will take this risk if the classroom discourse does not expect them to perform in the teacher's idiom, to quickly answer a fact question, or to absorb high culture as a standard of excellence. The third idiom is an invitation to students to experiment with language, thought, and the learning process. Some will be delighted at this opening; others will resist its challenge.

Openness is discouraged in authoritarian classrooms, where many students stop participating and eventually become anti-intellectual. The unproductive conflict of one-way classrooms can be witnessed when students create a sabotaging underdiscourse against teacher-talk. Their own private talk sometimes interrupts the teacher's lesson and sometimes proceeds alongside it. This is an unofficial discourse of jokes, personal advice, group laughter at the teacher's words, dress, or habits, whispered conversations about relationships, note passing, verbal help to other students trying to answer an exam or a teacher's question, calling out, sudden noises like sneezing or coughing or dropping a book, as well as playing dumb and getting by. In their discourse of resistance, students can more or less fight teacher-talk to a standoff.

Sometimes teachers and students develop vocal accommodations that help both get through the uninspiring discourse of teacher-talk. Teachers can give an extra verbal emphasis to some words while lecturing or giving instructions to students. This breaks up the droning quality of a narrating voice. It also emphasizes the few words worth remembering. Students can selectively listen for the teacher's extra pop of volume on the words that count. These key words may reappear as the correct short-answers in an exam coming up soon. The teacher who emphasizes the words worth memorizing often listens only for the right answer-words spoken by students.

On the first day of class, students expect to hear teacher-talk. To make their silence and sabotage less likely, a dialogic teacher begins the discourse immediately with student expression. Doing this well means balancing teacherly restraint and intervention. Problem-posing requires an active teacher to launch critical dialogue, but it also requires restraint to avoid creating too much verbal density around students. By posing problems, a teacher opens space for students to enter in their own words. By saying as little as needed, especially in the early weeks of the term, a teacher signals to students that their voices count.

Some teachers wonder how they will cover a syllabus if they restrain their voices. But, the key to learning is not how much the teacher says or covers; it is how much the students respond to. The myth of traditional schooling is that the more the teacher talks, the more the students learn. The reality of learning is a different equation. By restraining her or his lecturing voice, the dialogic teacher allows students' thought and language to engage the material, this engagement to be followed by the teacher's response to it. Further, restraint makes the teacher's voice more worth listening to. Regularly in class, students ask for my opinions and for me to read what I wrote in class in response to the problems posed. They often insist on knowing what I think as the dialogue evolves. After a lot of listening, I am ready to say a lot during the term. The best time to talk to students is after they engage a problem and dialogue on their understandings. When dialogue is under way, students have much to say and many questions to ask. Sometimes they demand that I say more, and sometimes they go right ahead with their own cross talk, bypassing me, so that I have trouble putting my two cents in.

Teaching Dialogic Habits: Breaking Eye Contact

Many times, old habits dominate an evolving dialogue, and I notice that a student is addressing remarks only to me, not to the whole class. When I observe this behavior, I break eye contact with the student as she or he speaks. I aim my eyes back to the class, away from the eyes of the speaking student, to encourage her or him to address the whole group or the student whose previous remarks are at issue. When not in eye contact with me, a speaking student may stop talking or may begin losing volume in her or his voice, thinking I am no longer paying attention. When I hear a student's voice declining, I turn my eyes back to her or him to reassure the student that I am still listening. The speaker's volume then usually goes back up. Some weeks of breaking eye contact, plus my requests that they speak to each other and the whole class, and my re-presenting student remarks as problems for discussion, can gradually desocialize the authority-dependence of only speaking to the teacher.

All in all, the third idiom is up against the habits learned in teacher-talk classrooms. These classrooms train students to respond briefly to the teacher's questions, not at length. Students expect the teacher to speak first, most, loudest, last, and always after a student has given a brief answer to a teacher's factual question. Students learn to speak least and lowest, between the teacher's question and evaluation of the student's answer. In this setting, it is up to the teacher to initiate the changes that make a mutual discourse possible. To do this, I modulate my voice into conversational styles, say only what is necessary, ask many thinking questions, refrain from replying immediately after a student speaks but rather pose her or his remarks to the entire class for response, break eye contact when required, backload my lectures dialogically, and share the last word with students at the end of the hour.

These practices contribute to inventing a third idiom, the democratic discourse that can ease student-teacher alienation and promote a critical learning process. That learning is a moment when inequality in school and society loses some power over the classroom, opening up cultural space to rethink knowledge and authority.

A Last Word

Empowering education is thus a road from where we are to where we need to be. It crosses terrains of doubt and time. One end of the road leads away from inequality and miseducation while the other lands us in a frontier of critical learning and democratic discourse. This is no easy road to travel. Any place truly different from the status quo is not close by or down a simple trail. But the need to go there is evident, given what we know about unequal conditions and the decay in social life, given the need to replace teacher-talk and student alienation with dialogue and critical inquiry. Fortunately, some valuable resources already exist to democratize school and society. That transformation is a journey of hope, humor, setbacks, breakthroughs, and creative life, on a long and winding road paved with dreams whose time is overdue.

References

Ada, Alma Flor. 1988. The Pajaro Valley experience: Working with Spanish-speaking parents to develop children's reading and writing skills in the home through the use of children's literature. In *Minority education: From shame to struggle*, ed. T. Skuttnab-Kangas and J. Cummins. Clevedon, Eng.: Multilingual Matters.

Ada, Alma Flor, and Maria de Olave. 1986. *Hagamos caminos*. Reading, Mass.: Addison-Wesley.

Adams, Frank, with Myles Horton. 1975. *Unearthing seeds of fire: The idea of Highlander*. Winston-Salem, N.C.: John F. Blair.

American Council on Education. 1990. *Community and junior colleges: A recent profile*. Washington, D.C.: American Council on Education.

Apple, Michael. 1979. *Ideology and curriculum*. Boston: Routledge and Kegan Paul.

———. 1982. *Education and power*. Boston: Routledge and Kegan Paul.

———. 1988. *Teachers and texts*. New York: Routledge and Kegan Paul.

Aronowitz, Stanley, and Henry Giroux. 1985. *Education under siege*. Westport, Conn.: Greenwood, Bergin-Garvey.

———. 1991. *Postmodern education: Politics, culture, and social criticism*. Minneapolis: University of Minnesota Press.

Ashton-Warner, Sylvia. 1979. *Teacher*. New York: Bantam. Originally published 1963.

Association of American Colleges. 1985. *Integrity in the college curriculum*. Washington, D.C.: Association of American Colleges.

Atwell, Nancie. 1987. Class-based writing research: Teachers learning from students. In *Reclaiming the classroom: Teacher research as an agency for change*, ed. Goswami and Stillman. Upper Montclair, N.J.: Boynton-Cook.

Auerbach, Elsa, and Nina Wallerstein. 1987. *ESL for action: Problem-posing at work*. Reading, Mass.: Addison-Wesley.

Bagdikian, Ben. 1987. *The media monopoly*. Boston: Beacon.

Banks, James. 1981. *Multiethnic education: Theory and practice*. Boston: Allyn and Bacon.

———. 1991. A curriculum for empowerment, action, and change. In *Empowerment through multicultural education*, ed. Sleeter.

Barnes, Douglas. 1976. *From community to curriculum.* Harmondsworth, Eng.: Penguin.

Bennett, Kathleen. 1991. Doing school in an urban Appalachian first grade. In *Empowerment through multicultural education,* ed. Sleeter.

Berlin, James. 1987. *Rhetoric and reality: Writing instruction in American colleges, 1900–1985.* Carbondale: Southern Illinois University Press.

————. 1988. Rhetoric and ideology in the writing class. *College English* 50 (September): 474–94.

Bigelow, William. 1985. *Strangers in their own country: A curriculum guide on South Africa.* Trenton, N.J.: Africa World Press.

————. 1987a. *The power in our hands: A curriculum in the history of workers in the United States.* New York: Monthly Review.

————. 1987b. *Witness to Apartheid: A teaching guide.* San Francisco: Southern Africa Media Center of California Newsreel.

————. 1989. Discovering Columbus: Rereading the past. *Language Arts* 66 (October): 635–43.

Bissex, Glenda. 1980. *Gnys at wrk: A child learns to write and read,* Cambridge: Harvard University Press.

Bloom, Allan. 1987. *The closing of the American mind.* New York: Simon and Schuster.

Boomer, Garth. 1987. Addressing the problem of elsewhereness: A case for action research in the schools. In *Reclaiming the classroom,* ed. Goswami and Stillman.

Booth, Wayne. 1989. Foreword. In *The English Coalition Conference: Democracy through language,* ed. Richard Lloyd-Jones and Andrea Lunsford. Urbana, Ill.: National Council of Teachers of English.

Bourdieu, Pierre, and Jean-Claude Passeron. 1977. *Reproduction in education, society, and culture.* Beverly Hills, Calif.: Sage.

Bowles, Samuel, and Herbert Gintis. 1976. *Schooling in capitalist America.* New York: Basic Books.

Boyer, Ernest. 1983. *High school: A report on secondary education in America.* New York: Harper and Row.

Britton, James, Tony Burgess, Nancy Martin, Alex McLeod, and Harold Rosen. 1975. *The development of writing abilities (11–18),* London: Macmillan.

Britzman, Deborah. 1986. Cultural myths in the making of a teacher: Biography and social structure in teacher education. *Harvard Educational Review* 56 (November): 442–56.

Brookfield, Stephen D. 1987. *Developing critical thinkers: Challenging adults to explore alternative ways of thinking and acting.* San Francisco: Jossey-Bass.

Brown, Cynthia. 1987. Literacy in thirty hours: Paulo Freire's process in northeast Brazil. In *Freire for the classroom,* ed. Shor.

Bruner, Jerome. 1959. Learning and thinking. *Harvard Educational Review* 29 (Summer): 184–92.

Cazden, Courtney. 1988. *Classroom discourse: The language of teaching and learning.* Portsmouth, N.H.: Heinemann.

Christensen, Linda. 1990. Teaching Standard English: Whose standard? *English Journal* 79 (February): 36–40.

Clark, Burton. 1960. The cooling-out function in higher education. *American Journal of Sociology* 65 (May): 569–76.

———. 1978. The cooling-out function revisited. In *New directions for the community colleges*, ed. George Vaughan. San Francisco: Jossey-Bass.

Cohen, Arthur, and Florence Brawer. 1982. *The American community college.* San Francisco: Jossey-Bass.

College Board. 1991. *College-bound seniors: 1991 profile of SAT and achievement test takers.* New York: College Board.

Comer, James. 1980. *School power.* New York: Free Press.

Cox, Murray. 1990. Paulo Freire: Interview. *Omni* 12 (April): 74–94.

Cross, Patricia K. 1971. *Beyond the open door.* San Francisco: Jossey-Bass.

Cummins, Jim. 1989. *Empowering minority students.* Sacramento: California Association for Bilingual Education.

Dewey, John. 1963. *Experience and education.* New York: Collier. Originally published 1938.

———. 1966. *Democracy and education.* New York: Free Press. Originally published 1916.

———. 1971a. *The school and society.* Chicago: University of Chicago Press. Originally published 1900.

———. 1971b. *The child and the curriculum.* Chicago: University of Chicago Press. Originally published 1900.

———. 1975. *Moral principles in education.* Carbondale: Southern Illinois University Press. Originally published 1909.

Digest of Education Statistics. 1989. Washington, D.C.: Department of Education.

Elbow, Peter. 1986. *Embracing contraries: Explorations in learning and teaching.* New York: Oxford University Press.

Elsasser, Nan, and Patricia Irvine. 1987. English and Creole: The dialectics of choice in a college writing program. In *Freire for the classroom*, ed. Shor.

Emig, Janet. 1987. Non-magical thinking: Presenting writing developmentally in schools. In *Reclaiming the classroom*, ed. Goswami and Stillman.

Fine, Michelle. 1987. Silencing in public schools. *Language Arts* 64 (February): 157–74.

Frankenstein, Marilyn. 1987. Critical mathematics education: An application of Paulo Freire's epistemology. In *Freire for the classroom*, ed. Shor.

———. 1989. *Relearning mathematics: A different third R—radical maths.* London: Free Association.

Frankenstein, Marilyn, and Arthur Powell. 1991. Ethnomathematics and Paulo Freire's epistemology. Paper presented at the research pre-session of the sixty-ninth annual meeting of the National Council of Teachers of Mathematics, 15 July, New Orleans.

Freire, Paulo. 1970. *Pedagogy of the oppressed.* New York: Seabury.

———. 1973. *Education for critical consciousness.* New York: Seabury.

———. 1978. *Pedagogy in process,* New York: Continuum.

———— (with David Dillon). 1985a. Reading the world and reading the word: An interview with Paulo Freire. *Language Arts* 62 (January): 15–21.

————. 1985b. *The politics of education: Culture, power, and liberation.* Westport, Conn.: Greenwood, Bergin-Garvey.

————. 1990. Interview. *Omni* 12 (April): 74–94.

Freire, Paulo, and Antonio Faundez. 1989. *Learning to question: A pedagogy of liberation.* New York: Continuum.

Freire, Paulo, and Donaldo Macedo. 1987. *Literacy: Reading the word and the world.* Westport, Conn.: Greenwood, Bergin-Garvey.

Fulwiler, Toby. 1987. *Teaching with writing.* Portsmouth, N.H.: Heinemann, Boynton-Cook.

Fulwiler, Toby, and Arthur Young, eds. 1982. *Language connections: Writing and reading across the curriculum.* Urbana, Ill.: National Council of Teachers of English.

Giroux, Henry. 1978. Writing and critical thinking in the social studies. *Curriculum Inquiry* 8 (Autumn): 291–310.

————. 1983. *Theory and resistance in education: A pedagogy for the opposition.* Westport, Conn.: Greenwood, Bergin-Garvey.

————. 1988. *Schooling and the struggle for public life: Critical pedagogy in the modern age.* Minneapolis: University of Minnesota Press.

Goodlad, John. 1984. *A place called school: Prospects for the future.* New York: McGraw-Hill.

————. 1990. *Teachers for our nation's schools.* San Francisco: Jossey-Bass.

Goswami, Dixie, and Peter Stillman, eds. 1987. *Reclaiming the classroom: Teacher research as an agency for change.* Portsmouth, N.H.: Heinemann, Boynton-Cook.

Gould, Stephen Jay. 1981. *The mismeasurement of man.* New York: W. W. Norton.

Greene, Maxine. 1988. *The dialectic of freedom.* New York: Teachers College Press.

Heath, Shirley Brice. 1978. *Teacher-talk: Language in the classroom.* Washington, D.C.: Center for Applied Linguistics.

————. 1982. What no bedtime story means: Narrative sills at home and school. *Language in Society* 11 (April): 49–76.

————. 1983. *Ways with words: Language, life, and work in communities and classrooms.* Cambridge: Cambridge University Press.

————. 1987. A lot of talk about nothing. In *Reclaiming the Classroom,* ed. Goswami and Stillman.

Highlander Education and Research Center. 1987. *Mission statement.* Newmarket, Tenn.: Highlander Education and Research Center.

Hirsch, E. D. 1987. *Cultural literacy: What every American needs to know.* Boston: Houghton Mifflin.

————, ed. 1989. *A first dictionary of cultural literacy: What our children need to know.* Boston: Houghton Mifflin.

Hirsch, E. D., Joseph F. Kett, and James Trefil, eds. 1988. *The dictionary of cultural literacy: What every American needs to know.* Boston: Houghton Mifflin.

Hirshon, Sheryl. 1983. *And also teach them to read.* Westport, Conn.: Lawrence Hill.

Hope, Ann, and Sally Timmel. 1984. *Training for transformation.* 3 vols. Illustrated by C. Hodzi. Zimbabwe: Mambo.

Horton, Myles, and Paulo Freire. 1990a. *We make the road by walking: Conversations on education and social change.* Philadelphia: Temple University Press.

Horton, Myles, with Judith Kohl and Herbert Kohl. 1990b. *The long haul: An autobiography.* New York: Doubleday.

Judy, Stephen. 1980. *The ABCs of literacy: A guide for parents and educators.* New York: Oxford University Press.

Kagan, Spencer. 1986. Cooperative learning and sociocultural factors in schooling. In *Beyond language: Social and cultural factors in schooling language minority students.* Los Angeles: Evaluation, Dissemination, and Assessment Center, California State University.

Kirkwood, Gerri, and Colin Kirkwood. 1989. *Living adult education: Freire in Scotland.* Milton-Keynes, Eng.: Open University.

Knoblauch, C. H., and Lil Brannon. 1984. *Rhetorical traditions and the teaching of writing.* Upper Montclair, N.J.: Boynton-Cook.

Koepke, Mary. 1991. The power to be a professional. *Teacher* 2 (August): 35–41.

Kohl, Herbert. 1969. *The open classroom.* New York: New York Review.

Kozol, Jonathan. 1987. *Illiterate America.* New York: Doubleday.

———. 1991. *Savage inequalities: Children in America's schools.* New York: Crown.

Kuhn, Thomas. 1962. *The structure of scientific revolutions.* Chicago: University of Chicago Press.

Ladestro, Debra. 1991. Making a change for good. *Teacher* 2 (August): 42–45.

Lankshear, Colin, with Moira Lawler. 1989. *Literacy, schooling and revolution.* Philadelphia: Falmer.

Lester, Nancy, and Cynthia Onore. 1990. *Learning change: One school district meets language across the curriculum.* Portsmouth, N.H.: Heinemann, Boynton-Cook.

Levin, Henry M. 1987. Accelerated schools for disadvantaged students. *Educational Leadership* 6 (March): 19–21.

———. 1988. *Accelerated schools for at-risk students.* CPRE Research Report Series RR-010. New Brunswick, N.J.: Center for Policy Research in Education, Rutgers University.

———. 1990. At-risk students in a yuppie age. *Educational Policy* 4 (November): 283–95.

McLaren, Peter. 1986. *Schooling as a ritual performance: Towards a political economy of educational symbols and gestures.* London: Routledge and Kegan Paul.

———. 1989. *Life in schools: An introduction to critical pedagogy in the foundations of education.* New York: Longman.

Mayher, John. 1990. *Uncommon sense: Theoretical practice in language education.* Portsmouth, N.H.: Heinemann, Boynton-Cook.

Mayher, John, Nancy Lester, and Gordon Pradl. 1983. *Learning to write/writing to learn.* Upper Montclair, N.J.: Boynton-Cook.

Meier, Daniel. 1990. "Take children's opinions seriously": A talk with Bruno Bettelheim. *Teacher* 1 (August): 6–7.

Meier, Terry. 1989. The case against standardized achievement tests. *Rethinking Schools* 3 (January–February): 9–12.

Meisenheimer, Joseph R. 1990. Black college graduates in the labor market, 1979 and 1989. *Monthly Labor Review* 113 (November): 13–21.

Miller, Valerie. 1985. *Between struggle and hope: The Nicaraguan Literacy Crusade.* Boulder, Colo.: Westview.

Monthly Labor Review. 1989. Selected issues, Washington D.C.: Department of Commerce.

Mortenson, Thomas G. 1991. *Equity of higher educational opportunity for women, black, Hispanic, and low income students.* ACT Student Financial Aid Research Report series, no. 91–1, January 1991. Iowa City: American College Testing Program.

Mortenson, Thomas G., and Zhijun Wu. 1990. *High school graduation and college preparation of young adults, by family income and background, 1970–1989.* Report no. 90–3, September 1990. Iowa City: American College Testing Program.

National Institute of Education. 1984. *Involvement in learning.* Washington D.C.: Department of Education.

Oakes, Jeannie. 1985. *Keeping track: How schools structure inequality.* New Haven: Yale University Press.

Ohmann, Richard. 1976. *English in America: A radical view of the profession.* New York: Oxford University Press.

Ooka Pang, Valerie. 1991. Teaching children about social issues. In *Empowerment through multicultural education,* ed. Sleeter.

Owen, David. 1985. *None of the above: Behind the myth of scholastic aptitude.* Boston: Houghton Mifflin.

Parenti, Michael. 1988. *Inventing reality: The politics of the mass media.* New York: St.Martin's.

Perr, Herb. 1988. *Making art together.* San Jose, Calif.: Resource Publications.

Peterson, Robert. 1989a. The struggle for a decent school. *Forward Motion* 8 (February–March): 26–29.

———. 1989b. "Don't mourn—organize": Teachers take the offensive against basals. *Theory into Practice* 28 (Autumn): 295–99.

———. 1991. Transforming school and community in Milwaukee. Speech delivered to the Institute in honor of Paulo Freire's seventieth birthday, New York, 7 December 1991.

Piaget, Jean. 1979. *Science of education and the psychology of the child.* New York: Penguin. Originally published 1969.

Pincus, Fred. 1980. The false promises of community colleges: Class conflict and vocational education. *Harvard Educational Review* 50 (August): 332–61.

Ravitch, Diane, and Chester Finn. 1987. *What do our seventeen-year-olds know?* New York: Harper and Row.

Sapon-Schevin, Mara, and Nancy Schniedewind. 1991. Cooperative learning as empowering pedagogy. In *Empowerment through multicultural education,* ed. Sleeter.

Schmitt, Carl. 1989. *Changes in educational attainment: A comparison among 1972* and 1980 and 1982 high school seniors. Report no. C589413, Office of Educational Research and Improvement, April 1989, Washington, D.C.: U.S. Department of Education.

Schniedewind, Nancy, and Ellen Davidson. 1983. Open minds to equality: Learning activities to promote race, sex, class, and age equity. Englewood Cliffs, N.J.: Prentice-Hall.

———. 1987. Cooperative learning, cooperative lives: A sourcebook of learning activities for building a peaceful world. Dubuque, Iowa: William C. Brown.

Shor, Ira. 1977. Reinventing daily life: Self-study and the theme of "work." College English 39 (December): 502–6.

———. 1986. Equality is excellence: Transforming teacher education and the learning process. Harvard Educational Review 56 (November): 406–26.

———. 1987a. Critical teaching and everyday life. Chicago: University of Chicago Press. Originally published 1980.

———, ed. 1987b. Freire for the classroom: A sourcebook for liberatory teaching. Portsmouth, N.H.: Heinemann.

———. 1988. Working hands and critical minds: A Paulo Freire model for job-training. Journal of Education 170:102–21.

——— (with David Dillon). 1990. Liberation education: An interview. Language Arts 67 (April): 342–52.

———. 1992. Culture wars: School and society in the conservative restoration, 1969–1991. Chicago: University of Chicago Press. Originally published 1986.

Shor, Ira, and Paulo Freire. 1987. A pedagogy for liberation: Dialogues on transforming education. Westport, Conn.: Greenwood, Bergin-Garvey.

Silberman, Charles. 1970. Crisis in the classroom: The remaking of American education. New York: Vintage.

Sizer, Theodore. 1984. Horace's compromise: The dilemmas of the American high school. Boston: Houghton Mifflin.

Slavin, Robert. 1987. Cooperative learning and the cooperative school. Educational Leadership 45 (November): 7–13.

———. 1988. Cooperative learning and student achievement. Educational Leadership 45 (October): 31–33.

Sleeter, Christine. 1991. Empowerment through multicultural education. Albany: State University of New York Press.

Smith, Frank. 1983. Essays into literacy. Portsmouth, N.H.: Heinemann.

Sola, Michelle, and Adrian Bennett. 1985. The struggle for voice: Narrative, literacy, and consciousness in an East Harlem school. Journal of Education 167:88–109.

Solorzano, Daniel. 1989. Teaching and social change: Reflections on a Freirian approach in a college classroom. Teaching Sociology 17 (April): 218–25.

Spring, Joel. 1989. The sorting machine revisited: National educational policy since 1945. New York: Longmans. Updated, original edition 1976.

Thompson, E. P., and Dan Smith. 1981. Protest and survive. New York: Monthly Review.

United States Census Bureau. 1989. Current population reports. Series P-60, no. 162. Consumer income. February. Washington, D.C.: Department of Commerce.

Vygotsky, Lev. 1962. *Thought and language*. Cambridge: MIT Press.

Wallerstein, Nina. 1983. *Language and culture in conflict: Problem-posing in the ESL classroom*. Reading, Mass.: Addison-Wesley.

Weiler, Kathleen. 1988. *Women teaching for change: Gender, class, and power*. Westport, Conn.: Greenwood, Bergin-Garvey.

Wertsch, J. V. 1985. *Vygotsky and the social formation of mind*. Cambridge: Cambridge University Press.

Williams, Selase W. 1991. Classroom use of African American language: Educational tool or social weapon? In *Empowerment through multicultural education*, ed. Sleeter.

Willis, Paul. 1981. *Learning to labor: How working class kids get working class jobs*. New York: Columbia University Press.

Zinn, Howard. 1980. *A people's history of the United States*. New York: Harper and Row.

Author Index

Ada, Alma Flor, 151
Adams, Frank, 194
American Council on Education, 107
Apple, Michael, 13, 14, 19
Aronowitz, Stanley, 190
Ashton-Warner, Sylvia, 101
Atwell, Nancie, 174
Auerbach, Elsa, 43

Bagdikian, Ben, 57, 81, 93
Banks, James, 14, 16, 34
Barnes, Douglas, 94
Bennett, Adrian, 98
Bennett, Kathleen, 140, 141
Bigelow, William, 69, 118–23
Bissex, Glenda, 21
Bloom, Allan, 32
Boomer, Garth, 170
Booth, Wayne, 146–47
Bourdieu, Pierre, 250
Bowles, Samuel, 19, 115, 141
Boyer, Ernest, 33
Brannon, Lil, 75
Brawer, Florence, 99
Britton, James, 187
Britzman, Deborah, 27
Brookfield, Stephen, 146
Brown, Cynthia, 46
Bruner, Jerome, 26

Cazden, Courtney, 94
Christensen, Linda, 53, 118–23
Clark, Burton, 18, 110
Cohen, Arthur, 99
College Board, 107
Comer, James, 140-41

Cox, Murray, 55
Cross, Patricia K., 99
Cummins, Jim, 50, 62, 112–13, 151, 202

Davidson, Ellen, 24, 140, 151–52, 179–82, 189
de Olave, Maria, 151
Dewey, John, 18, 23, 33, 47, 98–99, 136–37, 143, 177–78
Digest of Education Statistics, 106, 107

Elbow, Peter, 23
Elsasser, Nan, 48–49, 254
Emig, Janet, 174

Faundez, Antonio, 52
Fine, Michelle, 98
Finn, Chester, 32
Frankenstein, Marilyn, 58, 76, 147–50
Freire, Paulo, 12, 22–23, 29, 31, 33, 35, 47–48, 52, 59, 77–78, 86, 87
Fulwiler, Toby, 187

Gintis, Herbert, 19, 115, 141
Giroux, Henry, 14, 16, 22, 26–27, 57, 77, 141, 177, 190
Goodlad, John, 26, 33, 97, 101–2, 107, 196, 202
Goswami, Dixie, 173–74
Gould, Stephen Jay, 125

Heath, Shirley Brice, 92, 98, 175–77
Highlander Education and Research Center, 194

273

Hirsch, E. D., 32, 105, 119
Hirshon, Sheryl, 100
Hope, Ann, 100
Horton, Myles, 25–26

Irvine, Patricia, 48–49, 253–54

Judy, Stephen, 75, 177

Kagan, Spencer, 165
Kirkwood, Colin, 45, 100, 171, 192–94, 206–9
Kirkwood, Gerri, 45, 100, 171, 192–94, 206–9
Knoblauch, C. H., 75
Koepke, Mary, 172
Kohl, Herbert, 75
Kozol, Jonathan, 250
Kuhn, Thomas, 201

Ladestro, Debra, 173
Lester, Nancy, 187
Levin, Henry M., 140

Macedo, Donaldo, 52, 100
McLaren, Peter, 16, 109
Mayher, John, 187
Meier, Daniel, 11
Meier, Terry, 110
Meisenheimer, Joseph R., 107
Miller, Valerie, 101
Monthly Labor Review, 107
Mortenson, Thomas G., 106–7

National Institute of Education, 21–22

Oakes, Jeannie, 19, 115, 140, 141
Ogbu, John, 109
Ooka Pang, Valerie, 45–46
Owen, David, 110

Parenti, Michael, 128
Perr, Herb, 186
Peterson, Robert, 50-51
Piaget, Jean, 11–12, 17
Pincus, Fred, 74
Powell, Arthur, 58, 76
Pradl, Gordon, 187

Ravitch, Diane, 32

Sapon-Schevin, Mara, 23–24, 164–65, 166
Schmitt, Carl, 106
Schniedewind, Nancy, 23–24, 140, 151–52, 164–65, 166, 179–82, 189
Shor, Ira, 22–23, 86, 87, 131, 150, 166, 191, 239, 258
Silberman, Charles, 18, 97, 98
Sizer, Theodore, 97–98, 140, 142
Slavin, Robert, 140
Smith, Dan, 7
Smith, Frank, 21
Sola, Michelle, 98
Solorzano, Daniel, 182–84, 189
Spring, Joel, 19
Stillman, Peter, 173–74

Thompson, E. P., 7
Timmel, Sally, 100

Vygotsky, Lev, 203

Wallerstein, Nina, 43, 202
Wertsch, J. V., 21
Williams, Selase W., 49, 53
Willis, Paul, 137
Wu, Zhijun, 106–7

Young, Arthur, 187

Zinn, Howard, 124, 125

Subject Index

Ability grouping. *See* Tracking
Academic canons, 31–35, 103–5, 256.
    See also Transfer of information
Academic community
    resistance to critical pedagogy, 34–35
    scholarship, 170–71, 233, 235
Academic subjects
    placing in social context, 144–58
    teaching dialogically, 73–84, 89–90,
    103–5, 238
Academic themes, and dialogic pedag-
    ogy, 55, 73–84
Accelerated perception, in mass culture,
    131–32, 219
Accelerated Schools program, 140
Achievement tests, 106
Active modes of education, 17, 21–22.
    See also Participation
Activism, 17, 130, 188–99
    critical education as, 195–96
    obstacles to, 195–96
    student projects, 183–85, 252
    student resistance to, 6–7, 195
Ada, Alma Flor, 151
Adult Learning Project (Edinburgh),
    100, 171, 192–94, 206–10
Affective development, of students, 217–
    18, 223–24, 232
    integrating with cognitive develop-
    ment, 23–26
    role of dialogue in, 86–87
Affective environment, inequality in, 141
Affective value of empowering educa-
    tion, 17, 21–30
Affirmative action, student attitudes to-
    ward, 227

African-Americans
    access to education, 106
    dialects, 49–50
    early experiences with language, 175–
    76
    educational gains vs. economic stagna-
    tion, 107–8
Afro-Caribbeans, 48–50, 51–52, 253–54
After-class group, practicing democratic
    authority through, 161–63
Aggression, humor as, 257
Alternative media, 116–17, 189
American College Testing Program, 106
American Dream (literature course), 28–
    29, 242
Amplified perception, in mass culture,
    219
Animators, empowering educators as,
    100
Anthropological notion of culture, 58–
    60
Antidialogic styles. *See* Teacher-talk
Apartheid, as topical theme, 69–70
Apple, Michael, 19
Architecture, teaching, 37, 78
Art, teaching, 180–81, 186
Articulateness, of teacher, 234
Ashton-Warner, Sylvia, 101
Assessments. *See* Evaluation; Grades;
    Tests
Associated Press, 81
Association of American Colleges, 22
At-risk students, 165, 176–77
Attendance requirement, 27
Atwell, Nancie, 174
Auerbach, Elsa, 42–44

Authoritarian discourse. *See* Teacher-talk
Authority
  assertion of, by teachers, 102–3, 132,
    157, 234
  democratic (*see* Democratic authority)
  student resistance to, 137–39
  as theme, 43–44
  undemocratic, 18–21
Autobiographies. *See also* Personal narra-
    tives
  of students, 122–23
Avenue, 116

"Bananas for Breakfast," 181–82, 190
Banking model of education, 31–35
Banks, James, 16, 34
Bennett, Kathleen, 140, 141
Bettelheim, Bruno, 11, 27
Bidialectal education, 48–53, 253–54
Bigelow, William, 69–70, 118–23, 173
Bilingual education, 50–51, 151
Booth, Wayne, 146–47
Border culture, 201–6, 255–57
Bowles, Samuel, 19, 141
Boyz N the Hood, 117
Brazil, literacy programs, 46–48, 52, 58–
    60, 99–100, 197
Britzman, Deborah, 27
Bruner, Jerome, 26
Burnout, teacher, 20–21, 112, 233
Business
  goals for education, 143
  student attitudes toward, 231–32
Business news, critiquing, 39–41, 92,
    128–29

Caldicott, Helen, 68
Callenbach, Ernest, 250
Canons. *See* Academic canons
Capitalism
  as source of inequality, 141
  student attitudes toward, 231–32
Careerism, of students, 72–73, 74, 218
Career training, 143, 191–92
Caribbean dialects, 48–50, 51–52, 253–
    54
"Cash" language. *See* Standard English
Central bank of knowledge, 31–35
Change agency, 143, 190–94
  perceptions of, 126–28

Chapman, Tracy, 117
Cherokee Removal of 1832, 122–23
Chicanos, media stereotypes, 182–84
Children, early language development,
    17, 175–77
Christensen, Linda, 53, 70, 118–23, 173
CIO, 194
Citizenship. *See* Democracy
City University of New York, 1–9, 211–
    36
Clark, Burton, 18
Classroom events, using as themes, 258–
    59
Codes, 42–44, 208
Codeveloping the curriculum, 35–36,
    90–93, 240, 243–45. *See also* Par-
    ticipatory opening
  in academic subjects, 144–45
  in Adult Learning Project, 207–9
  with after-class group, 161–63
  in elementary grades, 151–52
Codifications, 42–44, 208
Cognitive levels, of students, 21, 217–
    18, 223–24
Coinvestigators, in community research,
    207–9
Collective text, 122–23
College graduation
  effect on income, 107
  rates, 106–8
College of Staten Island, 1–9, 211–36
College of the Virgin Islands, 48–52,
    253–54
The Color Purple, 82
Columbus, Christopher, 118–24, 173
Comedy. *See* Humor
Comer, James, 140–41
Common culture, academic canons as,
    256
Community coinvestigators, 207–9
Community colleges, 18–19, 99. *See also*
    College of Staten Island
  graduation rates, 107
Community idiom. *See* Dialects
Community research
  in Adult Learning Project, 171, 206–9
  by students, 180–85
  by teachers, 171–72
Community speakers, 49, 82, 253–54
Community speech. *See* Dialects

Commuting, 220–21
Competition, in classroom, 23–24
Competitive self-reliance. *See* Individualism
Composition classes. *See* Writing classes
Computer science, teaching, 36
Conceptual habit of mind, 112, 113
Conflict resolution, in classroom, 24–25, 210, 242–43
Congress of Industrial Organizations, 194
Consciousness, 126–30
Conservative reforms, 34, 105, 197–98, 215–16
Conspiracy for the Least, 142
Contending thought, in academic fields, 190–91
Context. *See* Situated learning
Contract grading, 159–61
Contras, as topical theme, 68–69
Control. *See* Authority
Convivality, as resource for teachers, 235
Cooling-out process, 18–19
Cooper, Vincent, 49, 253–54
Cooperative learning, 70–71
  as alternative to tracking, 140–41
  benefits for at-risk students, 164–65
  of literacy skills, 239–40
  in math classes, 150
Correction, of student papers, 163–64, 239–40
Counter-structure, problem-posing as, 260–63
Creole language
  Caribbean, 48–50, 51–52, 253–54
  in Guinea-Bissau, 52, 100
Critical consciousness, 126–30
Critical-democratic dialogue. *See* Dialogue
Critical-democratic pedagogy, defined, 15–17
Critical literacy
  defined, 129
  exercises in, 124, 186–87
Critical math, 58, 76, 147–50
  in elementary grades, 151–52
Critical paradigm, 200–204, 211, 216–23
Critical re-perception, 123–26
Critical transitivity, 126–30

Cross-cultural education, 123
Cross-disciplinary programs. *See* Interdisciplinary education
Cultural action for freedom, 188
Cultural inequality, 114–17, 201–2. *See also* Inequality
Cultural Literacy, 32, 105
Cultural literacy. *See* Academic canons
Cultural suicide, 109
Culture. *See also* Multicultural education
  Dewey's definition, 137
  dominant (*see* Academic canons)
  Freire's definition, 58–60
  integrating students' and teachers', 201–6, 255–57
  mass, 131, 219
  of students, 186, 202–4, 204–6, 211–16
Cummins, Jim, 62, 112–13, 202
Curiosity, as student resource, 17–18, 225–26
Cursing, as generative theme, 248–51

Daily life, use in curriculum. *See* Generative themes; Situated learning
Davidson, Ellen, 151–52, 171, 179–82, 185, 189, 190
Debate. *See also* Dialogue
  in academic fields, 190–91
  student resistance to, 72–73
  on topical themes, 64–65
Decelerating perception, 131–32, 219
Decoding, 208
Decontextualization, 175–76
Deficit model, 32–33, 200–201
Democracy
  effect of topical themes, 57–58, 62
  preparing students for, 16–18, 22, 143, 146–57
  as value in education, 16–17, 133–34, 135–37
Democratic authority, 16–17, 112–13, 135, 144–68
  in choosing topical themes, 55–57
  in leading dialogue, 87–93, 167–68
  lowering resistance to, 143–44, 157–58, 167
  in participatory opening, 237–39
  in problem-posing, 144–47
  structuring, 157–66, 260–63

Democratic authority (*continued*)
teacher resources for, 234–35
transition to, 184–85
Democratic values
in classroom, 166
of students, 226
de Olave, Maria, 151
Departmental structure, 233
Desocialization, 17, 114–18
and critical consciousness, 126–30
initiating, 133
permanent, 129–30
from received knowledge, 118–26
situated goals for, 130–33, 235
Deviance credits, 235
Dewey, John
on critical judgment, 177–78
on democracy, 136–37, 143
on participation, 18, 31
on "pouring in," 33, 47, 136
on subject-matter, 83–84, 145
on teaching language, 98–99
Dialects
excluding students', 95, 98, 100, 139, 221
including students', 48–52, 96, 253–54
Dialogic discourse. *See* Third idiom
Dialogic format, for tests, 178
Dialogic lectures, 246–52, 253–54
humor in, 257–58
Dialogue. *See also* Discourse
absence of, in classrooms, 96–98, 141
compared with teacher-talk, 93–96
conflict in, 210
democratic qualities, 87–88
in language teaching, 176–77
leading, 5–6, 113–14, 245–46, 261–63
models for, 88–93, 237–53
parent-child, 175–76
in social development, 86–87
student resistance to, 72, 93, 158–59, 167, 259–60
student resources for, 224
teacher resistance to, 99–105
teacher resources for, 112–14
third idiom, 77, 203, 254–63
undemocratic (*see* Teacher-talk)
as value in education, 17, 85–88

Dickens, Charles, 82
Dictation, as literacy exercise, 244
Dictionary of Cultural Literacy, 32, 105, 123–24
Didactic lectures, 74–75, 86, 96–97, 158–59, 246–47. *See also* Teacher-talk; Transfer of information
Digressions, as classroom obstacle to dialogue, 261
Directed Practice in Social Welfare, 182–84
Direct instruction, 96–97. *See also* Didactic lectures; Transfer of information
Disadvantaged students, 165, 176–77
Discourse. *See also* Dialogue; Teacher-talk
dialogic (*see* Dialogue)
politics of, 14–15
rules for, 160
in students' daily lives, 58, 68–69
styles of, 93–96
Discrimination. *See also* Inequality; Racism; Sexism
as classroom topic, 56, 151, 178–79
Discussion. *See* Dialogue
Distancing students, 102–3
Diversity, cultural. *See* Multicultural education
Domestication, 99
Domination of discussion
by students, 71, 95, 96
by teachers (*see* Teacher-talk)
Down These Mean Streets, 82
Dropout rates, 106–8, 109–11

Early development of children, 175–76
East Los Angeles Community College, 182–84
Economic policy, as topical theme, 64–66
Ecotopia, 250
Editing student papers, 132, 163–64, 239–40
Educational profession
research in, 170–71, 233
traditional training, 26–27, 232–33
Elementary grades
bilingual education, 50–51
critical math, 151–52
problem-posing, 45–46
Elsasser, Nan, 48–50, 51–52, 190, 253–54

Emerson, Ralph Waldo, 63
Emig, Janet, 174
Emotions. *See* Affective development
Employment, effect of education, 107–8
Empowering education
 defined, 15–17
 traditional educators' criticisms of, 105
Encyclopedic subject matter, 145–46
Endullment, 19–21
English. *See also* Language; Writing
 departments, 236
 dialects vs. standard, 48–53, 95, 96,
  139, 221, 253–54
 high-school classes, 118–23
 as interdisciplinary study, 75
 literature classes, 81–83, 152–56, 248–
  52
 remedial classes, 1–9
English as a Second Language, 42–44, 202
English Language Institute (College of
 Staten Island), 211
Entrance tests, college, 106, 212, 215. *See*
 also Placement tests
Environment, as topic, 248–51, 252
Equality. *See* Inequality
Errors, finding logic behind, 150, 172
Essential Schools, 140
Ethnomathematics, 147
Eurocentric canon. *See* Academic canons
Evaluation
 of course by students, 87, 162–63, 246
 of student learning (*see* Tests)
Examinations. *See* Tests
Experiential exercises. *See* Participatory
 experiences
Experientializing philosophy, 255–56
Experiential material. *See* Generative
 themes; Situated learning
Expository presentation. *See* Dialogic lec-
 tures
"Extraordinarily reexperiencing the ordi-
 nary," 122, 182
Eye contact, as classroom resource for
 problem-posing, 262–63

Failure rates, 107, 109–11
Fairness, as theme, 45
Family life
 of students, 222–23
 as theme, 248–51

Fate of the Earth, 68
Feelings. *See* Affective development
Feminism, of students, 229–31
Feminist studies, academic resistance to,
 34–35
Films, stereotypes in, 182–84
First day of class. *See* Participatory open-
 ing
A First Dictionary of Cultural Literacy, 32,
 105, 123–24
Focusing discussion, 113–14
Food industry, as topic, 149
Foreign policy, as topic, 67–69
For Whom the Bell Tolls, 82
Frankenstein, Marilyn, 58, 147–50, 185,
 187
Fratney School, 50–51
Freedom, fear of, 234
Freire, Paulo
 on activism, 188
 on "banking education," 31–35, 200
 on consciousness, 22–23, 126–28
 on culture, 58–60
 on dialogue, 86–87
 on generative themes, 55
 on joy, 25–26
 literacy programs, 46–48, 52, 58–60,
  99–100, 197
 on participation, 29
 on situating academic content, 77–78
 on summarizing, 166
 on teachers, 99–100
Frontal pedagogy, 96–97. *See also*
 Teacher-talk
Fundamentalist families, 176
Funding
 cuts in, 233
 inequities in, 15, 104, 105, 136–37

Gang Exploitation Film Committee, 183–
 84
Garbage, as theme, 258–59
General education, 145
Generation gap, 155
Generative themes, 46–48, 55
 examples, 2–5, 254
 leading to topical themes, 60–61
Generative words, 46–47, 58–59
Getting by, student resistance as, 132,
 138–39, 142

"Getting through the Day," 43–44
Gintis, Herbert, 19, 141
Giroux, Henry, 16, 22, 26–27, 57, 77, 141, 177
Goodlad, John, 26, 97, 101–2, 196, 202
Grades
    narrative, 132, 144
    negotiating, 159–61
    raising, 163
    student manipulation of, 138
Graduation rates, 106–8, 109–11
Grammar, self-correction of, 163–64, 244
Great equalizer, education as, 103–11, 141
Group reports, 70–71, 89, 240–41, 243
Groups of two, 2–3, 38, 39
Guinea-Bissau, literacy program, 52, 100

Hard Times, 82
Having the last word, as teacherly ritual, 132, 157, 166–67, 180–81, 208
Health, of students, 223
Health care, as topic, 46
Health science, teaching, 36–37
Heath, Shirley Brice, 98, 175–77
Hemingway, Ernest, 82
Henry IV, 82, 152–56
Henry V, 152–56
Hierarchy, in educational profession, 170–71, 233
Hierarchy of needs, 62
High achievers, from disadvantaged communities, 108–11
Highlander Center, 25–26, 194
High-school graduation rates, 106
Hirsch, E. D., 32, 105, 123–24
Hispanics
    access to education, 107
    stereotypes, 182–84
Historical perspective, on subject matter, 191
History
    critical re-perception of, 118–26
    mural project, 180–81
    problem-posing in, 76–77
    teaching through literature, 152–56
Honduras, 181–82
Hope, Ann, 100
Horton, Myles, 25–26, 194
Human agency, perception of, 126–28

Humor, 232, 257–60
Hunger, as topic, 181–82

Idiom. See Dialects
Impatience, 25
Income
    and access to education, 106–7
    effect of education on, 107–8
Individualism, 61, 63–64, 108–11, 118, 178–79, 190
Indoctrination, avoiding, 66–67, 196–97, 252
Inequality. See also Discrimination; Racism; Sexism
    in access to education, 18–19, 106–8, 114–15
    cultural, 201–2
    in early childhood experiences, 175–76
    education's failure to eliminate, 103–11, 141
    North-South, 181–82
    questioning, 178–85
    in social experiences, 114–17
    of tracking, 140–41
Injustice
    student experiences, 122–23
    as theme, 45–46
Institutional biographies of teachers, 27
Institutional work, 234
Instrument, knowledge as, 72–73
Integrated community-school approach, 140–41
Interdisciplinary education, 17, 185–88
    in academic courses, 75–76
    integrating language, 98–99, 187–88
Interruptions, by students, 95, 96, 221
Interventions, by teacher, 245–46
Intransitive consciousness, 126
Introductory courses, in academic subjects, 145–46
Irvine, Patricia, 48–50, 51–52, 190, 253–54

Job training, 143, 191–92
Journalism, teaching, 28, 79–81, 251. See also Mass media
Journal keeping
    by students, 131, 150
    by teachers, 173
Joy, as affective value in learning, 25–26

Judy, Stephen, 75, 177
Justice, as theme, 45–46

Kagan, Spencer, 165
Kalikow, Peter, 116
Key words, of student culture, 133, 241
Kirkwood, Colin, 45, 192–94, 206–9
Kirkwood, Gerri, 45, 192–94, 206–9
Kitagawa, Mary, 172
Knowledge. *See also* Academic canons;
    Transfer of information non-neutrality
    of, 12–14, 34–35, 41, 48
Kohl, Herbert, 75–76

Labor
    as information source, 192
    in news media, 40–41, 92, 128–29
    workshops for, 25, 194
Language. *See also* Dialects; English; Literacy; Writing
    critiquing, 120–21
    early childhood development, 17, 175–77
    integrating into curriculum, 98–99, 187–88
    politics of, 48–53
    scholarly, 170
    skills exercises, 176–77, 186, 239–40, 243, 244
    students', 221, 224
Language detectives, 177
Last word, as teacherly ritual, 132, 157, 166–67, 180–81, 208
Latinos, stereotypes, 182–84
Law
    interdisciplinary teaching, 185–86
    study in literature, 152–55
Laying down the law, as teacherly ritual, 132, 157
Leadership, of teacher. *See* Democratic authority
Learning community, 38, 259
Learning contracts, 159–61
Lectures. *See also* Teacher-talk
    dialogic, 246–54
    didactic, 74–75, 86, 96–97, 158–59, 246–47
Less than zero, as metaphor of obstacles to learning, 201, 210, 211, 217–23, 232–34

Levin, Henry M., 140
Liberation, Freire's definition, 33
Life experience
    in curriculum (*see* Generative themes;
    Situated learning)
    as resource for students, 224–25
Listening to students, 259, 262–63
Literacy. *See also* Language; Writing
    critical, 124, 129, 185–87
    cultural (*see* Academic canons)
    math, 148–50
    skills exercises, 186–87, 239–40, 243, 244
    of students, 221–22, 224
Literacy programs
    dialects in, 52
    dialogue in, 99–101
    generative themes in, 42–44, 46–48
    politics of, 197
    topical themes in, 58–60
Literature, themes in, 81–83, 152–56
Literature and Environment (course), 248–51, 252
Los Angeles Times, 182
Los Angeles Times Index, 183
Love of learning
    as student resource, 17–18, 225–26
    as teacher resource, 83–84, 234
Low achievers. *See* Disadvantaged students
Low performance. *See* Performance strike

McLaren, Peter, 16, 109
Madison Center, 34–35
Majoritarian interest, of dialogue, 110–11
Malraux, André, 82
Mann, Horace, 103
Man's Fate, 82
Maslow, Abraham, 62
Mass culture, effect on students, 131, 219
Mass education. *See also* Traditional education
    inequality in, 18–19
    as socialization, 115
    student resistance to, 135–37
Mass media
    course on, 39–41, 79–81, 89–93
    critiquing, 28, 128–29, 186, 249–50
    influence of, 115–17, 219, 222
    stereotypes in, 182–84

Math
  critical, 58, 76, 147–52
  literacy courses, 148–50
Media. *See* Mass media
The Media Monopoly, 93
Medicine, interdisciplinary teaching of,
    185–86
Military spending, as topic for math
    classes, 148–49
Miller, Valerie, 101
Minority students. *See also* Dialects; Rac-
    ism
  access to education, 105–10
  benefits of cooperative learning for,
    165, 176–77
  participation by, 6
  in school culture, 202
Mixed-ability groups, 140–41
Model, for problem-posing, 237–53
More than zero, as metaphor of resources
    for learning, 201, 210, 211, 223–32,
    234–36
Mortenson, Thomas G., 106–7
Multicultural education, 17, 46–53
  academic resistance to, 34–35
Mural project, 180–81
Murdoch, Rupert, 116
Mutuality, of dialogue, 85–87

Narrative grading, 132, 144
National Assessment of Education Pro-
    gress, 106
National Association of Scholars, 34–35
National Institute of Education, 21–22
Negotiation, of class requirements, 27,
    157–61
Neutral knowledge. *See* Knowledge, non-
    neutrality of
News media, critiquing, 28, 39–41, 79–
    81, 89–93, 128–29
Newspapers, 39–41, 90–93
New York Post, 115–16
New York Times, 68
New York Times Index, 183
Nicaragua
  Literary Crusade, 100–101
  as topical theme, 68–69
"Nightly Business Report," 40
Normative views, of students, 72
North-South inequality, as topic, 181–82

Nuclear arms race, as topic, 7, 68–69
Nuclear Madness, 68
Nutrition, of students, 223

Oakes, Jeannie, 140, 141
Obstacles, to empowering education,
    216–23, 232–34. *See also* Student re-
    sistance; Teacher resistance
Occupational training, 143, 191–92
Ogbu, John, 109
Ooka Pang, Valerie, 45–46
Open admissions, 213, 214–15
Opening classes. *See* Participatory open-
    ing
Organic readers, 101
Organizing. *See* Activism
Orthodoxy. *See* Academic canons
Orthography, for nonstandard languages
    and dialects, 48–52, 254

Paired discussions, 2–3, 38, 39
Paradigm shift, critical pedagogy as, 201
Parents, effect on early language develop-
    ment, 175–77
Participation
  statistics on, 97–98
  student resistance to, 6, 158–59
  as value in education, 17–23, 26–30, 33
Participatory academic problems, 79–81
Participatory experiences, 69–70, 120–21
Participatory opening in class, 26, 27–29,
    88–89, 146–47, 237–39
  examples, 120–21, 159–61
  for introducing topical themes, 60–63,
    67, 70–71
  for researching students, 172
Participatory research, 207–9
Passeron, Jean-Claude, 250
Passive absorption. *See* Transfer of infor-
    mation
Passivity, of students, 26, 72–73, 196–97
Patience, 25
Peer editing, 132, 164, 239–40
Peer evaluation, 164, 239–40
Peer pressure, and student resistance, 72,
    139, 167
People's History of the United States, 124, 125
Performance strike, student resistance as,
    20–21, 142–43, 223–24. *See also* Get-
    ting by

Permanent desocialization, 129–30
Permissiveness, 15–16, 160, 260
Perr, Herb, 186, 190
Personal growth, as theme, 62–64, 66, 178–79, 190
Personal narratives, 71, 148
Peterson, Robert, 50–51
Philosophizing experience, 255–56
Piaget, Jean, 11–12, 17, 31
Piercy, Marge, 82
Placement tests, 3–5, 9. *See also* Entrance tests
Play, 25–26
Playing dumb, as student resistance, 132, 135–39
Pledge of Allegiance, as topic, 45–46
Plots, reinventing, 155–56
"Political correctness," 34–35
Politics
  of education, 11–30 (*see also* Knowledge, non-neutrality of)
  introducing in classroom, 57–58, 62, 195–97
  in mass media, 91–93
  students' perception of, 91–93
Portfolio assessments, 144
Pouring in, 33, 136. *See also* Transfer of information
Powell, Arthur, 58
Power, in literature, 152–55
Power awareness, 129
Prereading exercises, 244
Price, Peter, 116
Primary sources
  in classroom research, 77, 177
  for community research, 207
Problem-posing, 17, 31, 35–54, 237–53. *See also* Participatory opening
  with academic subjects, 76–84, 89, 145–58
  democratic qualities, 144–47
  diagram of, 252–53
  models for, 2–3, 37–46, 237–53
  with participatory experiences, 120–21
  second-level, 241–43
  with topical themes, 60–61
Problem-solving, 43
Process, education as, 219
Process interventions, as function of dialogic teachers, 245

Product, education as, 219
Progressive education
  criticisms by traditional educators, 105
  Dewey's views on, 18, 47
  Protest and Survive, 7
Protests, student, 197–98
Public Broadcasting System, 40, 81
Public education. *See* Mass education
Publishing projects, student, 174
"Publish or perish," 233

Questioning schooling, 11, 114
Questionnaires, as used in classroom research, 68–69, 173
Question-response-evaluation pattern of classroom discourse, 98
Questions, asked by teachers, 94–95, 96, 98. *See also* Problem-posing

Racial subordination, 109, 202
Racism. *See also* Inequality; Minority students
  attitudes of students, 220, 226–29
  attitudes of teachers, 103
  of stereotypes in films, 182–85
  student experience of, 122–23, 126
  as topic, 63–65, 125–26
Radical democratic directiveness, 87
Readers, organic, 101
Readers' Guide to Periodical Literature, 183
Reading aloud
  as literacy exercise, 4, 131, 239–40
  to young children, 175
Reading matter, of students, 221–22
Readings. *See also* Textbooks
  integrating into curriculum, 6, 243–45
Reading skills. *See* Literacy
Reading the riot act, 132, 157
Rebellion. *See* Student resistance
Reflection, 22–23, 86
  on classroom dialogue, 113, 238–39
Reflective action, 86
Reflexive dialogue, 241–43
Reforms, conservative, 34, 105, 197–98, 215–16. *See also* Academic canons
Regressive values in mass culture, 114, 132–33, 219–20
Reinventing plots in literature, 155–56

Rejection
  students' right of, 57, 66, 133
  of topical themes, 65, 70–72
Remedial courses, 1–9, 233
Renegotiation of curriculum, 160–61
Re-presenting student responses, 113,
    241–43
Research, 169–85
  on community, 171–72, 180–85, 206–9
  as critical thought, 169, 177–78
  definitions of, 169–71
  scholarly, 170–71, 233, 235
  on student culture, 133, 202–6, 211–16
  by students, 171–73, 177–85
  on students, 90–91, 172–77, 241
  thematic, 178–85
  as value in education, 17, 169–71
  by young students, 151–52, 171, 176–
    77
Resistance. See Student resistance;
  Teacher resistance
Resources
  of students, 223–32
  of teachers, 113–14, 234–36
Responses, to dialogic lecture, 251–52
Restraint, of teacher's voice, 262
Rethinking Schools group, 50–51
Revision, of student papers, 163–64, 242
Richmond College, 211
Riot act, reading, as teacherly ritual, 132,
  157
Romeo and Juliet, 82
Roosevelt, Theodore, 63
Rules for speaking, 14–15, 160
Runaway shops, as topical theme, 64–66

Sabotaging education, 137–39, 261–62.
  See also Student resistance
Salic law, 152–53
Sapon-Shevin, Mara, 23–24
Sarcasm, 257
SATs, 106
Schell, Jonathan, 68
Schniedewind, Nancy, 23–24, 151–52,
  171, 179–82, 185, 189, 190
Scholarship, 233, 235
  traditional, 170–71, 233
Scholastic Aptitude Test, 106
Schooling, questioning, 11, 114

Science, teaching, 41–42, 78–79, 145–46,
  192
Scott, Sir Walter, 82
Secondary sources, for community re-
  search, 207
Second-level problem posing, 241–43
Sedimented histories, 26–27
Self-editing, 132, 163–64, 239–40
Self-education, 130
Self-esteem, of students, 225. See also Af-
  fective development
Self-reliance, 63. See also Individualism
Self-study, 90–91
Semi-transitive consciousness, 126–27
Setting, of classroom, 220–21
Sexism
  attitudes of students, 220, 229–31
  in classroom discourse, 8, 95, 96
  as topical theme, 65–66
Shakespeare, William, 82, 152–56
Short-answer questions, 94, 96, 98
Silberman, Charles, 18, 98
Silencing students, 93–101
Single issues, 92
Singleton, John, 117
Situated goals, for desocialization, 130–
  33, 235
Situated learning, 17, 42–53, 88. See also
  Generative themes
  of academic subjects, 76–84, 144–58
  of topical themes, 67–69, 70
Sizer, Theodore, 97–98, 140, 142
Skills exercises, 239–40, 243, 244
Skinner, B. F., 162, 242, 250
Slavery, 125
Slowing down, 131–32, 219
Social change. See Activism; Topical
  themes
Social development, role of critical dia-
  logue, 86–87
Social experience, 114–17
Social inequality. See Inequality
Socialization, 114–17. See also De-
  socializaton
  into democratic dialogue, 167–68
  education's role in, 11–14
  into inequality, 141
  resistance to, 116–17
  of teachers, 101–2

Social movements, 188–89, 197–99
Social Sciences Index, 183
Social welfare course, 182–84
Sociological Abstracts, 183
Sociology, teaching, 36, 182–84
Solorzano, Daniel, 182–84, 189, 190
South Africa, as topic, 69–70
Specialization, in academic community, 75–76
Standard English
 in bicultural education, 48–53, 96, 253–54
 as classroom language, 95, 139
Staten Island, 211–36
Stereotypes, in media, 182–84
Strangers in Their Own Country, 69
Structure, democratic, 158–63, 260–63
Student-centered pedagogy, defined, 15–17
Student protests, 197–98
Student resistance, 217
 to academic themes, 74
 to activism, 195
 dealing with, 143–44, 157–58
 to democratic authority, 143, 157–58, 167
 to dialogue, 93, 158–59, 167, 259–60
 getting by, 132, 138–39, 142
 playing dumb, 132, 135–39
 to topical themes, 65, 66–67, 70–73
 to traditional education, 20–21, 26
 to undemocratic authority, 135–39, 142, 261–62
 using as theme, 2–4
Students less than zero, as metaphor of resistance, 216–23
Students more than zero, as metaphor of participation, 223–32
Subject matter. *See* Academic subjects
Success, and education, 108–11
Summarizing. *See also* Having the last word
 of readings, 244
 with students, 96, 166–67, 180–81, 208
 by teacher, 95, 132
Syllabus, codeveloping. *See* Codeveloping the curriculum
Symbolic violence, 250–51

Synthesizing student responses, 113, 241–43

Talk. *See* Dialogue; Discourse; Teacher-talk
Taxes, as topic in math classes, 149
Teacher-centered education. *See* Traditional education
Teacher resistance
 to dialogue, 99–105, 256–57
 to empowering education, 232–34
Teachers
 discourse styles, 94–99
 education of, 26–27, 101–2, 232–33
 resources of, 113–14, 204, 234–36
Teachers less than zero, as metaphor of resistance, 232–34
Teachers more than zero, as metaphor of empowering resources, 234–36
Teacher-talk, 85, 93–101, 261–62. *See also* Didactic lectures; Transfer of information
 effect on students, 110–11, 112, 255–57, 261–62
 effect on teachers, 112
 reasons teachers use, 101–3
 student adaptations to, 138–39, 261–62
Telling. *See* Teacher-talk; Transfer of information
Tests
 college entrance, 106, 212, 215
 critical, 144, 178
 politics of, 15
 traditional, 144, 233
 of writing proficiency, 3–5, 9, 48–49, 50–51
Textbooks
 critiquing, 118, 119–24
 limitations of, 57–58, 221
Thematic interventions, 245
Thematic research, 179–85
Thinking examinations, 178
Thinking skills, of teachers, 234
Third idiom, 77, 203, 254–63
Thomas, Piri, 82
Time, allowed for classes, 87, 220–21, 234
Timmel, Sally, 100

Topical themes, 55–73
  discussion of in daily life, 58, 68–69
  introducing, 62–67, 70–71, 88–89
  student resistance to, 65, 66–67, 70–73
Tracking, 104, 105, 140–42
Traditional canons. *See* Academic canons
Traditional education. *See also* Teacher-
  talk; Transfer of information
  affective environment of, 23–26
  effect on students, 17–20, 218–19
Trail of Tears, 122–23
Transfer lectures. *See* Didactic lectures
Transfer of information, 31–35, 200–
  201. *See also* Teacher-talk
  in academic courses, 74–75
  authoritarianism of, 33–34
  inappropriateness for introductory
    courses, 145
  why teachers use, 103–5
Transformative intellectuals, 190

Unemployment, effect of education on,
  107–8
Upward mobility, effect of education on,
  107–11
Urban studies, teaching, 36
Usage, self-correction of, 163–64, 244
Usage interventions, as teacher's function
  in problem-posing, 245
Utopias (literature course), 27, 123–26,
  162–63, 242, 258–59

Values, teaching, 132–33, 166
Values for empowerment, 15–17
Vida, 82
Violence
  in mass media, 182–84, 249–51
  as theme in literature, 81–83
Virgin Islands, languages, 48–50, 51–52,
  253–54

Vocationalism, of students, 72–73, 74,
  218
Vocational training, 143, 191–92
Voicing exercises, 4, 240
Vulgarity, as theme, 248–51

Walden II, 162, 242, 250
Walker, Alice, 82
Wallerstein, Nina, 42–44, 202
Wall Street Journal, 40
War, as theme in literature, 152–55
Waverly, 82
West, Don, 194
What-questions, 98
Whole language, 40, 172–73
Whole-school reform approach, 140
Williams, Selase W., 49, 53
Witness to Apartheid, 69
Work environments, student research on,
  191–92
Writing. *See also* Language; Literacy
  integrating with academic subjects,
    187–88
  in participatory opening, 70–71, 238–
    39
  proficiency tests, 3–5, 9, 48–49, 50–51
  self-correction, 163–64, 244
  skills exercises, 163–65, 239–40, 243,
    244
Writing across the curriculum, 187
Writing classes
  bicultural, 48–53
  models for, 1–9
  participatory opening, 37–39, 88, 242
  teacher research in, 174–75
  topical themes in, 62–69
Wu, Zhijun, 106–7

Zero paradigm, 200–201. *See also* Transfer of information
Zone of proximal development, 203